P9-DHM-540

OTHER BOOKS BY WITOLD RYBCZYNSKI

Paper Heroes

Taming the Tiger

Home

The Most Beautiful House in the World

Waiting for the Weekend

Looking Around

A Place for Art

Witold Rybczynski

City Life

Urban Expectations in a New World

Scribner
New York London Toronto Sydney Tokyo Singapore

SCRIBNER
1230 Avenue of the Americas
New York, NY 10020

Manufactured in the United States of America

10 9 8 7 6 5 4 3 2 1

LIBRARY OF CONGRESS CATALOGING-IN-PUBLICATION DATA
Rybczynski, Witold.
City life: urban expectations in a new world / Witold Rybczynski.
p. cm.
Includes index.
1. Cities and towns—United States—History.
2. City planning—United States.
3. Architecture and society—United States.
I. Title.
NA9105.R93 1995
711'.4'0973—dc20
95-12648
CIP

ISBN 0-684-81302-5

To Shirley, Stacy, and Nan

Oft expectation fails, and most oft there
Where most it promises

—WILLIAM SHAKESPEARE

CONTENTS

PREFACE 11

1. *Why Aren't Our Cities Like That?* 15

2. *The Measure of a Town* 35

3. *A New, Uncrowded World* 51

4. *A Frenchman in New York* 84

5. *In the Land of the Dollar* 110

6. *Civic Art* 131

7. *High Hopes* 149

8. *Country Homes for City People* 173

9. *The New Downtown* 197

10. *The Best of Both Worlds* 218

NOTES 237

INDEX 247

PREFACE

When I was twenty-two, I made an urban tour. It was thanks to a traveling scholarship awarded by the Canadian federal government to one student from each of the country's six schools of architecture. Together we visited more than a dozen major cities in Canada and the United States. It was a memorable trip, not just because I made a lifelong friend—the Vancouver architect Bing Thom—but also because I was encouraged to look more closely at my urban surroundings.

The stated purpose of the scholarship was to study housing, and we visited an apartment building on Philadelphia's Rittenhouse Square, suburban houses in Marin County, public housing in Toronto and Chicago, and renovated slums in Baltimore. It made me appreciate the richness—and the complexity—of North

American cities. The previous summer I had been to Europe. I had been impressed by Rome, London, and Paris—especially Paris—but it was obvious that our cities were different from what I had seen there. If European cities seemed like beautiful architectural museums, our cities were more like unfinished building sites where each generation was free to try its hand.

We were eager to have our turn. I think the first book I read on urban planning was Victor Gruen's *The Heart of Our Cities.* I don't remember exactly what it was that prompted me to buy it—it wasn't a course text. The author's suggestion that downtown should be redesigned must have been appealing to a budding architect like me. I was probably also attracted by the dramatic combination of alarm and resolve in the subtitle: *The Urban Crisis: Diagnosis and Cure.*

In what follows I am more interested in looking at how our cities have become the way they are—or, more precisely, have not become what we expected them to be—than in looking for crises or imagining diagnoses and cures. This is a book about cities as they are, not as they might be. It is also about cities' evolution, for I'm convinced that our undistinguished record of the last fifty years in building cities and towns stems at least in part from a willful ignorance of our urban past. At the same time, this record is also the result of our inability to anticipate the new technological and social forces that came to bear on our urban condition: the automobile, air travel, electronic communications. There is no such thing as perfect foresight, of course, so we can never plan infallibly, but we can face the urban future with modesty and an approach tempered by a knowledge of earlier successes and failures. In order to understand where we're going, it's necessary to know where we've been.

The opportunity to write about urbanism was presented to me first by a number of editors whose encouragement I would like to acknowledge: William Whitworth of *The Atlantic Monthly* (in which a part of Chapter 9 originally appeared as an article); the helpful Robert Silvers of *The New York Review of Books; The Public Interest*'s Nathan Glazer, whose urban writings I have always admired; and Marilyn Minden of *The New York Times*. Some of the ideas in this book were initially explored in articles and reviews in *City Journal*, the *Times Literary Supplement, Queen's Quarterly*, and *Saturday Night*. Paula Deitz and Susan Cohen's kind invitation to speak at a Smith College symposium spurred me to reflect on the design of New England towns. Jerry Herron of Wayne State University invited me to Detroit to participate in a panel on "The City in the Twenty-first Century" that gave me useful firsthand experience of the volatile state of American urban politics.

The University of Pennsylvania has proved a congenial academic setting for pursuing my interest in urbanism; my thanks to Dean Patricia Conway of the Graduate School of Fine Arts and to Peter D. Linneman of the Wharton School. I would also be remiss in not acknowledging the support of two eminent urban scholars, Martin and Margy Meyerson, for whom the university chair I hold is named.

Shirley Hallam is my first and truest reader, and she has offered equal doses of skepticism and encouragement at the appropriate times. John Lukacs—now a neighbor—kindly reviewed my work, and his thoughtful observations were much appreciated. Stacy Schiff took time away from her own writing to cast a seasoned editor's eye on the manuscript. Carl Brandt, agent and friend, helped me to clarify my ideas when the book was still a vague intuition; he was a sympathetic sounding board throughout. Thanks to Iris Tupholme of HarperCollins in Toronto. At Scribner, the energetic Nan Graham provided sterling editorial advice and support, and got me out of a few dead ends; Nancy Inglis did a fine job of copy editing.

W.R.

Hemmingford, September 1992–
Philadelphia, January 1995.

ONE

Why Aren't Our Cities Like That?

I VISITED PARIS IN THE FALL OF 1992, AFTER AN ABSENCE of more than fifteen years. People had changed, of course. There were more nonwhite faces on the Métro, and, generally, many of the faces seemed less cheerful, or was that just my imagination? The subway cars themselves were much the same, with the flip-down seats near the doors, and places reserved for the elderly and for crippled war veterans—a grisly reminder of the 1914–18 conflict. There were no survivors of the Great War in evidence, but I didn't even see many people who looked, well, French. No elderly gentlemen wearing pale leather gloves and rosettes in their lapels, for example. No businessmen with those curious suits with short, ventless jackets and wide shoulders that I associated with actor Lino Ventura and French gangster movies. Workers were wearing nylon windbreakers rather than traditional blue overalls. Parisians, who had previously seemed to me, a North American, slightly old-fashioned, with their distinctive customs and elaborate courtesies, now appeared familiar.

Like young Germans and young Britishers, many young Frenchmen and Frenchwomen were wearing some combination of that now international uniform of jeans, sneakers, and T-shirts. People carried plastic shopping bags instead of the traditional stringed *filets*, and some wore Walkmans instead of berets. At first glance, I saw nothing that would look out of place in an American mall, or at least a New England mall, since fashionable young Parisians favor Ivy League styles—pressed chinos and penny loafers, for example, or button-down shirts and tweed sports jackets. On second glance, I realized that though the clothing was certainly inspired by American fashions, it was an imagined version of America, not the real thing. Like the imitation cowboy outfits—dude clothes, really—worn by French country-and-western singers. On the whole, there were, I thought, fewer fashionable women; perhaps in Paris it wasn't chic to be chic that year, I'm not sure. People appeared less formal, but they still spoke rapidly and they still smoked a lot. I was told that the government was instituting a ban on smoking in public places the following month; there seemed to be general agreement that such a ban would be ineffectual. Not that anyone thought smoking was good for you, but it was a personal decision, none of "their" business—this said with a great many *oufs* and shrugs. When the ban did go into effect, one restaurateur put up a sign saying, "We also welcome our nonsmoking patrons"; another, more direct, simply advertised "Smoking." At least the French attitude toward authority hadn't changed.

Everyone looked more prosperous—or perhaps I, with my less

valuable Canadian dollars, simply felt poorer than fifteen years earlier. The prosperity was evident in the generally high prices, the many new automobiles, and the expensive shops. For some reason, clothing boutiques in particular bore American names—Mister Cool, New York Jeans—or at least names that the French imagined sounded American. Some things in Paris were new, but many more were old: the names of streets were indicated by the familiar blue and white metal signs, some buildings still displayed those touching historical plaques (so-and-so lived here), and there were still standard stenciled warnings on walls proclaiming *Loi de 1881, Défense d'afficher* ("Posters forbidden"). As before, the sidewalks were crowded with café terraces, newsstands, and kiosks. I didn't see any smelly public pissoirs; these have been replaced by unisex cabins that look like enclosed telephone booths. There were still some subterranean public toilets with uniformed attendants and turnstiles; it cost me fifty cents to relieve myself.

The streets themselves were cleaner than I had remembered. Household garbage is picked up seven days a week and there were sweepers everywhere. The French have their own way of doing things—after all, who else would have gone to the trouble of designing plastic brooms to look like straw? In an attempt to keep things tidy, the municipality has installed curbstones with inlaid canine silhouettes to indicate appropriate places in the gutter for pets to defecate. From the evidence underfoot, this anti-poop campaign has not been a total success, but the effort impressed me. Public hygiene, as Eugen Weber, a historian of modern France, has noted, arrived slowly in France. It was the French, after all, who invented bottled mineral water because their tap water was not fit to drink, and who used to ridicule the American obsession with cleanliness. Weber recounts that when the Duc de Broglie, one of the richest men in France, bought what was considered to be a luxury mansion in Paris in 1902, the house had no bathrooms, no indoor toilets, and only one water tap per floor. This can be compared to George Vanderbilt's Fifth Avenue mansion, which contained a full bathroom as early as 1885; by the turn of the century, even ordinary middle-class Americans could enjoy "A Bed and a Bath for a Dollar and a Half" at the popular Statler Hotel in Buffalo, where every room had a private bathroom with a tub, sink, and water closet. The French, for whom such amenities were a novelty, often referred to them as "American comforts."

One Parisian comfort that is distinctly un-American was evident to me one evening, as I returned to my hotel from the opera. A month earlier I had walked late at night on the Upper East Side of New York, probably among the wealthiest urban residential neighborhoods in the world. It may have been the cardboard-shrouded figures sleeping in the darkened entrances of expensive stores selling ormolu clocks and handmade chocolates, or the almost continuous background whine of police sirens, but I couldn't shake a slight but persistent sense of wariness. Here in the Fourth Arrondissement, I didn't feel in the least edgy. Not that there were many people about at midnight—the boulevard Henri IV down which I was walking was quite empty except for passing cars—but the emptiness in the street felt pleasant, not threatening at all. That American cities now have homicide rates higher than those anywhere else in the Western world, sadly, goes without saying. That Paris felt and is safer, however, is not only the result of fewer social problems in what is still a relatively homogeneous culture. The City of Paris with its 2.3 million inhabitants is policed by 35,000 officers, the equivalent of more than 15 gendarmes per 1,000 citizens; New York City, on the other hand, fields only about 4 policemen per 1,000. By American standards, however, this is a high rate of policing (Los Angeles has about 2 officers per 1,000 citizens), which is probably why New York ranks relatively low in urban crime—thirty-eighth among large cities—according to the 1990 FBI Crime Index.

The day I arrived in Paris my publisher, Liana Levi, took me to lunch, and I was pleased to find that good food is still a part of French culture, although the cooking was nouvelle, not bourgeois, more Evian was consumed than wine, and the desserts were distinctly on the light side. Still, the excellent bread was unchanged, the coffee was as strong as ever, and the crowded restaurant was noisy and convivial. It was an atmosphere that I recalled from my earlier visits.

The conversation turned from matters literary—I was there to promote a new book—to architecture, and so inevitably to the *Grands Projets*. This refers to the monumental government-sponsored additions to Paris—there are nine buildings, thus far—that have been undertaken by President François Mitterrand. Mitterrand's architectural ambition vastly exceeds that of his three predecessors in the Fifth Republic. Charles de Gaulle, who ruled longest, built least—the undistinguished, doughnut-shaped Maison de la Radio—but he did leave one magnificent architectural legacy. In 1958, he ordered the *ravallement*, or cleanup, of the facades of Parisian public buildings, which dramatically altered the appearance of the capital, erasing centuries of accumulated dirt and grime. De Gaulle's successor, Georges Pompidou, was a mediocre president whose tenure was cut short by his death, but he managed to build a lot, most of it bad. He permitted the construction of the first skyscraper in Paris, the looming Tour Montparnasse, inserted expressways along both banks of the Seine, tore down the old market of Les Halles, and cleared a large residential area of the Beaubourg to make way for a multifunctional museum—now called the Centre Pompidou—which, paint peeling and steel rusting, today more than ever resembles an oil refinery (as its unkind critics originally nicknamed it). Valéry

Giscard d'Estaing, pointedly reversing Pompidou's policy of demolition, initiated the conversion of the vast Gare d'Orsay into a museum of nineteenth-century art, and at La Villette, on the northeast edge of the city, created a museum of science and industry to be housed in a beautifully restored nineteenth-century market building.

Although the record of presidential intervention in the architecture and urbanism of Paris is mixed, one must admire the sentiment embodied in this type of national leadership. The same kind of leadership is in play in Great Britain, where Prince Charles is an outspoken critic of modernist architecture and planning, and in Canada, where Prime Minister Pierre Trudeau played a personal role in the construction of several important public buildings in the national capital. In the United States, recent presidents have shown no interest in the art of building, beyond redecorating the White House.* An exception was Franklin D. Roosevelt, an amateur architect who largely designed his own presidential library in Hyde Park—a building of considerable charm—as well as several other projects. The lack of architectural awareness in the American presidency is striking, since the United States is probably the only country in the world that can boast a national leader who is also a celebrated architect, Thomas Jefferson. The contemporary lack of leadership in architecture appears to be a part of the modern technocratic presidency: the president's wife may attend to the arts, as Jacqueline Kennedy did; the president himself must be seen to be interested in touch football, cutting brush, speed-boating, or jogging, but not in culture, lest he be accused of elitism.

The French, on the other hand, see no difficulty in comparing their president to Louis XIV, who transformed the architectural

*Jimmy Carter's prominent involvement in building homes for low-income families occurred after the end of his presidency.

face of Paris; certainly, Mitterrand seems intent on emulating the Grand Siècle. So far not only has he moved the ministry of finance out of the Louvre and into a new building, renovated the Louvre itself, and endowed Paris with a brand-new opera house on the Place de la Bastille, but he has also built an Arabic institute, a music center, and a new public park at La Villette, and at La Défense in the northwestern suburbs, he has erected an unusual office building in the shape of a huge arch. This modern counterpart to the Arc de Triomphe will be overshadowed by his latest, and likely his last, project: an enormous new national library, a building that will add more than a billion dollars to the three billion that have already been spent on the *Grands Projets*.

"We will have achieved nothing if in the next ten years we have not created the basis for an urban civilization," President Mitterrand announced portentously after he was elected. It's fortunate that Paris was already the seat of a great urban architectural tradition, for Mitterrand's *Grands Projets* are not very good buildings. Even I. M. Pei's new glass pyramid in the courtyard of the Louvre is, finally, a timid gesture, and Jean Nouvel's Institut du Monde Arabe, while it fits well enough into its surroundings, is fussy and contrived in its details. What the *Grands Projets* chiefly exhibit is size—they are huge: the largest opera building in the world (almost three times the size of New York's Metropolitan Opera), the world's tallest habitable arch at La Défense, and Europe's biggest library. Judging from the published drawings, the latter will be a banal composition resembling four half-open books. Its glass-fronted stacks have already been the cause of controversy among bibliophiles: not only are all the books exposed to harmful daylight, but most of the public reading rooms are underground. The huge opera house reminded me of a supertanker that had been grounded in the newly restored seventeenth-century district in the east of Paris; the Parc de la Villette is a collection of goofy pavilions in an arid landscape; and the grandiose government office building at La Défense recalls less a triumphal arch than a huge marble-covered coffee table. Mitterrand is not Louis XIV, or rather his architects on the whole haven't lived up to the standards set by the Sun King's architects—Claude Perrault (designer of the east front of the Louvre), Jules-Hardouin Mansart (builder of the Dôme des Invalides), and André Le Nôtre (creator of the Tuileries gardens). Mitterrand has imported talent from around the world—the arch of the Défense was designed by a Dane, the Opéra by a Canadian—but instead of delicacy, refinement, and delight, there is bureaucratic heavy-handedness, technical gimmickry, intellectual pretension, and brittle modernism.

Nevertheless, despite the onslaught of new cultural monuments, and despite the modernization and the prosperity, the streets of central Paris that I saw had not changed all that much in fifteen years; indeed, the city remained in many ways as I remembered it from my first visit as a college student in 1964. Then, enchanted by this beautiful place (and also in love), I strolled the same tree-lined avenues, the same romantic *quais* along the Seine, and the same narrow streets in the Latin Quarter; sat on the same park benches and in the same noisy bistros, drinking the same café au lait. Being in Paris almost thirty years later brought it all back.

"Why aren't our cities like that?" asked my friend Danielle, who also had just returned from Paris, obviously impressed by what she'd seen. We were sitting around the dinner table in the Boathouse, our country home. The plates had been cleared away and our respective partners were engaged in close conversation nearby. What did she mean? I asked. Well, she answered, Paris had formal squares, stately parks, and tree-lined boulevards with wonderful vistas. I agreed that it was a beautiful city. Then why didn't we—Danielle is a Montrealer—have anything as elegant as the Place des Vosges, she wanted to know, or as stately as the Palais-Royal, as architecturally complete as the arcades along the Rue de Rivoli, as impressive as the *Grands Projets*? Where were the elegant avenues, the great civic spaces, and the impressive public monuments?

I sensed accusation in her voice. You architects, she seemed to be saying, have slipped up: You could have built a beautiful city like Paris. Why didn't you? I tried to explain the difference in history, in politics, and in economics that had formed the two cities. In any case, I argued lamely, this was North America, the New World; if our cities looked different, well, that was to be expected. I sensed myself getting defensive and I could see that I wasn't making much headway. Danielle regarded me with a tolerant but skeptical look. Thankfully—for me—our conversation was interrupted by a noisy dispute at the other end of the table on the merits and follies of Canada's ongoing constitutional crisis. Everyone in Quebec has an opinion on this arcane topic. The state of our cities was soon forgotten.

Though Montreal is sometimes described as the most European city on the North American continent, and though about half of Montrealers are descendants of immigrants from France and still speak French, no one could ever confuse Montreal with Paris.* Unlike Paris—and like all North American cities—Montreal is ringed by suburbs comprised mainly of individual houses, and it has a clearly defined commercial downtown of tall office buildings distinct from the residential neighborhoods of lower buildings that surround it. The center of Paris generally is made up of eight-story masonry buildings, which provide a pleasant uniformity of

*Montreal was for a long time the world's second-largest French-speaking metropolis after Paris, a distinction now accorded Kinshasa, the capital of Zaire.

color and scale. The center of Montreal is a typically North American free-for-all: tall buildings of various shapes, steel-and-glass buildings, brick buildings interspersed with empty lots and parking lots. The effect suggests happenstance and improvisation, not planning—a Monopoly board in midgame.

Paris, unlike almost all North American cities, shows evidence of having been planned according to an aesthetic vision. A tradition of building and city planning has guided the Parisian authorities for almost four hundred years. Despite the fact that this tradition is derived from building royal palaces and gardens, it has proved admirably adaptable to planning entire cities: instead of gravel walks, boulevards; instead of box hedges, residential blocks; instead of fountains, civic buildings. Moreover, this formal language of symmetry, vista, and the grand gesture has been adhered to with a consistency that is on the whole admirable. The Place de l'Etoile, for example, dates back to the seventeenth century; at that time the circle, built by Louis XIV, was merely a grandiose clearing in the countryside. In 1806 Napoleon decided to use the circle—now at the edge of the city—as the site for a great symbolic city gate, the Arc de Triomphe. This provided a termination to the vista from the courtyard of the Louvre, a vista that had been first established by Le Nôtre's remodeling of the Tuileries gardens in the 1660s, and reinforced by the majestic Place de la Concorde, which was begun in 1753. By the end of the nineteenth century, Baron Georges Haussmann had surrounded the Place de l'Etoile with buildings and extended the line of the Champs Elysées another two and a half miles to Neuilly on the Seine. More than three hundred years after Louis XIV, the project has finally been completed by Mitterrand in the shape of the arched office building at La Défense.

The idea of the urban axis appealed equally to king, emperor, and president, for it was and is a symbol, not of individual hubris, but of Frenchness. What is striking about this example is the consistency with which planning was carried out despite the different political ideologies of the planners. Equally striking is the degree of state intervention in urban development. When a shopping mall was built on the site of Les Halles in the center of Paris, the design had to be approved by President Giscard d'Estaing. When the authorities thought that the Champs Elysées was becoming too "American," they declared the boulevard a national landmark and forced it to be remade in a more acceptable, European manner. The same desire for explicit order is visible in the terminology of streets, avenues, and boulevards—indeed, the origin of the last two words is French. Avenues are important diagonal streets, usually linking two public squares; boulevards are broad promenades resembling linear parks that were originally built on the site of the old city walls and are heavily planted with trees.

Montreal, too, has boulevards, but they're boulevards in name only. René Lévesque Boulevard is a windy downtown artery whose chief adornment is a bleak concrete median strip. The city's best-known boulevard is Boulevard St-Laurent—the Main of Mordecai Richler's nostalgic and satirical novels of Jewish life in Montreal in the 1940s. The Main is a narrow commercial street whose most famous emporium is neither a haute couture boutique nor a luxury department store but Schwartz's Hebrew Delicatessen, a smoked-meat eatery of local renown but distinctly ungenteel. Montreal is not without charm, of course. The Main may not be a real boulevard, but it is a real shopping street, lined with Portuguese, Greek, and Italian produce stores that overflow onto the jammed sidewalks and recall nineteenth-century photographs of crowded immigrant neighborhoods in Philadelphia and the Lower East Side of Manhattan. Likewise old-fashioned are many of the residential districts of Montreal: ornate Victorian terraces, mountainside luxury apartment buildings, and turn-of-the-century middle-class suburbs that have grown in with large trees and lush gardens. Montreal working-class neighborhoods have long narrow streets flanked by three- and four-story walk-ups draped with steep exterior stairs and wrought-iron balconies that produce an atmosphere of tough, gregarious urbanity.

There have been attempts to make Montreal more like Paris. The most famous symbol of Paris is the Eiffel Tower, and in 1967, Jean Drapeau, the mayor of Montreal, tried to have a tower included in the World's Fair. He wasn't successful, but nine years later a tower was made part of the Olympic Stadium. It isn't as tall as Gustave Eiffel's 1,056-foot construction, but it is designed by a Frenchman, and because it is tilted and twenty stories high, it is taller than Pisa's Leaning Tower. The Montreal tower slants above the stadium and acts as a support for a huge, retractable fabric roof. The mayor's attempt to import Parisian grandeur and Parisian autocracy to Montreal proved problematic: the Quebec concrete industry was simply not up to the challenge posed by novel French engineering, and French engineering itself was confounded by the harshness of the Canadian climate. Cracks have appeared in the foundations of the tower, and recently a seventy-ton piece of the stadium fell to the ground. As for the retractable, tentlike roof, it has developed an unpredictable tendency to self-destruct, so much so that it was finally decided to replace it with a permanent structure. Montreal's now-superfluous leaning tower looks neither beautiful nor magnificent, only eccentric. When Eiffel's tower opened to the public in 1889, it was an immediate popular success, although intellectuals like de Maupassant and Zola hated it—but then Zola was wrong about Cézanne, too, whom he considered a failure. Nobody likes the Olympic stadium: it's a source of embarrassment and irritation, an expensive and irksome symbol of technical ineptitude and frustrated political dreams.

Most cities have places of which the visitor can say when he reaches them, "Now I'm *really* here." These hallmark places can be famous monuments like the Eiffel Tower and Berlin's Brandenburg Gate or famous buildings like Buckingham Palace. More often than not, they are large public spaces: the Piazza San Marco in Venice, Red Square in Moscow, Tiananmen Square in Beijing. Montreal is different. Ask people the location of the symbolic center of the city and the answer is likely to be "Peel and Saint Catherine." Other famous North American street corners include L.A.'s Hollywood and Vine, San Francisco's Powell and Market, Toronto's King and Bay, Winnipeg's Portage and Main, and New York's Times Square, which despite its name is really a street intersection, not a square. With very few exceptions—the Mall in Washington, D.C., a city planned by a Frenchman, and Pioneer Courthouse Square in downtown Seattle, Washington—we have made street corners, not plazas, into symbolic civic places. This suggests that if our cities are different—and clearly they are—it may be not only because we build them differently and use them differently but also because we imagine them in a different way.

The Paris that I visited as a college student in 1964 had not yet been subjected to the heavy hand of Georges Pompidou; there were no expressways along the Seine, no Tour Montparnasse, and no Centre Pompidou. But even with these unwelcome additions, and even after Mitterrand's monumental building spree, the center of the city—its Renaissance and Haussmannian character—remains essentially unchanged. On the other hand, if I was returning to a North American city after a twenty-eight-year absence, I would be most struck by how much *had* changed. During the last three decades, cities across the continent have retired streetcar systems, demolished railroad stations, and built new subways and urban freeways, not to mention airports. One of the major innovations in many cities has been the creation of what are in effect enclosed sidewalks. In Houston, Cincinnati, Milwaukee, and Minneapolis, one can now walk from building to building without ever going outside by using an elevated system of walkways and bridges; in Montreal, a subterranean pedestrian network has turned large parts of downtown into a huge underground shopping mall.

Downtown skylines have been altered by three generations of skyscrapers. First, the severe modernist flattops of the 1960s; then the more picturesque postmodern towers, spires, and turrets of the 1970s; finally, in the 1980s, neoclassical and neo–Art Deco high-rises. The downtown towers are the work of our captains of industry—captains of sinking ships, it often turned out—but our city fathers have been busy too, financing new stadiums, convention centers, world trade centers, symphony halls, and a host of new museums.

Where there were once buildings, there are now parking lots; where there were once vacant lots, new buildings have arisen. A few of the old buildings remain. Some, having succumbed to architectural face-lifts, have become eerily ageless; many have fallen to the wrecker's ball. Old family-owned businesses on the main shopping streets have been supplanted by neon-fronted franchise retailers and fast-food outlets. Landmark hotels disappear or are converted into condominiums; downtown movie houses, with rococo interiors and chandeliered lobbies, are subdivided into dull cineplexes; department stores are giving way to downtown shopping malls.

This building and rebuilding of North American cities since the 1950s demonstrates how much city planning is affected by changing fashions. One decade favors modernity and pulls down old buildings in the name of progress; the next decade discovers its heritage and promotes historic preservation. The artificial environment of tall buildings is a source of pride for one generation and a health hazard for another. A fad for closing streets and converting them to uniquely pedestrian use swept American and Canadian cities and towns in the 1950s; two decades later many of the so-called pedestrian malls had reverted to their original form. During the fifties and early sixties, progressive politicians replaced slums with public housing; their successors denounced "The Projects" as responsible for perpetuating poverty and promoting crime, and in several notorious cases public housing was torn down. Also during the fifties, downtown boosters welcomed federal highway construction funds; during the 1980s, they were more likely to be refusing them. In cities such as Miami, Minneapolis, Chicago, and New Orleans, proposed urban highways were rejected; some cities, like Toronto and Portland, Oregon, actually demolished sections of urban highway.

Mass transit has also been affected by fashion. Starting in Richmond, Virginia, in 1888, and until about the 1930s, virtually every large North American city and many small ones had electric trolley cars. In Los Angeles, the "Big Red Cars" of the Pacific Electric Railway operated on over one thousand miles of track.* When diesel-engine buses appeared, with a few exceptions—Toronto, New Orleans, San Francisco, parts of Philadelphia—most cities dismantled their trolley tracks. This was sometimes due to economic reasons (a drop-off in ridership), sometimes to political and lobby pressures, and sometimes simply to a feeling that trolleys were old-fashioned. Today trolleys are making a small comeback. Saint Louis has built an eighteen-mile line that connects downtown with Busch Stadium, the University of Mis-

*The interurban electric railway was spread over the entire Los Angeles basin, linking downtown to Santa Monica, San Fernando, Newport Beach, Pomona, San Bernardino, and Riverside. This is a reminder that it was the Pacific Electric, not the automobile, that created this sprawling metropolitan region.

souri, and the airport (the Saint Louis trolley, unlike most mass transit, has turned out to be extremely popular with the public). Buffalo has a six-mile system. Detroit has built a two-mile trolley along the waterfront, and New York City is studying a trolley line that would run along 42nd Street from one side of Manhattan to the other. The old interurban streetcars that used to run into the suburbs and which ceased operation during the early 1900s are being revived in the form of high-speed light-rail systems in cities like Portland and San Diego.

Changes in North American cities are often the result of what economists call market forces, a reminder that our cities are shaped not only by planners but also by the often idiosyncratic decisions of large numbers of separate citizens. *Money* magazine annually compiles a list of "The Best Places to Live in America." It is based on a survey of a cross section of readers who are asked to rate, on a scale of 1 to 10, forty-four variables that they feel are desirable in a community: plenty of doctors, many hospitals, good public schools, proximity to colleges, inexpensive living, low taxes, strong local government, and so on. These ranked preferences are then combined with statistical information describing the three hundred largest metropolitan areas in the United States to find how these cities correspond to people's current inclinations. What is surprising about the resulting list is its volatility. Only three of the top ten cities in 1991 made the top ten in 1992; on the other hand, Minneapolis/Saint Paul, which reached only sixty-third place in 1991, jumped to fourth in 1992, and the first and second places in 1992 were occupied by Sioux Falls, South Dakota, and Columbia, Missouri, which had ranked twelfth and twentieth the year before.

This rise and fall reflects not only changes in the cities themselves but also changes in what matters to people when choosing a place to live. Although the public's chief concerns remained stable between 1991 and 1992—clean air and water, low crime rate, and quality of health care—other preferences varied. For example, proximity to skiing areas was less important in 1992 than in the year before, and received a ranking of only 4.1 out of 10, much lower than proximity to lakes or ocean (7.4), or sunny weather (6.4). Which may explain why Billings, Montana, slipped from sixth place to seventy-third, and why Honolulu jumped to seventh place from twenty-seventh. In 1992, Americans gave more importance to living close to good colleges, which helped to raise the ranking of northwestern New Jersey and Philadelphia.

It is unlikely that Sioux Falls will turn into the hub of a prairie megalopolis merely because it happens to have clean air, clean water, and a low crime rate, but the factors that made it number one on *Money* magazine's list are real enough, and they have had real effects. Compared to number three hundred on the list—Waterbury, Connecticut, a city of roughly the same size (about 100,000 inhabitants)—Sioux Falls has a higher per capita income, more doctors, twice as many college-educated people, a 50 percent lower unemployment rate, and a 50 percent lower crime rate (hence needing a much smaller police force, which results in lower taxes). Does all this make it a more attractive place to live? Apparently so: Sioux Falls is growing by almost 20 percent annually according to 1990 figures; the population of Waterbury, on the other hand, shrank by almost 1 percent the same year.

The history of American cities has always been marked by citizens voting with their feet, but never more so than in the twentieth century. People decide they like living in houses with gardens, and inner-city neighborhoods shrink while outer-city neighborhoods expand. Shopping habits change, with drastic effects on the department stores that were once the largest downtown buildings. Young couples develop a taste for Victorian houses and run-down streets acquire new life—and the previous rooming-house tenants are obliged to move on. Corporations decide that it might be a good idea to relocate nearer the highway, and so-called office parks spring up on what had been farmland. Air travel becomes cheaper, more people fly, new airport terminals are built, and new warehouses appear around them; inevitably, old warehouse districts are abandoned. Industry relocates factories to the Sunbelt, and Phoenix and Dallas boom while Flint, Michigan, and Youngstown, Ohio, suffer. Or people are simply attracted by safe, clean, and prosperous cities, and Sioux City grows while Waterbury declines.

In his 1992 Nobel Lecture, Derek Walcott described the sunny, pretty market towns of his native Caribbean and observed that these picture-postcard places appear frivolous and shallow to outsiders, who find them hard to take seriously. "Ours are not cities in the accepted sense," he admitted, "but no one wants them to be. They dictate their own proportions, their own definitions in particular places and in a prose equal to that of their detractors." No one would describe most North American cities as picture-postcard places, but they too are not cities in the accepted sense, or at least not in the traditional sense. Socially fragmented, recklessly entrepreneurial, relying almost completely on the automobile, and often lacking a defined center, they are without many of the conventional trappings of urbanity that have characterized cities in the past. According to their detractors, they are not real cities at all. At least they are not real cities if one assumes that real cities have cathedrals and outdoor plazas, not parking garages and indoor shopping malls; that they have sidewalk cafés, not drive-through Pizza Huts, and movie theaters, not cineplexes; that real cities are beautiful, ordered, and high-minded, not raucous, unfinished, and commercial.

No, our cities are definitely not like Paris. But then what *are* they like? And how did they get that way? If the City of Light can be described as a stage on which the dreams of emperors and kings and presidents are played out, the American city is more difficult to characterize. No kings, certainly, nor emperors, although there have been individual dreamers, men such as William Penn, the founder of colonial Philadelphia, which was the most ambitious planned city of its day; or William Levitt, the home builder who pioneered the model postwar suburb on Long Island and set an example that altered urban history; or William Zeckendorf, a property developer of the 1960s whose real estate ventures transformed the downtowns of many North American cities then caught up in the process of urban renewal. But above all, the American city has been a stage for the ideas of ordinary people: the small business man on Main Street, the franchisee along the commercial strip, the family in the suburbs. It all adds up to a disparate vision of the city. Perhaps the American urban stage is best described as cinematic rather than theatrical. A jumbled back lot with a cheek-by-jowl assortment of different sets for different productions—the dusty back alleys of *High Noon* next to the tree-lined small-town streets of *It's a Wonderful Life* beside the drive-in highway strip of *American Graffiti* around the corner from the metropolitan nightmare of *Blade Runner*.

The cinematic analogy is apt because there is something fleeting about the American city, as if it were a temporary venue for diversion, a place to find entertaining novelty, at least for a time, before settling down elsewhere. The historian John Lukacs has written about Americans' restlessness: the tendency to want to move around, not only from one part of the country to another, but from one neighborhood to another, even from one house to another. For such a mobile people, street corners would be appealing. The permanence of residence that was and is the stable foundation of European cities has always been absent in America, and accommodation to this transience has had an effect on the way that cities evolve and are altered. Lukacs speculates that this restlessness may have something to do with the vast, open continent itself. The architectural historian Vincent Scully agrees. Scully cites two examples of American peoples who voluntarily gave up their sedentary life in the face of a new mode of transportation: the Plains Indians, when confronted by the horse, and twentieth-century Americans, when confronted by the automobile. "Similar, too, are the human qualities which brought the primitivistic and nomadic patterns forth, alike among post-conquest Plains Indians and contemporary Americans: a sense of open horizons, an impatience with communal restraints, an instinct for the continuation throughout life of childish joys, a taste for violence, hard use, quick turnover, lonely fantasies, eternal change."

Eternal change is certainly the hallmark of American urban history, which, as we shall see, is the story of a series of urban ideals—some mundane, some high-minded, some wonderful, some wrongheaded, some elitist, some popular—that were often interrupted by unforeseen events, interruptions frequently accompanied by calamitous consequences. What is surprising is the continuing sense of public optimism throughout. Despite the setbacks, urban expectations go on unabated. Sometimes the past is impatiently discarded, sometimes it's resurrected, sometimes it's ignored, but throughout the making and unmaking of cities, there is evidence of a constant striving to correct and improve, of an attempt finally to get it right.

TWO

The Measure of a Town

CITIES ARE ARTIFACTS. THEY ARE NOT THE BIGGEST man-made objects in the world—they are not as big as works of pure engineering like the Great Wall of China or the Panama Canal or the continental telephone system—but what they lack in extent they make up for in conscious impact. The telephone system is huge but largely invisible, and only a part of the Great Wall or the Panama Canal can be seen at a time; the immensity of these creations makes itself felt only in the imagination. But a city can be experienced all of a piece. That is why city views, whether of Paris spread out below the heights of Sacré-Coeur or of lower Manhattan from the Staten Island ferry or of the crowded island of Hong Kong from Kowloon, are so moving. Such views are also a potent reminder that cities represent great human achievements. "It was divine nature which gave us the country," wrote the Roman scholar Marcus Terentius Varro, "and man's skill that built the cities."

It would be logical to assume that because cities are man-made and not accidental creations, they follow discrete patterns, and hence can be described and catalogued according to some simple scheme. Canals can be categorized according to length or depth or lock capacity, say, and telephone systems can be rated by technical sophistication or by the number of calls carried or the distance covered. Since cities are above all concentrations of people, population suggests itself as the simplest measure. Yet to begin with, there is no strict, or even loose, definition of just how many heads it takes to make a city. In the United States, "city" has been used to identify settlements of almost any size. The grandly named Dodge City, laid out in 1872, was described by a contemporary visitor as "about a dozen frame houses and about two dozen tents, besides a few adobe houses." Even in its heyday, when Dodge City had a reputation as the western frontier's wildest town, rivaled only by Deadwood and Tombstone, the permanent population was probably well under 1,000 people. Plattsburgh, New York, which is near where I used to live, had 7,446 inhabitants when it was incorporated as a city in 1902. When Miami was officially declared a city, it had only 343 voters. In Canada, the provinces of Ontario and Quebec require that a town have a population of 15,000 before it can incorporate itself as a city, but British Columbia does not use the official designation "town" and calls anything larger than a village a "city."

The idea of what constitutes a city has varied greatly in the past. Aristotle thought that the ideal city should contain not more than 5,000 citizens (he did not count women, freemen, or slaves), which he considered was the largest number of people who could conveniently meet together to govern themselves. This was an implicit criticism of Athens, since it is estimated that at the time of Pericles the city contained about 40,000 citizens. Although it was probably smaller when Aristotle lived there, it was obviously much larger than he judged fit. What would he have thought of ancient Rome, which reached a million inhabitants at its peak, although it shrank to less than 100,000 during the Middle Ages? One hundred thousand was still exceptionally large for the time. In medieval Germany, settlements of 3,000 inhabitants were granted the status of cities, and in medieval France, there were numerous examples of walled cities with as few as 200 or 300 households, probably 2,000 or 3,000 people. Such small, compact cities would have functioned like modern neighborhoods: one walked everywhere and knew everybody.

There were many different ways of referring to cities and towns. In the Middle Ages in Europe, walled, self-governing towns were usually called boroughs or burghs, from the German *burg*, originally meaning a fortress or castle; whence also the terms burghers, burgess, and bourgeois. Bourgeois now refers to a social class rather than place of residence, but borough continues to be used in England (and in some American states) to denote self-governing towns. In New York City, borough refers to the five administrative units that constitute the city. *Bourg*, in French, means a market town, and burg has survived in its many forms in the names of cities around the world: Strasbourg, Salzburg, Nuremberg, and Edinburgh. There are so many burgs in the United States—Pittsburgh, Saint Petersburg, Gettysburg, Vicksburg—that beginning in the nineteenth century, "burg" became a colloquial term signifying town. "Urban," from the Latin *urbs* for city—as distinct from *rus*, or rural—has survived in English and has produced urbane, which implies refined behavior, clearly derived from life in towns.

The word "town" comes from the Old English *tūn*, and originally meant a fence or an enclosure. During the Middle Ages it became a generic term for large and small urban settlements, which were usually walled; even as late as the nineteenth century in Scotland and northern England a group of farm buildings was referred to as a town. In the United States, on the other hand, a town or township can be a large administrative area that often has a rural character. As for the word "city" (derived from the Old French, *cité*), it originally signified towns that were the seat of a bishopric. This had nothing to do with population—cathedral towns were not necessarily larger than others—and eventually, important boroughs were also granted the title of city. The city was thought of as the seat of authority. National capitals were called cities, as were the traditional centers of old towns: the City of London or the Ile de la Cité in Paris. City was also used to distinguish special religious places—Rome was the Eternal City, Jerusalem the Holy City; heaven was the City of God.*

Perhaps one should not make too much of the distinction between city and town, for it is not present in all languages. In Spanish, *ciudad* can be used to describe both a city and a town; in Italian, *cittá* likewise blurs the distinction. In German, Russian, Polish, and Hungarian, although there are special words to denote a village, the same word is used to describe both a city and a town. In French, a single word, *ville*, refers both to Paris and to small country towns. The need English speakers uniquely felt to distinguish towns from cities may have been simply a linguistic accident. As a result of the Norman Conquest, modern English is an amalgam of Old English and Old French, and sometimes this results in different roots for words with related meanings, like house

*The use of the word "city" to denote a special place, rather than an urban center, still occurs in building names like New York's Radio City, and Chicago's Marina City, as well as in commercial names like Toyota City or Circuit City.

(Old English) and mansion (Old French), or rope (Old English) and cord (Old French).

Whatever the reason, the presence of the two different words, town and city, has allowed English speakers to draw subtle distinctions. Today, to call a place a town implies that it has close economic and emotional ties with the surrounding countryside. A city, on the other hand, while it may appropriate natural areas for weekend recreation, is considered to be self-sufficient, and if it depends on natural resources, these are likely to come from far away, not from its immediate surroundings. Thus, to say that one place is a large town and that another is a small city is to insinuate that while their population sizes may be similar, their character is not. To call a place a small town evokes an image that is not merely demographic. Big city, city slickers, and fighting city hall all connote a certain way of life, just as town hall and town meeting suggests a smaller, more intimate scale, which is why the notion of a "national town meeting" is an oxymoron.

For a long time, it was the largest cities that set the tempo for entire eras, and being number one in population counted for something. This was true of imperial Rome and Constantinople, medieval Baghdad, fifteenth-century Nanjing, and nineteenth-century London. London was number one, demographically speaking, from 1850 until 1950, when it was overtaken by New York City. When Tokyo displaced New York as the world's largest city in the 1980s, it was taken as a sign of Japan's industrial prowess. But a list of the world's six largest metropolitan areas today would include not just Tokyo and New York City but also São Paulo, Mexico City, Shanghai, and Bombay. While it could be argued that the presence of Shanghai reflects the arrival of the People's Republic of China as a world economic power, the same can hardly be said of São

Paulo, Mexico City, or Bombay, which are all situated in countries with troubled economies. Indeed, of the twenty-two so-called megacities, cities whose population is expected to exceed 10 million by the year 2000, none is in Europe, only two are in the United States, two are in Japan, one is in South Korea, and the rest—seventeen of them—are in poor countries in Asia, Africa, and Latin America.

Even among rich, industrialized nations, the size of a city is no longer a measure of its importance. A ranking of cities by population situates Chicago above Paris; yet whereas Paris, like London and New York, is a city of global influence, Chicago, despite an outstanding university, a famous symphony orchestra, and one of the world's busiest airports, is not. An important banking center like Zurich is in the same population rank as Buffalo, which is not an influential city. Rotterdam, which handles the most cargo of any ocean port in the world, is lower on the population scale than the port city of Valencia. Jerusalem, a city that dominates Middle Eastern politics and is a holy place for three world religions, is side by side with Manchester, England, a city whose glory days ended a century ago.

The size of a city's population is a crude measure of urbanity, for it reveals nothing of the wealth or poverty of the citizens, of their education or lack of it, of their level of culture and degree of accomplishment. When Vienna, the city of Mozart, was a sophisticated imperial capital, it contained only slightly more than 200,000 people. The population of Venice peaked at about 180,000 in the seventeenth century, yet this small city (about the size of present-day Little Rock, Arkansas) was home to a host of creative individuals: Titian and Veronese, Monteverdi and Jacopo Sansovino, as well as, of course, their many enlightened patrons. Venice's legacy was not just artistic; the city also gave Europe such varied inventions as glass mirrors, income tax, gambling casinos, government bonds, and the term "ghetto." In 1516 the New Ghetto (literally, New Foundry—*getto* means "to cast metals") was set aside for German and Italian Jewish refugees from the mainland; the district was surrounded by a wall and locked up at night. Venice has grown almost not at all since the seventeenth century, and the modern visitor can still experience the pleasure of a small and concentrated city that can easily be grasped in the mind's eye, unlike the behemoths that we call cities today.

By the eighteenth century, the largest city in Europe was London, with a population of about three-quarters of a million. In population, that is roughly the size of present-day Phoenix or Edmonton, but the cultural resources of these provincial centers cannot be compared with those that flourished in eighteenth-century London: the dozens of locally published journals and newspapers, the hundreds of theaters and music rooms, and the almost 2,000 coffeehouses, where literati could go for gossip, political debate, and reading material. "When a man is tired of London," said Samuel Johnson, "he is tired of life; for there is in London all that life can afford."

Nor does the measure of the population of a city disclose what came before or what is to come. It does not indicate whether a city is growing or stable or shrinking. Detroit and San Diego presently have about the same number of inhabitants, but one city, a former giant, is a troubled company town whose industries are in retreat and whose population is contracting (about 175,000 people less in 1990 than in 1980), and the other is an up-and-coming regional powerhouse, international in language, culture, and orientation, whose population is growing rapidly (an increase of 235,000 people in the same decade).

Detroit and San Diego are a reminder that the fortunes of cities change. Venice started as a European banking center and has become a tourist city; Miami started its urban existence as a tourist city and may eventually become a tropical Zurich. Miami was incorporated in 1896 and, thanks to a combination of surrounding citrus groves and the railroad, by 1920 it had grown to about 30,000 people. Then, two years later, the South Florida land rush began. The boom lasted five years, and at its height people from across the United States were arriving at the rate of more than 6,000 a day. It was an extraordinary spectacle, as people rushed in, often to discover that their dream home was half an acre of the proverbial swampland. Most stayed, however, and by 1926, the population of the city stood at a remarkable 130,000. The next great period of expansion did not occur until after World War II, when Miami became predominantly a winter holidayers' and a retirees' city. A mixture of beachside hotels and inland mobile-home parks accommodated both groups. Between 1940 and 1950, the city's population almost doubled; since then, its growth has been less dramatic, except for sporadic bursts of immigration from Central and South America. The greater Miami area, including Fort Lauderdale, is now among the ten largest metropolitan areas in the United States, and functions as the chief shopping and banking center for the well-heeled (including the drug-cartel managers) of the Latin American countries of the Caribbean. What is also dramatic is the change in the character of the city, half of whose population is now of Hispanic origin, predominantly Cuban.

The American city planner Kevin Lynch suggested that there have always been distinct ways of thinking about cities, and that all cities could be described as having been built following one of three conceptual models. He called the first model "cosmic" to denote cities whose spatial layouts symbolically represented specific rituals and beliefs. These beliefs could be religious, as in the case of ancient India, where cities were laid out like huge mandalas; in traditional Chinese capital cities, which were planned as perfect squares, the twelve gates, three on each side, represented the twelve months of the year. When the ancient Romans laid out new towns, the two intersecting main streets stood for the solar axis and the line of the equinox. In Japanese cities the central location of the emperor's palace symbolized the preeminence of imperial rule. Sacred or cosmic aspirations were also expressed in the location of buildings. Hilltops were reserved for temples and other buildings of religious importance. In some Asian cities man-made temple-mountains were intended to recall Mount Meru, the mountain at the center of traditional Indian cosmology.

Symbolic urban layouts are not necessarily religious or ancient. Washington, D.C., where the separation of White House and Capitol symbolizes the separation of executive and legislative powers, was planned at the end of the eighteenth century. Washington obviously influenced Albert Speer when he redesigned Berlin for the Third Reich: a grand boulevard was to terminate in a huge domed hall. Speer's plan was never realized, but there have been other symbolically charged capital cities built in the twentieth century. New Delhi, begun in 1911, has a great east-west processional way leading to a hill on which sits the domed viceroy's residence. Canberra, Australia, planned in 1912 by the American Walter Burley Griffin, is less formal, but likewise establishes a symbolic axis between two hills, Parliament Hill and Capitol Hill. The plan of Brasília (1957–1960) resembles the outline of an airplane, with the main government buildings located in what would be the pilot's cockpit.

Lynch's second model is the "practical" city—that is, the city imagined as a kind of machine, chiefly a machine for commerce. Such cities are pragmatic and functional; they grow according to material needs, as new parts are added and as old parts are altered. Their urban form derives from simply the addition of undifferentiated parts; they have, Lynch writes, no wider significance. This does not mean that practical cities are urbanistically inferior, but unlike cosmic cities they are not subject to a single overriding philosophical guiding principle.

The streets of the practical city have typically followed an orthogonal grid. The oldest gridded cities were colonies of preclassical Mesopotamia and Assyria. Grid planning has often been associated with colonization, since standardized, orderly, rational layouts appeal to the military mind; grids also can be devised in advance and imposed on different terrain. The Laws of the Indies, codified by Philip II in 1573, mandated that Spanish colonial towns in the New World (at least the civil settlements—the laws did not govern forts and mission towns) follow a standardized grid plan that incorporated sensible ideas about orientation and zoning (slaughterhouses and tanneries, for example, were separated from residential areas) and provided shaded arcades on the main streets. The main public area in these towns was a large central plaza surrounded by the chief colonizing institutions: the royal council, the town hall, and the main church.

The most recent examples of grid planning on a huge scale are found in the cities of the Third World. In the suburbs of Djakarta, Calcutta, Nairobi, Mexico City, and Lima are so-called sites and services projects, large tracts of land subdivided into small rectangular plots onto which poor families move and erect their own dwellings. The systematic, orderly layouts of these new planned neighborhoods are in marked contrast to the apparent chaos of the unplanned slums and squatter settlements they replace. This geometric order is not merely the result of engineering considerations and a rationalized sewerage layout, but also represents a kind of colonization, the colonization of traditional cultures by modern state bureaucracies. The political persuasion of the bureaucrats is irrelevant; similar sites and services layouts are imposed by Asian autocracies, African dictatorships, and Latin American oligarchies.

North American cities, with their regular grids of intersecting streets, are typical examples of Lynch's practical model. This does not necessarily mean that the apparently mechanical grid lacks poetic character, however. When the grid meets the natural landscape, it produces special lakeshore and harborside conditions (Chicago); it can be fractured by ravines (Los Angeles) and protruding hillocks (Montreal); and the view of distant mountains (Seattle) inevitably introduces a picturesque element to the practical city. Grids are lifeless only when seen from the air. They assume a different bearing on the ground, where topography asserts itself as it does in Cincinnati, where the mechanical mating of grid and hills produces amazingly steep streets. Buildings on higher ground inevitably assume greater importance, as does the Cathedral of Saint John the Divine in Morningside Heights, seven miles north of City Hall and the old downtown in New York City. Even a gentle slope significantly modifies the experience of the simple grid as some streets climb hills and others run across the slope. In San Francisco the unusual combination of practical grid and dramatic topography has produced one of the most beautiful cities in the world.

Grids are usually homogeneous checkerboards, but not always. The 1811 gridiron plan of midtown Manhattan, for example, incorporates a clear hierarchy, with broad, short-block avenues for large buildings and narrow, long-block streets for smaller rowhouses. An extra-wide avenue like Park introduces yet another differentiation to the grid; so does the occasional open square like Gramercy Park, or the slanted slash of Broadway across the regular gridiron. Like the angled meeting of different grids in Atlanta, Seattle, and New Orleans, diagonal streets produce odd-shaped building plots and odd-shaped buildings. There is one American city whose grid could accurately be described as cosmic: Salt Lake City. What appears to be merely an unrelieved crisscrossing of streets is actually based on the "Plat of the City of Zion," devised by Joseph Smith in 1833 following what is said to have been a divine revelation.

The third type of urban model Lynch called "organic." As the name suggests, this is the city considered as a kind of organism: cohesive, balanced, indivisible. Medieval towns are organic—their layouts look natural rather than man-made. Streets vary in width, they are rarely straight, and they wind sinuously throughout the town. Many traditional Islamic cities likewise consist of a convoluted web of streets and dead-ending alleys. To the visitor who wanders away from the main town square, the Islamic city is perplexing. There are no simple axes, no vistas or replicated geometries. In fact, the labyrinth contains a carefully organized hierarchy of spaces, from public avenues to private, family compounds. A larger-scale example of an organic city is London, whose sprawling street layout, unlike that of Paris or Berlin, defies easy characterization. It is a result of centuries of addition, as different neighborhoods, or boroughs, gradually knitted together to form a whole. Most organic cities seem to have been planned around meandering pedestrian movement, or, as in the case of Los Angeles, around the meandering line of an electric railway. One exception is Venice. The city grew by the accretion of parts—islands—that were expanded and combined as need dictated; additional canals were built to provide access by watercraft.

Lynch describes three historical urban models. It's necessary to add a fourth, to reflect the momentous change that affected cities at the beginning of the twentieth century: the automobile city. The city planned for cars and trucks resembles the organic city, inasmuch as it is chiefly a pragmatic expression of personal mobility. Just as the medieval city enabled its inhabitants to walk easily from place to place, the automobile city enables people to drive. Since drivers move faster than pedestrians, however, the horizontal extent of the automobile city is vastly greater; it is spread out. A small medieval city could be traversed on foot in about fifteen minutes. A fifteen-minute drive at low speed, on the other hand, covers about five miles. The requirements of automobile movement also impose their own peculiar geometry, producing cities like Houston and Phoenix, whose gently curving freeways resemble arteries or rivers, or indeed, canals. The other difference in the automobile city is the presence of large numbers of vehicles. Buildings in cities have always needed coach houses and stables, but their number was limited by the high cost of owning and maintaining horses. The large number of privately owned cars, as well as the size of trucks and buses, has vastly increased the amount of land devoted to parking, an unproductive but crucial function in the automobile city.

Lynch's scheme describes what cities look like, but cities are also historical creations. The French historian Fernand Braudel has identified three distinctive stages in the early history of European towns: the open town, the closed town, and the subjugated town. According to him, the ancient Greek and Roman settlements were examples of open towns. The line between town and country—and between townsman and countryman—was not rigidly drawn, although citizenship itself was exclusive (even when democracy was introduced, not all free persons were citizens—not women, for example, nor many traders and craftsmen). This openness was reflected in the fact that Sparta never built town walls, and Athens did so only after the Persian invasions. Lewis Mumford used the term "open" in reference to the Pharaonic towns of ancient Egypt, which were also unwalled.

The open town was succeeded by the closed town, a classic example of which was the medieval walled town, or burg. The burg was closed in many senses: not only military and social, but economic and political as well. Legal distinctions as well as the imposing walls that surrounded all towns separated the townspeople, or burghers, from the serfs. It was true that "*Stadtluft macht frei*" (the town air makes you free), as a famous German saying went, but this freedom was not for all. It was severely circumscribed by the powerful ruling merchant families and the members of the fiercely monopolistic guilds. In some towns a countryman became a city man—that is, a citizen—only after ten years of residence, property ownership, and a local marriage, practices that still exist in parts of Switzerland. In the eighteenth century when the first suburbs began to grow outside the city walls, it was, among other things, as places where the so-called free crafts could escape the constraints of the traditional guilds. A different type of closed town was found in Russia (and in China): here it was only the compound of the rulers that was walled; outside the Kremlin or the Walled City, the ordinary people lived in a more or less suburban sprawl. This is undoubtedly why, as Braudel notes, Russian towns did not dominate the countryside as did their counterparts in Europe.

At the beginning of the sixteenth century, some European towns started to lose their independence and to come under the authority of the aristocracy. This is what Braudel calls the subjugated town. The Medicis, the German princes, Louis XIV, and the Hapsburg emperor controlled Florence, Munich, Paris, and Vienna, respectively. They built their grand palaces (the Nymphenburg, Versailles, Schönbrunn) on the outskirts of the walled cities and slowly but inexorably imposed their royal will on the town. By the Baroque period, this will was evidenced physically in huge urban construction projects: squares, avenues, promenades. But the major change was political: citizenship, which had originally meant allegiance to the town, was transformed into allegiance to the state, which eventually replaced the monarchy as the leading urban power.

This takes us up to the seventeenth century, but what of the modern city? The industrial city of the nineteenth century was more akin to Braudel's closed town of the Middle Ages. There were no walls and gates, to be sure, but the line between city and country was just as firm. A city was distinguished by industrial employment, access to power sources (steam, gas, and eventually, electricity), pollution, literacy, technological innovation, unemployment, social reform. The countryside had few of these things, and the character of rural life (with the exception of coal-mining communities) remained largely preindustrial. The postindustrial city of the late twentieth century, on the other hand, may be a throwback to the open town of antiquity. The physical distinction between the city and its surrounding territory—that is, between central cities and suburbs—is blurred; the legal definition of the city remains, but the reality of metropolitan life has become mobile and decentralized. Will history repeat itself, and will the open, postindustrial city be followed by the information-age city, dominated by the multinational corporations who are increasingly locating their headquarters in suburban areas? Will these suburban cities with their gated communities and security-conscious office parks be the model for a new kind of "subjugated" city?

Whatever future cities look like, they will still be cities. According to Braudel, "A town is always a town, wherever it is located, in time as well as in space." He goes on, "I do not mean that all towns are alike. But over and above their distinctive and original features, they all necessarily speak the same basic language: common to them all are the continuous dialogue with their rural surroundings, a prime necessity of everyday life; the supply of manpower, as indispensable as water to the mill; their self-consciousness—their desire to be distinguished from the others; their inevitable location at the centre of communications networks large and small; their relationship with their suburbs and with other cities." At the same time, Braudel does not lose sight of the fact that cities are always a reflection of the culture of a particular period. "Urban development," he writes, "does not happen of its own accord: it is not an endogenous phenomenon produced under a bell-jar. It is always the expression of a society which controls it from within, but also from without."

It's useful to keep both Lynch's and Braudel's ideas in mind when looking at our own cities and how they have developed. Lynch is right: there are only a certain number of ways that streets and buildings can be organized in space. Cities are man-made things, and because they are man-made, we can recognize a continuity of the ideas that went into their making. When I walk down a street in Philadelphia, I see many elements—streets, sidewalks, street corners, blocks of buildings—that were present in ancient Pompeii. Philadelphia and Pompeii are both gridded cities, so in that sense they represent a similar model. But we must see cities in their cultural and historical context. Philadelphia and Pompeii adopted the grid plan for different reasons and used it in different ways. Cities and towns, like customary dress and food, have always been local responses that incorporate local needs and local dreams. In order to understand our own cities—to understand why they are not "like Paris"—we need to examine our own urban past.

THREE

A New, Uncrowded World

TO DISCERN THE ROOTS OF THE DEVELOPMENT OF towns in the New World, one must distinguish between Hispanic, French, and English colonial urbanization. The sixteenth-century Spanish conquest of Mexico and Central and South America required an extensive administrative, military, and missionary network whose nodal points were towns: civil settlements for Spanish colonists (*pueblos*), fortified garrison towns (*presidios*), and mission towns, which were administered by the church and settled by Indian converts. The Spanish founded many settlements, and most eventually grew into large, well-known cities: inland towns like Guadalajara and Guatemala City, coastal ports like Veracruz and Panama City, island citadels like Havana and Santo Domingo, and, of course, Mexico City, the capital of the viceroyalty of New Spain. In the case of Mexico City, "founded" is not the right word, since there was already a large Aztec city on the site—Tenochtitlán. The Spanish towns were often prosperous, but with the exception of Mexico City, they remained small during the colonial period, since they contained little commercial activity. Their wealth came from exploiting the resources of the hinterland, chiefly silver, and to a lesser extent, from ranching and growing sugarcane (all activities based on an indigenous labor force).

Farther north, the first European settlements also depended on the exploitation of local resources—fur, in the case of New France, and tobacco and rice plantations in the Carolinas—but there was no attempt to urbanize the native population by establishing mission towns. This would in any case have been difficult, for there was no extant flourishing indigenous urban culture, and there were no real towns, certainly nothing on the scale of Tenochtitlán. The Algonquian tribes of the Northeast inhabited an area stretching from the Carolinas to Labrador, and practiced a mixture of hunting, fishing, and agriculture. Since the Algonquians were semi-nomadic, changing their place of dwelling according to the seasons, the wigwams of frames made out of bent saplings covered with bark were put up and taken down several times a year; only the bark covering and reed floor mats were reused. Although the small, informal groups of wigwams are sometimes termed villages, they are probably better described as temporary campsites.

The settlements of the people of the Iroquois Confederacy, the League of Five Nations, were more impressive. Formed during the seventeenth century, the league was a military and economic federation of the Seneca, Mohawk, Onondaga, Cayuga, and Oneida tribes that covered most of present-day New York State. The Iroquois called themselves "people of the longhouse," and communities were organized into clans, each occupying a communal structure, or longhouse. The largest longhouses were four hundred feet in length and housed more than two hundred persons. Iroquois towns, some as large as four thousand people, consisted of longhouses surrounded by tall palisades of sharpened logs with parapet walls from which the defenders could shoot arrows and throw projectiles. This gave the longhouse communities a resemblance to medieval fortified burgs; in fact they were sometimes described as castles by European observers. But Iroquois towns were surrounded by wilderness, not by feudal domains, and they were not primarily centers of manufacturing or trade but rather home bases for hunting and raiding parties. Drawings made by French explorers show the longhouses lined up side by side in rows in a fashion that looks like the functional layout of a modern mobile home park. These towns were impermanent and were rarely used for more than a decade or two. By then the adjacent tillable soil and sources of firewood and construction material were depleted; rubbish had piled up; and the houses had become infested with rats and fleas. The occupants abandoned their old dwellings to establish a new settlement nearby.

The native inhabitants of the southern coast followed a more stable, agricultural way of life and consequently built more permanent towns. Excavations in Florida, Louisiana, and Mississippi, as well as in Ohio and Missouri, have uncovered monumental earthworks that suggest the early presence of developed urban civilizations. The most impressive of these was the Mississippian culture, whose chief metropolis was the city of Cahokia, near present-day Saint Louis. It is estimated that at its peak in the twelfth century Cahokia was home to about 40,000 people, which would have made it about the same size as medieval Florence, although smaller than the largest city in Europe at the time,

Paris, which already numbered about 100,000 inhabitants. Florence and Paris in the Middle Ages were walled and extremely compact; Cahokia, by contrast, was a sprawling city that covered close to six square miles. It contained six ceremonial plazas and about a hundred earthen mounds analogous to the stone pyramids found in Aztec cities. The evidence of how ordinary people lived has long since disappeared, which suggests that houses were probably built of impermanent materials: wood posts supporting roofs covered in bark, or perhaps log cabins. The city appears not to have been fortified, except for a small ceremonial area in the center.

Cahokia is an exceptional case of a major urban development north of the Rio Grande. Despite its imperial trappings and unlike Tenochtitlán, it was not the seat of an empire, although it seems to have served as a religious and trading center for outlying villages and towns. The city-building Mississippian culture flourished several centuries before the arrival of the Europeans, and by the time that Hernando de Soto visited the region in 1539, the cities had disappeared. The layout of the small towns he described was informal, although important public buildings were sometimes located on raised mounds that recall Cahokia, and the towns were surrounded by wood palisades.

Another later town-building people was the Creek Confederacy, which included the Creek, Cherokee, Choctaw, and Chickasaw tribes and occupied a region that included northern Florida, the Carolinas, and Georgia. Creek towns were planned around a public center that included a ceremonial plaza, a large, swept ball court (for a ritual sport similar to field hockey), and a meeting structure (called the Square Ground); there were no mounds. William Bartram, a traveler who visited these towns in the late eighteenth century, recorded that houses were "placed with considerable regularity in streets or ranges," and his sketches show a layout that resembles a grid. The Creeks occupied such towns until the early nineteenth century, when they were evicted in the infamous deportation to Oklahoma known as the Trail of Tears.

The Southwest was the site of another urbanized Indian culture, the Anasazi, who built some extraordinary towns, the most famous of which are in Mesa Verde and Chaco Canyon. Mesa Verde, in southwestern Colorado, contains several spectacular cliff towns. The most famous is known as Cliff Palace and is tucked under an overhanging canyon wall. (The overhang actually shades the settlement from the summer sun, while permitting the sunlight to warm the stone walls during the cool winter.) There are no streets—people walked from one roof to another—and the square and circular rooms and towers are piled up like a child's blocks. Chaco Canyon is the site of nine so-called Great Houses, each a stepped-back communal structure of interlocking rooms, usually focused on a central plaza, which is likewise oriented to the sun. The urban form is extremely compact, almost like a very large horizontal apartment building with stepped-back terraces in front of each dwelling. Pueblo Bonito, which seems to have been the capital town of Chaco Canyon, rises to four stories at the rear. It is not clear if these structures were built for defensive reasons or whether they merely reflected a close-knit social organization. These small settlements, located roughly in the region where present-day Utah, Colorado, New Mexico, and Arizona meet, probably numbered fewer than 2,000 persons each, and were the centers of what archaeologists speculate was a successful regional trading and water management economy.

The Anasazi towns flourished between about 1100 and 1300, long before the arrival of the Spaniards, and so were unknown to the early European settlers except as ruins. The Anasazi culture collapsed abruptly in the late thirteenth century, whether as a result of drought or of decimation by aggressive invaders is unclear.

However, the Pueblo villages of the Anasazi's descendants—the Acoma, the Hopi, and the Zuni—have survived to the present day. The layouts of Taos and Santa Clara, both in New Mexico, do not exhibit the architectural refinement of the Great Houses, and the adobe buildings lack the technological sophistication of the beautiful stone architecture of Mesa Verde. But the pueblos of southwestern New Mexico do incorporate such subtle adaptation to their surrounding topography that some observers have likened their siting to that of the palace of Knossos in Crete and of ancient temples in Greece. The location of towns like Acoma, on the summit of a 375-foot-high mesa, is breathtaking. Whether such pueblos would have developed into larger towns or even cities will never be known, since their evolution was interrupted and finally brutally truncated by the arrival of the Spanish in the sixteenth century. Nevertheless, even in their ruined state, they are testimony to a vision well suited to the terrain and the climate.

Native American settlements, especially those of the Southwest, represent a different, non-Western urban model. "The architectural principle at work in these individual dwellings, therefore, is that of imitation of natural forms by human beings who seek thereby to fit themselves safely into nature's order," Vincent Scully writes. "When the resources of large populations made it possible to build monumental architectural forms of communal function and at the landscape's scale, exactly the same principle was brought to bear." If ever we are to consider an environmentally conscious architecture, these are buildings that merit intensive study. The lesson we might learn is of a way of building that makes little distinction between individual structures and the collective whole, just as it makes no sharp division between the man-made and the natural worlds.

To the early European settlers, however, with their desire to separate private from public property, these settlements were inappropriate models. They could not appreciate the subtle and sophisticated use of local materials and adaptation to local conditions. The more or less temporary towns of the Iroquois Confederacy, too, would have appeared crude and unimpressive to European eyes. At best, existing Indian encampments might influence the choice of a site for a new town, since a well-known gathering place was a useful location when the chief function of the European settlement was fur trading. Thus Montreal was built near the site of the abandoned Iroquois town of Hochelaga; Toronto (which means "the meeting place") replaced a French fort which itself had been situated on the site of an Indian summer camp; and Detroit was built across the river from a Huron village.* Just like the Iroquois towns that preceded them, the trading posts of the French colonists were fortified; in both cultures military considerations led to the choice of easily defensible locations like islands, hilltops, and clearings.

The oldest European town in the United States and Canada is Saint Augustine—originally San Agostín—in northern Florida, founded by the Spaniards on the site of a Timucua Indian village in 1565. San Agostín was a small garrison town—even after a hundred and fifty years its population was less than fifteen hundred—whose chief function was as a military outpost to protect the passage of Spanish ships carrying cargo through the Straits of Florida to and from Havana and Veracruz. The town, surrounded

*There are many city names derived from Indian words. However, only a few—Toronto, Chattanooga, Chicago, Milwaukee—are original place names; most, like Kansas City, Ottawa, Omaha, Cheyenne, Manhattan, Miami, Peoria, Sioux Falls, and Wichita, are the names of tribes. Nineteenth-century Americans, in particular, favored Indian names: New Amsterdam was renamed Buffalo, Commencement City became Tacoma.

by a wood palisade, was divided by narrow streets lined with walled gardens and small houses whose facades were interrupted by loggias and overhanging balconies. At one end was a small citadel that commanded the entrance to the harbor from the sea. The streets of San Agostín are laid out in a rectangular grid, and in the center there is a plaza faced by the main church and the governor's house. This sounds very much like the Laws of the Indies, with their insistence on gridded streets and a central square. But in fact the Laws were formulated eight years after the town was founded, which suggests that they only codified what was becoming to be standard planning practice. This charming town can still be visited today but it is largely a reconstruction, since San Agostín suffered periodic devastation: it was put to the torch first by Indians, later by Francis Drake in 1586; sacked by pirates; burned by Carolina colonists in 1702; and bombarded by the British navy in 1740. In 1763 the town was ceded to the British. Twenty years later it returned to Spanish hands, and in 1821 changed hands again when Florida became a part of the United States.

San Agostín was the first town built by the Spaniards north of the Rio Grande; the last, Sonoma, in California, was founded in 1835. In the two hundred and seventy intervening years many pueblos, presidios, and mission towns were built in the Southwest, along the Gulf Coast, and along the entire California coast. A few cities, like Sonoma, preserve traces of the regular gridded street layout and the large central plaza that characterized Hispanic urbanism, but in most cases, evidence of the settlements has disappeared. For despite the fact that many of these towns later became the basis for huge cities like Los Angeles, San Francisco, and San Diego, during the Spanish rule these were not impressive towns. Although the Laws of the Indies were more or less adhered to, the buildings were usually of poor quality, there was little local economic activity, and the population of these towns grew slowly. As the urban historian John W. Reps points out, "The North American settlements of the Spanish colonial empire were always frontier outposts far removed from the prosperity that characterized the cities at the heart of Spain's colonial enterprise in the Western Hemisphere." He adds, "Spanish colonial efforts rarely were regarded in the home country as more than marginal activities. Undermanned and underfinanced, the Spanish reach always exceeded its grasp, and the results were meager."

At the other end of the continent was the French colonial citadel of Quebec, which was founded by Samuel de Champlain in 1608 and became the capital of the French colony of New France. Quebec City is located on magnificent heights commanding the broad Saint Lawrence River. The city was made up of two parts. At the level of the river, against a rising cliff, was the so-called Lower Town, which contained the original settlement as well as boatyards, docks, and storehouses. The main city, including the citadel, the cathedral, the bishop's palace, as well as numerous religious buildings, was in the Upper Town, on the heights. Although the Lower Town was laid out on a more or less regular grid, the Upper Town grew uncontrolled and resembled a medieval "organic" plan, an impression heightened by the city wall that circled it on the landward side.

Farther up the Saint Lawrence River was the missionary outpost of Ville-Marie de Montréal. When Ville-Marie was founded in 1642, the population was only fifty; a hundred years later it had grown to four thousand, although that was probably not many more than had lived in the original Iroquois town that had preceded it. Like Quebec City, Montreal, as it was now called, was surrounded by defensive fortifications and remained so until the eighteenth century. The walls offered protection against attack by a variety of enemies: first the Iroquois, who were allied with the British and staged regular raids; later the British themselves, with whom the French were at war; and lastly, after New France passed into British hands, the Americans during the Revolutionary War and the War of 1812.

The walled towns of New France were different from the neat, gridded towns of New Spain. An engraving of Montreal made in 1760, when the population had grown to about five thousand, shows a lively landscape of closely packed house roofs and church and convent spires, all peeping out from behind a stone wall. The presence of the encircling fortifications gives the town a medieval air. Medieval, too, was the street layout. The shape of the walled town was roughly a long rectangle, divided lengthwise by two wide, main streets and crisscrossed at random angles by numerous narrower streets. There were several open spaces: a parade ground and a market square, a cemetery, and the gardens and orchards belonging to the five religious orders (Jesuits, Sulpicians, Recollets, Sisters of Notre-Dame, Sisters of Saint Joseph) headquartered inside the town. The residential plots were of different shapes and sizes, and like the streets, displayed little geometrical regularity. The effect was casual, almost haphazard. As in the Middle Ages, the houses of the poorer people were outside the walls, situated in what was called the faubourg (from the Old French *forsbourg*, meaning the town outside the wall); by 1765, almost half of the population of Montreal lived in these incipient suburbs.

New France was distinctly old-fashioned, almost medieval. Land was granted to prominent individuals who assumed the role and title of seigneur, together with the rights and privileges of a feudal lord. Equally old-fashioned was the city planning. Montreal's Place d'Armes was an unprepossessing open area of beaten earth, awkwardly flanked by the side wall of the parish church. A Parisian visiting Montreal in 1760 would not have been impressed by the latest civic improvement, the newly completed fortification (a fourteen-foot-high masonry wall, a ditch, and a glacis) that replaced an earlier wood stockade. By then, Paris's ramparts had long since been converted into tree-lined promenades and Louis XV was building the expansive Place de la Concorde. While in London, English aristocrats were turning their estates into upper-class residential developments like Leicester Square and Grosvenor Square, with grand houses facing a landscaped square, and in Friedrichstadt, a planned extension to Berlin, Friedrich Wilhelm I of Prussia had started to lay out a series of square, circular, and octagonal plazas, in Montreal, people huddled close together in little houses crowded behind the protective town walls.

There was a single short-lived example of innovative town planning in New France: Louisbourg, on Cape Breton Island. This fortress town was begun in 1712 and took twenty years and thirty million francs—a vast sum—to complete. The plan reflected the latest version of a French approach to building fortified towns that had been evolving since the middle of the seventeenth century. Louisbourg bears a close resemblance to the plan that the famous military engineer Sébastien Le Prestre de Vauban devised in 1704 for the fortified town of Neuf-Brisach, near Strasbourg. The perimeter of the town resembles a starburst and is made up of several layers of bastions linked by zigzagging walls. Inside the star shape, Vauban laid out a perfectly orthogonal grid of streets and square blocks, with a central open parade ground. Unlike Neuf-Brisach, however, and despite its incorporation of the latest in fortification technology, Louisbourg turned out to be militarily ineffective. It was captured twice: once by American colonists in 1745 and again by the British in 1758, who a few years later, in a fit of vindictive pique, razed it to the ground.

The French established a network of forts in the interior of the continent, as far west as Manitoba and as far south as Texas: Fort

Du Quesne (Pittsburgh), Fort Rosalie (Natchez), Fort Rouge (Winnipeg), Fort Nécessité (Uniontown, Pennsylvania), and many others. Some of these outposts, such as Fort Pontchartrain du Détroit, Saint Louis des Illinois (Saint Louis), and Louis de la Louisiane (Mobile), also included small towns. There was no French equivalent to the Laws of the Indies, but these foundations did follow a pattern: the towns were built beside rivers, they were fortified, and their plans, like that of Montreal, were more or less elongated and orthogonal. Mobile (1710) and Saint Louis (1762) were carefully gridded to accommodate future expansion, although neither settlement experienced much growth during French rule, each remaining a large village with only one or two hundred houses. Detroit (founded in 1701) was a walled settlement, a tiny version of Louisbourg, surrounded by farmsteads. Nothing remains of the original layout, however, for in 1805, after it passed into American hands, Detroit was destroyed by fire and was rebuilt according to a new plan.*

Generally, the French efforts at town building suffered from the same constraints as those of the Spanish: not enough support from the mother country, not enough immigration to promote rapid growth, and too much dispersal in the vast continent to allow towns to establish trade links with one another. The largest and most successful of the French river towns was New Orleans, whose construction began in 1722. This was to be the capital of the province of Louisiana, and its founder, Jean-Baptiste Le Moyne, adopted a similar plan to one that he had used a decade

*The new plan for Detroit was devised in 1807 by Judge Augustus Woodward, a friend of Jefferson. His novel proposal was based on a triangular system of land division that resembled a honeycomb, and combined elegance with utility. This experiment in city planning was short-lived and was abandoned in favor of a simple grid; only Grand Circus Park and Campus Martius remain today as reminders of the city that might have been.

earlier at Mobile, although at New Orleans there was no fort—the entire town was walled. The streets divided the town into regular square blocks, exactly fifty French *toises* (about 300 feet) on each side; the town measured eleven blocks long by four deep (later expanded to six deep). As in Mobile, the central block facing the river was a formal parade ground (today, Jackson Square) and the block behind it was reserved for institutional buildings, including, at the center, in the place of honor, the parish church.

The street layout of New Orleans has proved remarkably durable, although most of the architecture of the so-called French Quarter really dates from the Spanish period (1762–1801), when the wooden French buildings were destroyed in two calamitous fires and the town was rebuilt in brick. Under Spanish rule, New Orleans grew slowly, and it was only after the Louisiana Purchase in 1803 that the city began a period of steady urban expansion. Nevertheless, the plan put in place by Le Moyne proved to be an excellent model. When new districts, or faubourgs, were laid out, they included similarly proportioned blocks and central squares, but instead of simply extending the French grid, the American planners adjusted the angle of the new gridded areas to follow the curve of the Mississippi, which created interesting relationships between the different districts where the grids intersected. As the entire geometry shifted, the early inhabitants of New Orleans knew they were passing from one faubourg to another; arriving at the square they knew they were in the heart of the district.

The British colonies of North America grew more quickly than those of the French, and by the middle of the eighteenth century their combined population was more than twenty times larger than that of New France. The towns were bigger, too. In 1750, when the population of Quebec was about 8,000 and that of

Montreal less than 4,000, Boston's had already reached 15,000; Philadelphia and New York, 14,000; and Charleston, 12,000.

New York was founded in 1623—only fifteen years after Quebec—but by 1664, when the Dutch handed over what was then called New Amsterdam to the British, the walled town contained 10,000 persons. The influence of old Amsterdam was evident in the canal that led into the center of the town, the brick construction, and the gable-fronted houses; behind the houses were large garden plots and orchards. There was a fort and a governor's palace. The great expansion that transformed old Amsterdam from an essentially medieval town to a planned city of radiating streets and great concentric arcs of canals was begun in 1607, but it had no influence on the planning of New Amsterdam. New York continued to expand under British rule; the name was changed, but its street layout continued to be informal, at least until 1811, when the Commissioners' Plan divided the rest of Manhattan into a gridiron.

Nor was civic grandeur to be found in Boston, which was founded in 1630 and was the largest city in North America throughout the first half of the eighteenth century. Its planning, too, followed the organic model: winding, narrow streets, irregular plots, vaguely defined public spaces. Boston was located on a peninsula, protected by the invincible British navy on the sea and by Iroquois allies on the land. Like all the northern British colonial towns, it was not fortified. Nevertheless, its buildings, as one urban history puts it, belonged to the Middle Ages: the plain houses were built of timber frames infilled with rubble, brick, and stucco; their second stories overhung the cramped and winding streets.

The medieval similarity was more than superficial. Although there was no equivalent to the self-governing free towns of the Middle Ages, towns in the New World were far away from one another and were obliged to develop a similar self-suficiency with regard to trade. There was another similarity to the Middle Ages: relatively few people in the New World lived in towns. In 1700, North American urbanization was just beginning and only about 10 percent of the population was urbanized, a figure comparable to English urbanization at the beginning of the sixteenth century. European cities were passing from their closed phase to one of aristocratic control, but the isolated towns of the New World seemed to be a throwback to an earlier period.

The first colonial towns were on their own in terms of design. There were few contemporary European models for city builders to follow. All the great European cities—Paris, Vienna, Berlin, and Amsterdam—had grown from medieval roots; in the case of Rome and Naples, the roots went back to ancient times. After the sixteenth century, no large cities were founded in Europe, and the new towns that were built were usually Renaissance fortress-towns such as Vauban's Neuf-Brisach. Philippeville in Belgium, built in 1555, and Palmanova in Italy, designed in 1593, were both fortified towns, but their streets radiated from the central squares like the sun's rays. The unusual plans were chiefly dictated by the shape of the fortifications, as well as by their autocratic builders' interest in geometry. In any case, these towns were intended to remain small: the constraints of the surrounding walls and the lack of any real economic base guaranteed that they rarely grew to more than a few thousand people.

The influence of continental European town-planning theories was evident in the New World in the towns of the Laws of the Indies, and to a lesser extent in French settlements like Louisbourg and Detroit, but French and Spanish urban theories had little or no impact on the British colonies of North America. Moreover, there was no strong English tradition of formal town planning. English towns and cities remained unaffected by Renaissance planning concepts and continued to grow according to the old and well-established medieval patterns. This was partly the result of the emphasis that the wealthy English placed on the countryside, where they had their primary homes, and partly of an innate conservatism. This conservatism is apparent in the reconstruction of the City of London, much of which was destroyed by the Great Fire of 1666. English architects saw this as an opportunity to refashion the cramped medieval street layout. Some proposed perfectly regular square grids; others, like John Evelyn and Christopher Wren, devised plans that were obviously influenced by Continental ideas and incorporated Baroque devices like diagonal avenues and circular piazzas. These would have transformed the City into a version of sixteenth-century Rome, which was replanned by Sixtus V in 1585–90. Had one of these plans been adopted, it is likely that the history of American urbanism would have taken a different course. But when London was rebuilt in 1666, it largely followed the earlier medieval street layout, and although historians have speculated about the possible transatlantic influence of the unbuilt proposals, there is little evidence that these plans inspired city builders in the New World. There was one important influence of post–Great Fire London on the New World, however. Although the city was rebuilt as before, it was used differently: the business section, or the City, was separated from the surrounding residential districts. This novel idea probably played a role in the development of an important characteristic of later American cities: the commercial downtown.

The first generation of American towns—New York (founded in 1623), Boston (1630), Cambridge (1636), Providence (1638), Newport (1639), and Hartford (1640)—reflected the traditional English preference for informality and improvisation, and a casual approach to planning. The layouts of these towns followed one of three general patterns: angled and winding streets, as in Boston, resembling Lynch's organic model of a town that grows informally over a period of time; orthogonal and roughly gridlike plans with occasional open squares, like Cambridge and Hartford; and linear layouts, that is, towns organized along a main or "high" street, like Providence. Some towns combined two or more patterns. When villages grew into towns or towns into cities, the street pattern was simply expanded.

New Haven, founded in 1638, was an exception to this pragmatic approach. Here the plan resembled a ticktacktoe diagram: nine perfect squares, 825 feet on each side, with the central square a town green and the site of the market, meetinghouse, courthouse, school, and jail. This scheme is unusual not only because of its strict geometry (still visible today) but also because of its scale. A plan of New Haven, drawn in 1748, shows that houses formed an almost continuous frontage along the streets, and that the large square blocks, without lanes or intermediary streets, created extremely deep gardens in the rear. Thus although the plan appears urban, the density is what we would call suburban. The green itself is huge, larger than the maximum size dictated by the Laws of the Indies, and suggests a park rather than an urban square. The regularity of the plan (it may have been prepared in advance in England) could have been influenced by Vitruvian principles, as one historian has argued, but the effect on the ground is much more open—and much greener—than anything the ancient Roman architect would have designed. The farsighted decision to create such a generous town green is a mark of the ambition of New Haven's founders and makes the center of New Haven particularly appealing to this day. On the other hand, since the nine-square plan made no provision for future expansion of the town, as the population grew, the residential squares filled up and were further subdivided, losing much of their green character in the process.

Charleston (originally named Charles Town, in honor of Charles II), the capital of Carolina, was established on its present site in 1680, and became the largest city of the southern colonies and probably the richest city in all of British America. (Through its port flowed American rice to Europe and African slaves to America.) It was the only major fortified town built by the British in America, and remained walled until 1717. Charles Town was also the first British colonial town in America laid out on a grid. This was done specifically to "avoid the undecent and incommodious irregularities which other Inglish Collonies are fallen unto for want of any early care in laying out the Townes," wrote Maurice Mathews, a contemporary observer, who must have been thinking of the "irregularities" of New York and Boston. Charleston's street grid, not as geometrically perfect as that of New Orleans, which was planned almost fifty years later, was differentiated by two major streets crossing in a central square (built over by 1788). The site of the city, a point at the confluence of the Ashley and Cooper rivers, was particularly attractive and permitted a pleasant promenade along the water's edge. The width of the chief streets (60 feet), allowed room for tree planting, and the generous blocks (about 500 feet by 600 feet) produced a sense of breathing space that is still noticeable in this charming southern city.

After Charleston came a spate of gridded towns in Virginia: Yorktown, Tappahannock, and Marlborough, all laid out during the 1680s and all consisting of blocks crisscrossed by a simple street grid. Unlike Charleston, however, the blocks were small—in the case of Tappahannock and Marlborough, each block contained only four half-acre plots and measured 230 feet by 265 feet. There were advantages to such small blocks—all the houses were situated on corner plots—but these diagrammatic plans demonstrate little artistry. There is no public green as at New Haven, no river's edge promenade as at Charleston, and there are no special sites for civic buildings. This is surveying, rather than town planning; the chief virtue of this approach was simplicity and speed of execution, which is perhaps why, fifty years later, new Virginia towns like Fredericksburg and Alexandria were still being laid out this way.

Farther north, Annapolis experimented with a different sort of town plan. At the mouth of the Severn River on Chesapeake Bay, the town was founded in 1694 by Francis Nicholson, a governor of Maryland, who is believed to have devised the plan. Although Annapolis, which Nicholson designated the new capital of the colony, incorporated not much more than a hundred building plots, it was laid out like a miniature perfect city. Nicholson knew Paris and incorporated such Baroque planning devices as radial and diagonal streets and four public open spaces: two large circles, the larger one reserved for the statehouse and the smaller for the church, a market square, and a London-type residential square, which he called Bloomsbury Square. What is unusual is not only the provision of such a variety of public spaces but also, as in New Haven, their generous dimensions: the market square was 100 feet on each side, the residential square measured 350 feet on each side, the church circle about 300 feet in diameter, and the grand public circle, located on a slight rise, was more than 500 feet in diameter. Unlike the layouts of the earlier-established Virginia towns, the plan of Annapolis provided a variety of sizes and shapes of plots; there was even a group of twenty smaller plots on the outskirts of the town for tradesmen whose industrial activities might disturb the townspeople. The greatest benefit of Nicholson's plan was to provide for special locations for public buildings in the great circles, which create a useful balance to the relatively straightforward grid layout of the residential streets.

Such planning did not necessarily make Annapolis functionally more successful than other colonial towns, but the modern visitor—and thousands come yearly, merely to stroll in these charming surroundings—can only conclude that it is considerably more attractive. Annapolis has that rarest of urban qualities, a distinctive sense of place due in part to its setting on Chesapeake Bay, in part to the comfortable scale of its streets and buildings, and in part to Nicholson's sophisticated planning.

Annapolis had no precedent in the British colonies; indeed, this kind of Baroque town layout would not reappear in America for another hundred years, with L'Enfant's plan for Washington, D.C. It has been suggested that perhaps Nicholson knew of Wren's unrealized proposal for London, although it was almost thirty years old by then and, in any case, the scale of the two projects is quite dissimilar (the reconstruction of London involved about 500 acres, or three times the area of Annapolis). More than likely, just as many English gentlemen used their extensive libraries and foreign travel as the basis for designing country residences, Nicholson, who was largely self-taught, went one step further and designed an entire town. Annapolis was the work of an amateur, and it is easy to point out its shortcomings: some radial streets arrive at the circles at odd angles, there are occasional awkward intersections, and as so often happens in Baroque plans, the shapes of some of the building plots make design and construction difficult. But Nicholson was a gifted amateur, as evidenced by Annapolis today, which in large measure has fulfilled its planner's ambition.

Shortly after laying out Annapolis, Nicholson was appointed governor of Virginia and decided to move the capital from its swampy location at Jamestown to Middle Plantation, henceforth to be called Williamsburg. The same ambition and amplitude is visible in Williamsburg as in Annapolis, although the plan is quite different. In Williamsburg, Nicholson adhered to strictly orthogonal geometry, avoiding Annapolis's impractical wedge-shaped plots, caused by the intersection of many differently angled streets. Still, this was anything but a simple grid. The chief element of the plan was Duke of Gloucester Street (which in the eighteenth century was also called Main Street), ninety-nine feet wide and three-quarters of a mile long, with lines of catalpas trees separating the broad sidewalks from the thoroughfare. Today, the effect is less of a street than a long park. As in Annapolis, the houses along the street are built far apart on large garden plots (half an acre) and, as if that were not greenery enough, the lots are interrupted by shallow ravines left in their natural state.

The plan of Williamsburg was more than a two-dimensional document. Nicholson prepared an architectural code that dictated building lines and setbacks, required houses on Duke of Gloucester Street to be provided with fences, and also spelled out in detail the location and general configuration of the public buildings. As in Annapolis, public buildings were assigned important locations. The House of Burgesses was placed at one end of Duke of Gloucester Street, and the College of William and Mary at the other; at the midpoint of the street, it was intersected by a broad (210 feet wide) green, at the head of which stood the Governor's Palace. The civic buildings gain prominence from their advantageous positions and are always approached from a distance; the houses play a distinctly secondary role and define the edges of the main street. A small grid of residential streets continues behind Duke of Gloucester Street.

When I first visited Williamsburg, I was not struck by its strenuous "historical" character, despite the employees costumed in colonial garb and the carefully restored buildings, but rather by how familiar it seemed. Here were all the hallmarks of the American small town: the spatial liberality; the large plots and broad streets; the dependence on landscaping, especially large trees, which create a natural atmosphere in the very center of the town.

Main Street, in what would become a common American practice, is a mixture of commercial establishments and private homes, the houses standing free and surrounded by large gardens. In Williamsburg the American town was born, incorporating all the ingredients that would set it on a course independent of its European counterpart.

Williamsburg was intended to reach a population of about 2,000; like Annapolis, it was never meant to be a large town. The plan of Philadelphia, on the other hand, devised by William Penn and Thomas Holme in 1681–83, was intended to accommodate a very large city indeed. It measured two miles long and one mile across, about the same size as contemporary London or Paris (it took a hundred years to fill out this immense area). The rectangle lay almost exactly on an east-west axis and stretched between two rivers, the Delaware and the Schuylkill. Philadelphia was a city of orthogonal streets, but unlike Alexandria or New Orleans, it was not a repetitive grid but a finite composition. The city was divided in four by two intersecting main streets, and at the center of each quarter was a square. The grid was not exactly square (the blocks were 425 by 675 feet and 425 by 500 feet); the majority of the plots fronted on the east-west streets that traversed the city. Rationalism governed the organization of the city, including two novelties that would become an American habit: streets named after trees, and numbered streets (an idea Penn may have derived from Amsterdam, which was the first European city to have numbered houses).

It was a generous plan. The two main streets—Market and Broad—were one hundred feet wide (by comparison, Montreal's main streets, laid out at roughly the same date, were only thirty feet wide, and no street in New Orleans exceeded sixty feet). At the intersection of Market and Broad was a ten-acre park; the four squares were each eight acres. The straight streets were lined with trees, and the smallest plot was half an acre. If today the four scattered squares seem insufficient for a city of this scale, it is because Penn's vision was of an entire city as a garden. "Let every house be placed, if the person pleases, in the middle of its plat," he specified to his surveyors, "as to the breadth way of it, that so there may be ground on each side for gardens or orchards, or fields, that it may be a green country town, which will never be burnt, and always be wholesome." This spread-out and expansive urban vision would have made Philadelphia unlike any city then known in England, or indeed, anywhere in Europe.

Penn, who once said of his creation that "The Improvement of the place is best measur'd by the advance of Value upon every man's Lot," was not innocent of the speculative nature of town building, but he seriously miscalculated the economic forces that came to bear on his endeavor. The original plan showed a variety of building plot sizes: the larger plots on Market Street, and the smaller on the narrower streets. But the true commercial center of gravity of the town was neither along Market Street nor at the intersection of the two avenues, which was nothing more than a crossroads in the forest. It was on the banks of the Delaware River, which was then the chief transportation route. This is where the city began to grow. The side of Front Street facing the river, which was to have been left open to create a pleasant esplanade, was soon crowded by warehouses of merchants who wanted to be as close to the river as possible. Most dramatically, instead of implementing Penn's idea of detached houses surrounded by gardens, the practical Quakers subdivided the generous building lots into narrow slivers and filled them in with rowhouses. As land values rose, they cut narrow lanes through the back gardens and crammed in rental units: the tiny three-story townhouses (often no more than one room per floor) called Trinity houses. Brick, not foliage, became the defining element of Philadelphia.

It took only two decades for commerce and cupidity to compromise Penn's plans. Penn had intended that important public buildings would surround the main central square, but because the real center was the commercial waterfront, that was where the public buildings were built. The State House (now Independence Hall) for the province of Pennsylvania was located on Chestnut Street—one of the narrow streets, not one of the broad avenues—and it faced a row of small houses, not a square; the hospital, the Quaker meetinghouse, and the many churches were likewise scattered throughout the city without being given favorable locations. This was a common situation in gridded towns like Alexandria or Yorktown, where similar plots were allocated to public and private buildings. A citizen of Philadelphia in 1750 walked down streets along which commercial, residential, and institutional buildings stood side by side, none preeminent over its neighbor. When the land around the squares was finally occupied, it was by private residences, not public buildings. (The main square did become the site of a new city hall, but the building, completed in 1901, was crudely located within—rather than facing—the square.)

Penn's original plan was thwarted by the dulling impact of land speculation and commerce and by the dynamics of growth. It was one thing for aristocrats and military engineers to lay out perfect little garrison towns in Europe, and quite another for a British proprietor, whose powers were severely limited, to attempt to do so in the wilderness of Pennsylvania. Moreover, Penn faced something that didn't exist in Europe—brisk immigration. Many American towns grew quickly, but the rate of Philadelphia's expansion was extreme. Attracted by the promise of prosperity and civic and religious tolerance (not for nothing was this called the

City of Brotherly Love), which Penn actively advertised throughout Europe, immigrants flowed to the city from Great Britain, Ireland, Germany, Holland, and Scandinavia. Philadelphia grew quickly: in 1684, only a year after the town was officially founded, there were already 600 houses; in 1698 there were 2,000; in 1750 the city had attained a population of about 20,000; and by 1800, with a population of 41,000, it surpassed New York as the largest city in the United States.

Philadelphia did not grow according to Penn's vision, but it was still an impressive accomplishment. A young Bostonian visiting the city in 1773 wrote: "The streets of Philadelphia intersect each other at right angles; and it is probably the most regular, best laid out city in the world." So it must have seemed to many, and the prosperous city became a model for new towns around the country. In some situations, as in the case of Raleigh, North Carolina, or Tallahassee, Florida, the five-square plan was replicated; in others, it was simply the idea of an open square in the middle of a grid that was followed. The original plan for Philadelphia was almost certainly an influence on a remarkable group of towns built in the 1730s in Georgia. The towns of Savannah, Ebenezer, and New Darien were the work of General James Oglethorpe, perhaps the most gifted of the colonial city planners. Oglethorpe actively promoted the idea of the new colony of Georgia, and he accompanied the first colonists and personally supervised the laying out of the new towns. Their ordered, rational urbanism recalls Roman camps and reflected his military background, but their political organization, much more sophisticated than anything that Nicholson or Penn imagined, reflected his practical experience as a member of the House of Commons and as an active social reformer.

Savannah, begun in 1733, was the largest town, and the model for the other two. The town was divided into wards—neighborhoods—of forty households. At the center of each ward was a large public square, approximately 300 feet by 300 feet; four lots on the opposite sides of the square were set aside for institutional and commercial uses (church, school, stores). The building plots were 60 feet wide and 90 feet deep (about the size of a typical suburban plot in the 1960s, and much smaller than the half-acre plots that were typical in most colonial cities). Unlike those in Charleston or Philadelphia, the blocks were shallow, only two hundred feet deep, and they were bisected by alleys. Alleys had been used in Europe since the Middle Ages, but they generally had extremely small houses (for poor people) facing them, a pattern that was continued in Philadelphia. The alleys in Savannah were not designed for dwellings; they were intended only to provide access to the rear of the houses for service deliveries. Service alleys were not a common feature of colonial towns—they do not appear in French or Spanish plans at all—and Savannah probably represents their first use in America.

Although alleys were incorporated into the layouts of all the new towns of the Georgia colony, it was some time before they were used elsewhere. Ebenezer Zane's 1799 plan for Zanesville, Ohio, did include service alleys, and a few years later they were part of the plan for another Ohio river town, Columbus. Woodward's 1807 plan for Detroit also included alleys, and they did become a standard feature of later nineteenth-century plans for cities such as Indianapolis, Cleveland, and Chicago. The service alley is a useful urban device that has almost disappeared from the modern planner's lexicon. It was originally used for the delivery of heating and cooking fuel as well as for the collection of night soil, and was later adapted for such diverse functions as garbage collection and automobile parking.

Savannah's plan was not a simple grid like that of Alexandria, nor a picturesque approach to town building, like Annapolis or

Williamsburg, nor a finite composition like Philadelphia; the ward blocks of Savannah comprised a fine-grained system that could be incrementally extended, ward by ward, as the city grew. This sounds mechanical, but it was tempered by many subtle devices. For one thing, the grid was not homogeneous: a historic central axis, Bull Street, led inland from the river and passed through a series of squares to terminate in Forsyth Place, a much larger square measuring 700 feet on each side. Moreover, the squares differed in character, depending on the types of public buildings that fronted them: the hospital on Forsyth Square, the barracks on Madison Square, the market on Ellis Square. Some squares were strictly residential. As the town grew, wide, tree-lined boulevards parallel to the river were introduced at intervals.

The resident of Savannah could read the social structure of his city in the location of the fashionable houses lining the squares, separated from more modest dwellings on the side streets. Like Charleston, Savannah reflected a southern sense of gentility and refinement that was absent in many of the pragmatic northern gridded layouts. The chief streets linked the leafy squares, although they did not traverse them; vehicular traffic occurred on the secondary streets between the wards. Built almost two centuries before automobiles became commonplace in American cities, Savannah incorporated a carefully ordered traffic system of tree-lined boulevards, through-traffic streets, neighborhood streets, and back lanes. Oglethorpe's farsighted plan proved enduring. Savannah started with four wards; two years later there were six; by 1790, eight; in 1801, thirteen; and fifty years later there were twenty-six wards. This pattern of growth lasted until the Civil War.

In Williamsburg, Philadelphia, and Savannah, there is already a clear expression of what made American towns different. In the

New World real estate was cheap, population was sparse, there was plenty of empty land, and colonial town builders took advantage of these conditions to spread out. There were also practical considerations. Fire, for one: anyone, like William Penn, building a city after 1666—the year of London's calamitous Great Fire—could hardly ignore the advantages of keeping buildings well apart. Food production, for another: Williamsburg was surrounded by forests, not tended fields, and the land provided for gardens was for vegetables, not flowers, since unlike European towns, New World towns, at least at first, could not count on the surrounding countryside for food. This gave American towns an independence of spirit, but also reinforced the general assumption that urban self-sufficiency was the normal state of affairs. This was fine in good times, but proved to be a problem when cities encountered difficulties, not always of their own making. This attitude persists today; whether it relates to immigration, poverty, or industrial unemployment, cities are expected to solve their problems themselves.

Looking at the broad streets and ample public squares of American towns, it is obvious that there was also an enjoyment of open space for its own sake. According to Lukacs, it is part of the American character to be stingy with time but spendthrift about space. Whence came this profligacy? Was it the open, apparently limitless land itself? Was it a reaction to the generally crowded conditions of towns and cities in Europe? Or will people always seek elbow room and spread themselves out? Whatever the reason—probably a combination of all three—spaciousness in the towns of the New World became a habit almost immediately. Baron Christopher von Graffenried, who founded the town of New Bern in Carolina in 1710, wrote that "Since in America they do not like to live crowded, in order to enjoy a purer air, I accordingly ordered the streets to be very broad and the houses well separated one from the other." The baron was Swiss, but his intuition about his adopted land was absolutely correct: the spread-out towns of the New World were not simply functional products; this was the way people *wanted* to live.

The common desire for openness that Graffenried observed was easily achievable because American cities lacked walls. This circumstance had several important consequences. It meant that the definition of exactly what was city and what was not—and consequently also of who exactly was a city dweller—was inexact, or at least blurred. There was no American equivalent of the medieval tradition of exclusive urban citizenship, in which the privileges of town life were jealously guarded, or of the customs boundaries that most European cities maintained well into the nineteenth century. City walls created inflexible limits, but the edges of American cities were easily movable: what was wilderness one day could be suburb the next, and what was suburb one decade might be city the next. This sense of infinite possibilities and of rapid and continual change became a hallmark of the North American city (and it did so well before the automobile).

The need to build cities quickly and to provide for almost continual growth led to a reliance on grid planning, a type of planning that would characterize city building throughout the New World. Grids were a convenient way to lay out plots for future sale, an important consideration in all the new towns that depended on immigration for their economic well-being. Rectangular plots were easy to build on, could be combined to form different-sized parcels, and could accommodate different uses; the first towns were not zoned according to different functions, as cities are today, but were, in the jargon of the planner, mixed use. Mixed, too, was the community that they contained, for the American grid also had a philosophic dimension that is not immediately apparent.

Colonial America was not, of course, a democracy, but prerevolutionary towns did incorporate traits that can be called democratic. The degree of religious tolerance, for example, was unusual. In Charleston the established religion was the Anglican Church, but other Protestants, including Baptists, Quakers, French Huguenots, and various Dissenters, all had their own places of worship; so did Jews, who established a congregation in 1749, and forty-three years later built the largest synagogue in the United States. Although the official nature of the Church of England was recognized by the naming of Church Street (on which the Anglican Saint Philip's was located), the sites of the different houses of worship were really comparable. Charleston's openness reflected its merchant founders' laissez-faire attitude and an easygoing English Restoration tolerance that also extended to social behavior (prostitution and gambling were tolerated). Philadelphia's tolerance had its roots in Penn's experience of religious persecution in England, and the greater measure of privileges and powers that were accorded to individual colonists was grounded in his own idealism. A 1762 map of the city shows meetinghouses for Quakers, Moravians, Anabaptists, and Presbyterians; churches for Anglicans, Lutherans, and Calvinists; and a "Popish Chapel."

These were secular and diverse cities in which there was a place for all. They did not require a single focus like the cathedral square or the royal precinct of the European town; it would have been difficult to make a single, grand urban gesture that reflected and incorporated such a wide variety of beliefs. The anonymous American grid was not chosen for military convenience, as in the ancient world, or bureaucratic standardization, as in the Laws of the Indies. It was initially adopted for easy and rapid real estate development, but it also turned out to be an ideal accommodating device for a more tolerant society.

Seventeenth-century grid planning did incorporate a new type of urban space for which there was no contemporary European precedent: the broad, tree-lined residential street. This emphasis on trees was distinctive, and was epitomized by the characteristic American habit (popularized, if not invented, by William Penn) of naming streets after trees. Surrounded by nature, American town builders reacted not by emphasizing the contrast between the natural and the man-made, but by incorporating natural elements in the town as much as possible, whether as green squares, tree-lined streets, or ample gardens. There were practical reasons for this interest in greenery. The summers of the eastern seaboard of North America were extremely hot and humid, more so than those of northern Europe, first home to most of the early immigrants. Spacing houses far apart and planting large trees for shade created a more comfortable town. The desire for cooling greenery continued in the nineteenth century in enormous undertakings to build large urban parks (New York's Central Park, Montreal's Mount Royal Park) and to create urban lakes (Minneapolis, Denver, Seattle), urban wilderness areas (Philadelphia, Toronto), and urban lakeside recreation areas (Chicago). It is also part of the motivation that produced nineteenth-century garden suburbs. In some way this "naturalization" of the city represents an unconscious move away from the man-made and toward the natural—that is, away from Europe and toward the American Indian urban model, in which architecture was subordinated to the landscape.

The most important architectural element of these leafy colonial towns was not a royal palace or a cathedral or even the statehouse; it was, rather, the humble individual abode. According to the American architect Jaquelin Robertson, the colonial urban vision was of "an idealized, even mythic, domesticity, with the individual house not only as the center of urban life, but as the city's most representative secular temple." To say that houses were secular temples is going too far, but Robertson has a point: these towns are, first of all, a celebration of the house. This celebration is apparent in the way residences stand side by side with civic monuments on New England town greens, or the way that in Charleston, as in Savannah, the houses, rather than public buildings, occupy center stage. It is also visible in the hundreds of small-town Elm Streets, with their canopies of trees (often, sadly, no longer elms), their green borders of front yards, and their porch-fronted houses.

This domestic ideal had its origin not in the New World but in the old. The establishment of Annapolis, Williamsburg, Philadelphia, and Savannah corresponds roughly to the period when the cult of the house became an established part of British—and hence Anglo-American—culture. The chief expression of this cult was the British (and Dutch) preference for owning individual houses. The situation on the rest of the Continent was different; in Paris, Naples, and Vienna, the bourgeoisie were likely to occupy apartments in multistory buildings. The relationship between dwelling and street was different, too. The front door of the Anglo-Dutch house faced the street directly, whereas one entered the French or Italian apartment house via an inner, private courtyard. Thus, the street in front of the private house acquired some of that privacy; the street in front of the apartment building was purely public.* This produced two distinctly different types of cities: the Continental model, dense, communal, and oriented to life in the square and in the street; and the Anglo-Dutch model, more spread out, more private, and socially focused on the family house. Some historians have speculated that the roots of this difference may be religious: in Catholic cities, traditional, extended families lasted longer and people became used to living in buildings that accom-

*In Holland, the stoop outside the front door is maintained by the householder, just as in many American towns, home owners are responsible for cleaning the sidewalk in front of their houses.

modated several generations, whereas in Protestant countries, like Holland and England, the nuclear family developed earlier, and with it the ideal of living in private, single-family homes.

The Anglo-Dutch ideal of domesticity was adopted in colonial America, and consequently, American towns, like English towns, were made up mainly of houses containing single families rather than of buildings shared by several households. In London, however, only a few rich people lived in their own houses; in America, real estate was cheap and ordinary people could afford to be property owners. Another difference was that in London and Amsterdam, houses, even houses of the wealthy, were usually built with common walls; in America, people could spread out. The American idea that cities could be made almost entirely of freestanding private houses with their own gardens was an original notion, at least in Western culture.* It was a powerful cultural ideal that would later create all sorts of difficulties as urban areas spread ever more widely to accommodate this desire, but it was an ideal that, against many odds, would never be completely abandoned.

*Cities composed of private houses with gardens were not unknown elsewhere. Traditional African cities consisted of houses surrounded by agricultural plots, and Chinese and Japanese cities were made up of one- and two-story houses with walled gardens.

FOUR

A Frenchman in New York

On May 9, 1831, Alexis de Tocqueville and his friend and traveling companion, Gustave-Auguste de Beaumont de la Bonninière, disembarked from the sailing ship that had brought them from France to the New World. The town in which they landed—Newport, Rhode Island—contained several notable public buildings: the State House at the head of Washington Square, a synagogue, the Redwood Library, and Trinity Church, with its graceful spire. But it was the tiny, toylike rowhouses along the narrow streets climbing the hill behind the long wharf at the water's edge that made the strongest impression on Tocqueville. "We went to see the town," he wrote in a letter to his mother, "which seemed to us very attractive. It's true we weren't difficult. [It had taken thirty-seven days to make the trip from Le Havre, and a severe storm had forced them away from their original destination, New York.] It's a collection of small houses, the size of chicken coops, but distinguished by a cleanness that is a pleasure to see and that we have no conception of in France. Beyond that, the inhabitants differ but little superficially from the French."

When the two young Frenchmen arrived—Tocqueville was twenty-five, Beaumont three years older—Newport was, in a sense, between roles. No longer a commercial powerhouse, it was still one of the two capitals of Rhode Island, with an architectural heritage that announced its earlier prosperity. Newport had been established in 1639. Its founders, a group of religious freethinkers driven out of the Massachusetts Bay Colony, picked a propitious site. Thanks to its well-protected harbor and advantageous location at the head of Narragansett Bay, the small settlement grew into a major colonial port and, by the middle of the eighteenth century, was handling more international cargo than New York. Newport shipped rum to Africa, where it was exchanged for slaves, who were transported to Barbados and traded for sugar, which in turn was brought back to Newport to be made into rum. This profitable triangular commerce was disrupted by the Revolutionary War, during which the town spent five years under the occupation of the English and then the French. Although it never again recovered its commercial preeminence, Newport did not fade into obscurity. During the late 1800s and early 1900s it became a fashionable summer and autumn resort for the New York rich, after World War II it was a navy port, and today it continues as a summer resort and a destination for tourists.

Tocqueville and Beaumont were in the United States as representatives of the French minister of the interior; their official purpose was to visit prisons and penitentiaries in order to make a study of reforms in the American penal system. That, at least, was the project that the two lowly *juges-auditeurs* (assistant magistrates) at Versailles had proposed to their government, and the idea was accepted, although evidently not with great enthusiasm, as most of the travel expenses were borne by the young men's families. But Beaumont and Tocqueville had grander ambitions than merely the study of prisons. They planned to use the opportunity of visiting the United States to write a book together. Perhaps Tocqueville was influenced by his distant relative, Chateaubriand, who had earlier written *Voyage en Amérique.* France had just undergone the Revolution of July 1830, which expelled Charles X, the last of the Bourbon kings, and installed Louis-Philippe (the Citizen King) on the throne as a sort of constitutional monarch. The two young Frenchmen hoped that a book on the world's only mass democracy would attract readers and make their fortunes.

And so it did, although their joint writing project foundered and each wrote separately (they nevertheless remained lifelong friends). Beaumont published a well-received abolitionist novel, *Marie, ou l'esclavage aux Etats-Unis (Marie, or Slavery in the United States*); and Tocqueville pursued the original project. The first volume of *De la démocratie en Amérique* (as the title suggests, his main subject was democracy rather than the United States) appeared four years after his return to France (the second volume was published in 1840). The book (that is, the first volume) was a popular success, printed in thirteen French editions during the author's lifetime. With honesty and intelligence, Tocqueville described the effects of Jacksonian democracy not only on political institutions but also, especially in the second volume, on everyday life, on the family, on social customs, on public and private behavior, and on literature and the arts. *Democracy in America* established his reputation in England, where John Stuart Mill wrote a favorable review in the *London and Westminster Review*, and in Europe. Tocqueville went on to a political career, was elected to the Chamber of Deputies, wrote the constitution of the Second Republic, served briefly as minister of foreign affairs, and resigned because of Louis-Napoléon (later Napoléon III). As a result of his public protest following the latter's coup d'état of 1851, Tocqueville was briefly imprisoned, but unlike his illustrious great-grandfather, Malesherbes, who was guillotined during the Revolution, Tocqueville was set free in a few days. Withdrawing from public life, he spent his last eight years living on his ancestral estate in Normandy writing a history of the French Revolution; he died at the relatively young age of fifty-four. He traveled widely during his life, and although he had many American correspondents he never returned to America.

Tocqueville and Beaumont spent slightly less than nine months in North America. Their travels consisted of two major swings. On the first, they went from New York by steamboat up the Hudson to Albany, by stagecoach to Buffalo, a stop at Niagara Falls, and then by water as far west as Michigan, in what was then called the Northwest Territory; then after a side trip to Montreal and Quebec City, they visited Boston and returned to New York, traveling through Massachusetts and Connecticut. This journey lasted about four months. The second trip, slightly shorter, took them to Philadelphia, Pittsburgh, down the Ohio Valley to Cincinnati and Memphis, on the Mississippi River to New Orleans, overland to Norfolk, Virginia, and up to the capital, Washington.

Armed with official letters of introduction, they dutifully visited penal establishments such as Philadelphia's brand-new Eastern State Penitentiary, where all prisoners were kept in round-the-clock solitary confinement, and the New York state penitentiaries at Auburn and Sing-Sing, where some common activities were allowed but all speech was forbidden. Tocqueville, who spoke English well (and later married an Englishwoman), interviewed people in all walks of life—government officials, politicians, businessmen, farmers, trappers, and Indians. He also met such notables as Daniel Webster, Sam Houston, the recently defeated President John Quincy Adams, and Charles Carroll, the last surviving signer of the Declaration of Independence. The young Frenchman had a wide-ranging intellect, a keen sense of observation, and a journalist's curiosity. Consequently, one can pick almost any subject—religion, education, slavery—and find that Tocqueville had something interesting to say about it.

Tocqueville filled fourteen notebooks during his travels, and it is these, as well as his letters, that are the best source for his opinions of American cities and towns. Generally, he admired small towns. Traveling through Massachusetts, he writes: "Almost all the houses are charming (especially in the villages), and there prevails a height of cleanliness which is something astonishing."* Tocqueville considered the New England small town to be an exemplary democratic institution, since it involved a large number of citizens in managing their own affairs; he called the town "the ultimate *individual* [emphasis in original] in the American system." He was also astute enough to note that the political independence of these small towns lay in what he called their municipal spirit. "Americans love their towns," he wrote, "for much the same reasons that highlanders love their mountains. In both cases the native land has emphatic and peculiar features; it has more pronounced physiognomy than is found elsewhere."

At first glance, these charming and picturesque towns seem more like the products of happy accidents than achievements of

*The cleanliness of towns that Tocqueville refers to several times was probably chiefly due to large lots and wide streets, something that most European towns lacked.

urban planning. The eminent urban historian John Reps agrees. Discussing Woodstock, Vermont, which was founded in 1768 and is similar in layout to the towns that Tocqueville visited, Reps concludes that there is no hard evidence that the town was built according to a predetermined plan. Its layout was characterized by curved and doglegged streets that seem to follow no regular geometry; in fact, there was only one intersection that formed a ninety-degree angle. There were no rectangular blocks in the conventional sense; none of the streets were even parallel. At its heart was a park or green. The shape of the green was roughly oval, with a sort of prow at one end. According to local tradition, the green represents the main deck of a ship once commanded by one of the town fathers. A charming story about a charming place, but surely it is no more than that? Surely, the shape of the green, like the rambling layout of the streets, was no more than chance? Reps appears to think so, but thoughtfully adds: "The visual satisfaction one discovers there is no accident. . . . The plan alone cannot convey the pervading qualities of fitness, serenity, and congruity one encounters on the spot."

A visit to Woodstock bears out Reps's observation: topography, views of the surrounding landscape, and shifting prospects do seem to have been taken into account by the builders of the town. The streets provide interesting views of buildings. Nothing is centered or quite lined up, but this does not produce visual confusion. Is all this accidental? The overall plan seems to have been dictated by the site: a narrow, flat valley hemmed in by the sweeping curve of the Ottauqueechy River on one side and a small creek on the other. The green was laid out lengthwise on the narrow peninsula between the river and the creek, allowing for many plots to have rear gardens running down to the riverbank. At each end of the green, two streets fan out at an acute angle. The town has a small extension, a sort of suburb, across the river, which is spanned by a covered bridge approached from one side of the green. Beyond the extension was the line of the Rutland and Woodstock Railroad, an important ingredient to the growth of the town.

The builders of Woodstock were aware that important buildings needed important sites. The Episcopalian church is at the head of the green, the Methodist farther down, and the Congregationalist church artfully closes the vista of Pleasant Street where it dead-ends into Elm Street. Two lesser churches, the Universalist and the Church of Christ, occupy lesser sites. The pride of place, on the green, is shared by private homes on one side, and the courthouse and the Eagle Hotel on the other. Stores, banks, the post office, and other businesses are located on two streets adjacent to but not actually on the green. This is a subtle sort of urban design, but it is design, design that proceeds not from a predetermined master plan, but from the process of building itself. A rough framework is established, with individual builders adapting as they come along. If Parisian planning in the grand manner can be likened to carefully scored symphonic music, the New England town is like jazz. Admittedly, it's a very restrained jazz—pianist Bill Evans, say, not Fats Waller. But like jazz, it involves improvisation, and as in jazz, this does not mean that the result is accidental or that there are no rules.

Tocqueville considered the New England town an exemplary democratic institution. Yet the visual impact of a town like Woodstock suggests a very different urban response to democracy than our own. Woodstock grew according to a set of rules—not all written down, perhaps, but nevertheless widely understood. For example, buildings were erected on a line located close to the street, either along the sidewalk, in the case of commercial buildings, or ten or fifteen feet behind it, in the case of houses. It is this proximity that defines the streets in such a pleasant way. That is why the Woodstock Inn, which replaced the Eagle Hotel but relocated the main building some distance back from the street, is so disturbing. Even though the parking lot in front of the building is attractively landscaped, the effect of the empty space on the street is deadening—it has broken one of the key rules. Another rule involved the shape of the plots, which were narrow and deep. This meant that buildings, too, were narrow and deep; a larger house extended farther back but kept roughly the same frontage as its more modest neighbor. Only the most important public buildings, like the churches or the courthouse, were meant to be experienced as freestanding "objects." The public library, a stone building of the late 1800s in a robust, neo-Romanesque style, successfully followed this rule. The commercial buildings, on the other hand, were built side by side and were meant to be experienced as a continuous series of fronts.

Another rule, which is less obvious and was certainly unwritten, was that as buildings were added and the overall composition enlarged, builders were expected to take these changes into account. The intersection of Elm and Central streets, for example, acquired a special character, with commercial blocks rather than freestanding structures. This development left the green largely unaffected and still provides an interesting double focus between the busy shopping area and the quiet park. An accident? Perhaps. But if this is considered in terms of jazz, each solo player in succession built on what came before, added his own interpretation, and passed on the altered piece to the next soloist.

Here is another aspect of Woodstock that lends itself to the musical analogy. In a classical symphony orchestra, the musicians are placed in discrete groups: strings over here, woodwinds over there, violins in the front, brass in the back. In jazz, the instruments are more or less mixed up, and the musicians, at least those with portable instruments, have no predetermined spots and are free to walk around; what is important is that they stay close enough together for eye contact. From an extant map of the town as it was in 1869, one can tell that apart from the concentration of the commercial blocks, functional zoning didn't exist in Woodstock. There were a few exceptions: the gasworks and the slaughterhouse were kept well back from the street; the wool mill was on the outskirts of the town and drew power from the river; but on the whole, buildings with different functions sat—and still sit today—side by side on the same streets. We live in a period when it is felt that streets—indeed, entire neighborhoods—must be either exclusively residential or exclusively commercial or industrial. (Manhattan and central Paris are exceptions to this rule.) It's worth noting that Elm Street, arguably Woodstock's toniest residential street, contained not only houses but also a little office block, the post office, a livery stable, a dry goods store, the probate office, and a church. All this on a street that is about a thousand feet long. Since the houses belonged to the town's most prominent citizens, chiefly doctors and lawyers, the mixture of functions must not have been considered a drawback, nor, indeed, is it today. Instead, it provides variety and vitality to the town, a vitality that is often absent in modern single-use neighborhoods.

The 1869 map of Woodstock shows a proposed street drawn in dotted lines at the south end of town. Now this cannot be called a historical accident or an improvised street or a donkey track—it is clearly a planned street. But it is neither parallel to adjacent South Street nor even perfectly straight. Since the proposed street cuts through several properties in an awkward way, its imperfect course does not appear to have been governed by legal constraints, nor can its slight irregularity be explained by topography. It is the way it is because that is the way its makers wanted it to be. One can only surmise that the people who built these towns liked slightly twisted, angled streets, or it might be more accurate to say that they dislike geometrical regularity in city planning.*

There are not more than 250 houses on the 1869 map of Woodstock, a reminder that during most of the nineteenth century New England towns remained small. They rarely had more than two thousand residents, which undoubtedly facilitated the democratic government that Tocqueville so admired. These were communities in the Aristotelian model, where everyone knew each other and communal decisions could easily be made. But in the early nineteenth century such small settlements were no longer typical of the United States. In the American interior a very different sort of town was coming into being—the boomtown. Tocqueville passed through a number of these towns: Rochester, whose population had increased from 150 to 15,000 in the decade between 1820 and 1830; Memphis, only four years old but already a busy cotton port; and Louisville, where a local merchant proudly told him that the town had grown from 3,000 inhabitants to 13,000 in only seven years. The fastest-growing inland city was undoubtedly Cincinnati, where Tocqueville and Beaumont spent three days in December 1831.

The birth of Cincinnati was typical of nineteenth-century real estate finagling. John Symmes, a New Jersey congressman, bought one million acres in southwestern Ohio, the so-called Miami pur-

*In his famous book *The Art of Building Cities*, published in 1889, the Viennese urban theorist Camillo Sitte, who attempted to uncover the principles that governed the design of streets and squares in medieval and Renaissance towns, wrote: "Technicians of today take more trouble than is necessary to create interminable rectangular streets and public squares of impeccable symmetry. These efforts seem misdirected to those who are interested in good city appearance. Our forebears had ideas on this subject quite different to ours."

chase, from the federal government. Symmes, who eventually defaulted on his payments and lost everything, sold a large parcel of land on the bank of the Ohio River to Matthias Denman, a New Jersey speculator, who in turn sold shares to two promoters from Kentucky. They quickly laid out building plots and set about attracting buyers, chiefly from Kentucky and New Jersey, to what they called Losantiville. When Tocqueville arrived, the now-rechristened Cincinnati was only forty-three years old, but thanks to the opening up of the river to steamboat traffic in 1816, it had grown to a busy city of about 30,000 people.

"Cincinnati presents an odd spectacle," Tocqueville recorded in his notebook. "A town which seems to want to get built too quickly to have things done in order. Large buildings, huts, streets blocked by rubble, houses under construction; no names to the streets, no numbers on the houses, no external luxury, but a picture of industry and work that strikes one at every step."* An extraordinary photographic panorama of Cincinnati taken around 1865 by a traveling photographer named Henry Rhohiler illustrates the effect of this pragmatic approach. The horizontal photograph, which is five feet long, is composed of four overlapping plates and shows the entire sweep of what had become a city of more than 100,000 people along the curve of the Ohio River. It is an impressive sight, the hills girdling the city, the mighty river, the riverbank lined with more than a dozen steamboats; the tall stone tower of a partially finished suspension bridge (built by John Augustus Roebling, who later designed the Brooklyn Bridge) domi-

*Tocqueville was wrong about the lack of street names—there were simply no signs. According to contemporary city maps, Cincinnati streets parallel to the river were numbered; the cross streets, likewise following the example of Philadelphia, were Sycamore, Walnut, Vine, Plum, and Elm. There was a Front Street, but its view of the river was blocked by commercial buildings; there was also a Main Street running inland from the river.

nates the foreground. Paradoxically it is the bridge, a work of engineering, that is the one lyrical gesture in the picture; otherwise, the city has all the poetry of a parking lot, with rows and rows of three- and four-story buildings instead of cars. One can feel the untrammeled commercial life of this boomtown that is bursting at its seams. The riverbank is lined with the backs of warehouses and ramshackle sheds and outbuildings, regularly interrupted by the dead ends of dusty streets that stop just short of falling into the river. This cavalier—or rather commercial—treatment of the waterfront was typical of cities in North America. (The river promenade of Charleston, a genteel southern city, was an exception.) In a vast land with few roads the rivers provided the chief means of transportation and appeared to push their way through cities in the insistent manner of interstate highways today. Only after rivers were supplanted by railroads and highways did urban waterfronts come to be seen as potential amenities, places where it might be pleasant to stroll, play, or even live.

The most prominent city being built in the United States at the time of Tocqueville's visit was the new capital, Washington; the two Frenchmen spent about two weeks there meeting public officials and consulting government archives. Construction of the city had begun forty years before their visit, according to a master plan devised largely by Tocqueville's countryman, Pierre Charles L'Enfant, an architect and engineer who had established a practice in New York. This made Washington the first example in the United States of a city planned by a trained professional. The skilled L'Enfant merged practicality with grandeur by overlaying a straightforward grid with large diagonal avenues that created vistas and monumental axes. He set aside special sites for the president's house, Congress, a national church (now the site of the National Portrait Gallery), several commemorative monuments, and five grand fountains. At the intersections of the avenues there were to be fifteen squares, one for each of the states in the union.

The plan of Washington effectively combined European and American ideas of planning: the diagonal avenues and axial composition of Versailles with the grid of Philadelphia (it was the practical Jefferson who had insisted on the grid). The mall, which L'Enfant called the Grand Avenue, was the equivalent of Williamsburg's Main Street, but 400 feet wide and about a mile long; an equestrian statue of George Washington was planned for the site where the great obelisk, the Washington National Monument, now stands. The complete plan was roughly four miles across, which dwarfed William Penn's Philadelphia and was also larger than any new city being planned in Europe, including even Peter the Great's Saint Petersburg on the banks of the Neva.

When Tocqueville and Beaumont stayed in Washington, the population was less than 20,000, and the city was growing slowly. Unlike nearby Baltimore, which had already surpassed 80,000, Washington lacked a good port—Jefferson had misjudged the depth of the eastern branch of the Potomac River, which silted up and soon became unusable. Moreover, the new capital had a particularly unhealthy climate; from August to October, the so-called sickly season, Congress adjourned and those who could moved inland to avoid malaria. Compared with the carefully drafted plans made by L'Enfant (and by his successor, the surveyor Andrew Ellicott), the reality was almost comical. The largest building, after the Capitol and the White House, was a lowly tavern. The mall was used as a cow pasture; the *rond-points* scattered throughout the city were planted with vegetables. There was no indication in L'Enfant's plan of how the city might grow in phases, so major avenues had been built in their entirety, with building construction taking place in a scattershot manner. The plan may have been Parisian in inspiration, but it gave Tocqueville the impression of a town composed of five or six villages, with groups of buildings here and there. The monumental avenues (130 to 160 feet wide) that L'Enfant had created to link important sites were flanked by cleared forest, not by buildings. There was disbelief in Tocqueville's voice when he wrote that "They have already rooted up trees for ten miles around, lest they should get in the way of the future citizens of this imagined capital." In fact the trees were probably removed as part of an effort to dry up the mosquito-ridden swamp.

L'Enfant's plan may have struck Tocqueville as hopelessly ambitious, but it has turned out to be a success. The symbolic iconography of the city's plan has become a part of the national imagination: the Mall representing the Constitution, and the locations of the White House and the Capitol representing the separation of powers. The monumental buildings have taken their intended places, and at the same time, the plan has proved adaptable, as evidenced by the addition of the Lincoln and Jefferson memorials and the extension of the Mall in 1901. The combination of grid and diagonal avenues has also proved amenable to automobile traffic. The only thing that L'Enfant did not foresee was the growth of the public bureaucracy—"ten miles around" was nowhere near enough.

Tocqueville and Beaumont visited all the major cities of eastern North America with the exception of Charleston and Savannah. Altogether, their impressions were mixed. In eastern Canada, where the presence of a French-speaking majority made him feel at home, Tocqueville wrote admiringly of the countryside and the villages but observed that Montreal and Quebec City (which then each had about 28,000 inhabitants) reminded him of ugly French provincial towns. He was favorably inclined toward smaller towns like Utica ("a charming town of ten thousand"), and Detroit ("a fine American village"). He passed New Year's Day in New Orleans, but was unimpressed by its squares and jotted in his notebook: "External appearance of the town. Beautiful houses. Huts. Muddy, unpaved streets. Spanish architecture: flat roofs; English: bricks, little doors; French: massive carriage entrances. Population just as mixed." The two Frenchmen spent several weeks in Philadelphia, whose extreme regularity they found oppressive. "All the edifices are neat, kept with extreme care," wrote Beaumont in a letter. "Its sole defect I repeat is to be monotonous in its beauty." Tocqueville commented again on the numbered, nameless streets, an American custom to which he could not adjust. He liked Boston, "a pretty town in a picturesque site on several hills in the middle of the waters." Boston was one of very few American cities that did create a civic waterfront, which happened shortly before Tocqueville's visit—Quincy Market was opened in 1825. The city was then the cultural center of the United States and the heart of the architectural Greek Revival that was sweeping the nation, and the young French aristocrat (Tocqueville was a count) appreciated Boston society, which he compared favorably with the upper classes in Europe. "One feels one has escaped from those commercial habits and that money-conscious spirit which makes New York society so vulgar," he wrote.

Tocqueville spent a total of two months in New York, since it was the base from which he and Beaumont set out on their several trips, but he never warmed to the city. In a letter to his mother, he wrote: "To a Frenchman the aspect of the city is bizarre and not very agreeable. One sees neither dome, nor bell tower, nor great edifice, with the result that one has the constant impression of being in a suburb. In its center the city is built of brick, which gives it a most monotonous appearance. The houses have neither cornices, nor balustrades, nor *portes-cochères*. The streets are badly paved, but sidewalks for pedestrians are to be found in all of them." Writing to his friend Ernest de Chabrol, he described the island site of New York as "admirable" but complained about the lack of noteworthy public monuments and added that "it does not resemble in the least our principal cities in Europe." To Tocqueville, it was obvious why New York wasn't like Paris. It lacked architectural refinements—cupolas, carvings, and ornamentation—and grand civic buildings. These would come. Tocqueville hardly suspected that in less than seventy years New Yorkers would start building public monuments at least as grand as anything in his native city—the New York Public Library, the Metropolitan Museum, Pennsylvania Station, and Grand Central Terminal.

But in 1831 New York was a dismal place. Large sections of the city had been destroyed during the British occupation by two disastrous fires, and after the Revolutionary War the population shrank to 10,000. Eventually the city regained its trade, and by 1825, with the completion of the Erie Canal, it was once again the largest and busiest city in the nation. New York was certainly a city ruled by the "commercial and mercantile spirit." It was also a newly growing, hurriedly built place, which, combined with the lack of an architectural heritage, gave it a makeshift, insubstantial air. The monotony that Tocqueville commented on was also the result of the Commissioners' Plan of 1811, which divided almost the entire island of Manhattan north of Washington Square into a regular gridiron consisting of 155 parallel east-west streets at regular 200-foot intervals, linking the two rivers, and a dozen 100-foot-wide north-south avenues more than seven miles long. Three large open spaces were set aside for public uses—a parade ground, a market, and a reservoir—and there were four small parks, almost afterthoughts. (In any case the open spaces were soon built over; Central Park was not inserted until 1858.) The blocks were subdivided into standard plots, 25 feet wide and 100 feet deep. "As an aid to speculation the commissioners' plan was perhaps unequaled," Reps observed wryly in *The Making of Urban America*, "but only on this ground can it be justifiably called a great achievement."

In 1811, with the population of New York at about 50,000, laying out such a vast gridiron must have appeared hopelessly optimistic. Twenty years later, when Tocqueville stayed there, less than a third of the grid was filled in, despite the city having mushroomed to over 200,000. In another twenty years, the population would more than triple. A city of 200,000 doesn't seem like a major center today (it's smaller than Anchorage, Alaska), but at the beginning of the nineteenth century 200,000 people meant a city the size of Amsterdam, Vienna, or Berlin.

One should not imagine Tocqueville's New York as a more livable version of today's metropolitan behemoth. This was a premodern city lacking most of the urban technologies we take for granted. There were no underground sewers to carry off household wastewater, for example. The fecal matter of 200,000 people was either collected by night-soil scavengers and carted to the countryside to be used as fertilizer or was deposited directly into pits and cesspools; household slops were dumped into the street. Since there was no municipal water supply, backyard wells were easily contaminated. New York was no different than other American cities and towns in this regard, but it was much more densely occupied, and it is little wonder that the first cholera epidemic in the United States (brought over from Europe) broke out here in 1832. As Tocqueville noted, most streets were unpaved and crowded with thousands of wagons and carriages. The mud in the street was mixed with horse manure, and domestic waste was scattered everywhere, for there was no trash collection. Garbage simply accumulated outside and was trampled into the street, which explains why the oldest Manhattan streets are anywhere from six to fifteen feet higher than their original levels. Scavenging pigs wandered the streets and sidewalks. There was no mass transportation, although a horse-drawn omnibus on rails—the first trolley car—was introduced along the Bowery in 1832. There were few building regulations and such poor fire protection that a great fire destroyed more than fifty acres in lower Manhattan only three years after Tocqueville's departure. Life in the big city was dangerous, uncomfortable, and unhealthy.

When Tocqueville and Beaumont first arrived in New York, the steamboat in which they were traveling from Newport came through Long Island Sound and down the East River. They passed what is today the Upper East Side but what was then the suburbs, and admired a number of private mansions ("big as boxes of candy") whose gardens came down to the water's edge. Tocqueville was so intrigued by this pretty sight that the following day he set out to look at the houses more closely. He describes his disappointment at discovering that these classical buildings were not built of marble, as he had expected, but of whitewashed brick, and that the columns were not stone, but painted wood. They were, in his eyes, fakes.

Tocqueville recounted this story in the second volume of *Democracy in America* in a chapter he entitled "In What Spirit the Americans Cultivate the Arts." The spirit, according to him, was distinctly shaped by the political system: that is, in sharp contrast to an aristocratic society, in which the fine arts were a prerogative of a privileged few who could be counted on to maintain a high level of craftsmanship and taste, a democracy left the patronage of the arts in the hands of wealthy but untutored patrons, or what was worse, at the mercy of the masses. "Quantity increases; quality goes down," he observed mercilessly. "Appearance counts for more than reality." This encapsulated the dilemma of the American city, which aspired to the artistic accomplishments of the aristocratic European city—to be "like that"—but was reluctant to deny participation to the mass of its citizens.

Tocqueville was skeptical of America's artistic prospects. "Democratic peoples . . . cultivate those arts which help to make life comfortable rather than those which adorn it," he wrote. "They habitually put use before beauty, and they want beauty itself to be useful." However, although the architecture of New York might appear crude and functional to a sophisticated Frenchman like Tocqueville, for the previous hundred years everyday life in the United States had in fact been undergoing significant change precisely in the direction of adornment and beautification. There is evidence that beginning in the 1720s, the lives of at least some Americans were becoming more genteel. This was manifested in manners—using knives and forks instead of eating with the hands, for example—and in a rising interest in personal hygiene. More elaborate dress and an awareness of social etiquette were further evidence of the process of refinement.

A desire for elegance manifested itself in people's heightened awareness of their physical surroundings. True, in some cities, like Philadelphia, commercial instincts overwhelmed civic aspirations, and instead of green amplitude there was congestion and overbuilding. But as we have seen, in many colonial towns, squares, parks, and ceremonial civic spaces appeared during the early eighteenth century. Boston started to build Long Wharf, which extended the main street straight into the harbor, in 1710, and located a new statehouse in a civic square the following year; Newport's grand wharf, modeled on Boston's, was built in 1739; Hartford added a new statehouse to its central square in 1718.

Perhaps the most striking illustration of the quest for beauty is the domestic American architecture of the first half of the eighteenth century. The townhouses of the gentry became larger, more ornate, more embellished, and painted. (During the seventeenth century, houses were usually left unpainted.) Interiors acquired grand staircases, plastered ceilings, and larger windows. Their architectural style, derived from the English Georgian, was refined but not ostentatious, with simple exteriors and more elaborate interiors. It continued well after the break with England as the Federal style, allowing prosperous citizens to privately enjoy their homes without jeopardizing republican ideals by an ostentatious display of wealth on the exterior of their houses.

The colonial gentry as well as their postcolonial successors, with their fine houses and clothes and manners, set themselves apart from the common folk. It was inevitable, after the War of Independence, that American gentility should democratize itself and broaden its base, and by the end of the eighteenth century, it did so. Refinements that were previously reserved for the gentry—the planters and successful merchants—began to spread to the middle class—those in the professions, industrial entrepreneurs, artisans, and shopkeepers. Such people could rarely afford a mansion, but they could have at least a front parlor; even modest houses could acquire a coat of paint (usually white), a front garden, and a picket fence. People could also change their manners: popular novels assisted readers in developing a more delicate sensibility; cookbooks promoted more elaborate recipes; self-help guides advised on etiquette and interior decoration; pattern books assisted carpenters in building more elegant houses. Briefly put, the quest for gentility was commercialized. This produced the first stirring of a mass consumer culture in dress, furnishings, and domestic architecture, and led to the inevitable cheapening of previously aristocratic fashions, as Tocqueville had noted on his visit to the East River mansions.

It proved easier to commercialize colonial architecture (the Georgian style is based on the use of standardized elements and relatively simple conventions) than to commercialize colonial town planning. Annapolis and Williamsburg, with their Baroque-inspired vistas and ceremonial promenades, might have offered a graceful example to city builders, except that their plans were ill suited to rapid growth, and their attractive, studied layouts had none of the advantages of gridded towns when it came to real estate development. Only Savannah, with its regular geometry, its standardized neighborhoods, and its handsome squares and tree-lined avenues, offered a balance between practicality and civic beauty. But Savannah, located far from the great population centers of the Northeast, had no influence whatsoever on American urbanism in the eighteenth century or later.

There was another indisputable fact that prospective city builders could not afford to ignore—Annapolis and Williamsburg were commercial failures. The development of the port of Annapolis was overshadowed by the phenomenal success of its upstart neighbor, Baltimore. By 1850, the population of Baltimore reached 150,000 and that city was second only to New York, while Annapolis, the capital of the state, remained a small town. Williamsburg did not fare any better. It was one of the few colonial towns not located on water; rather, the site was equidistant from two rivers, the James and the York. Nicholson intended Williamsburg to have not one but two ports, one on each river (with characteristic grandiloquence he named them Queen Mary's Port and Princess Anne's Port, after the late British queen and a Danish royal). It was hardly a practical solution. The ports were several miles from the town, and to make matters worse, the rivers were only navigable at high tide. Williamsburg therefore remained chiefly an administrative center. When the capital of Virginia was moved to Richmond in 1779, Nicholson's town went into decline until it became an out-of-the-way country village whose only livelihood was the College of William and Mary. This is a reminder that in urban design, good aesthetic intentions are not enough.

A point must be made about the difference between American and European capitals. In Europe a capital city was not merely the seat of political power, but provided commercial, cultural, intellectual, and social leadership. This is what economists call a primate city. Englishmen looked to London, Frenchmen to Paris, Spaniards to Madrid, and Prussians to Berlin for ideas about what to wear, who to read, and how to build. Braudel has called the great European capitals of the eighteenth and nineteenth centuries "hot-houses," fostering innovation and sometimes upheaval in all fields, including urbanism. Things were different in the New World. "America has not yet any great capital whose direct or indirect influence is felt through the length and breadth of the land," Tocqueville observed. New York was the most important city commercially, but Boston was predominant culturally and Washington was the seat of government. This diffusion of powers was not accidental. It was a question of the country's size. Many individual states were the size of European countries; hence no single city could be expected to dominate. Furthermore, as Tocqueville pointed out, many rural Americans were indisputably suspicious of the political influence of large cities; no less than Thomas Jefferson had proclaimed: "I view great cities as pestilential to the morals, the health, the liberties of man." State capitals were often located in secondary, out-of-the-way towns: Albany, not New York; Harrisburg, not Philadelphia, Annapolis, not Baltimore. (Only in the New England states of Massachusetts, Connecticut, and Rhode Island was the capital also the largest city.) Of course, the federal capital was moved from New York to a backwoods location.* Ostensibly, this placed the capital closer to the center of the state or of the country, but curtailing the powers of the largest cities was undoubtedly a consideration.

If Washington, D.C., had been the commercial and cultural capital of the United States, American urbanism might have taken

*Interestingly, the same pattern was followed in Canada. Of the largest cities, neither Montreal nor Vancouver is a seat of government. Toronto, an exception, is a provincial capital and the financial and media center of the country; this would qualify it as a European-style capital were the national capital not located in Ottawa.

a different turn and L'Enfant's planning ideas might have spread across the country. But the city that provided the ready example for prospective city builders was not Washington but New York, the largest and most commercially successful city on the continent; what worked there was good enough for everyone else. New towns had to deal with furious growth, and a simple subdivisible planning system was imperative. The no-nonsense Commissioners' Plan of 1811 provided exactly that, and it became the model for almost all new North American cities: Chicago (planned in 1830), San Francisco (founded in 1839, and vastly extended in 1849), and Toronto (which started to grow in earnest after 1812). Occasionally, modifications were made to the simple grid: the Philadelphia central square showed up in Ohio towns like Columbus and Cleveland; the diagonal avenues of Washington are visible in the plans of Indianapolis and Madison, Wisconsin; the extensions to New Orleans were gridded but incorporated open squares based on the old French model. But generally the grid prevailed. The Land Ordinance adopted by the Continental Congress of 1785 also assured its continued widespread use. This legislation effectively divided all unsettled land in the United States into a vast grid of regular six-mile-square townships, each subdivided into a checkerboard of square-mile sections. Since country roads were usually located along section lines, and towns tended to spring up at crossroads, it was convenient and natural that their streets should follow the same orthogonal geometry.

"Money is the only form of social distinction; but see how arrogantly it classifies itself," Tocqueville observed caustically. That social refinements in the form of fine clothes and fine houses could now be purchased sounds democratic, but it did not apply to most of the poor. Gentility, even in its diluted, commercialized form, naturally erected barriers between the middle class and working poor that flew in the face of democratic ideals. Nowhere was this contradiction more evident than in the city itself. Eighteenth-century Europeans dealt with social distinctions by creating segregated "public" spaces. The pleasure gardens of the Palais Royal in Paris, for example, which was still operating when Tocqueville was a young man, were open to aristocrats and the bourgeoisie, but were off-limits to the common classes (who were invited in on only three special days of the year). Paris and London both had fashionable promenades (the Cours la Reine, the Tuileries gardens, the Mall in Saint James Park) to which only "respectable" people were admitted; these areas were fenced, with guards posted at the gates to keep out the riffraff. Many of the residential squares in the fashionable districts of London are still surrounded by iron fences and have locked gates, with keys available only to the householders living around them. There were some American attempts to create analogous restricted urban spaces, particularly in New York City, where there were several private residential squares like Union Square, Irving Place, and Gramercy Park (which remains fenced and gated to this day). But New Yorkers had no equivalent to the Mall or the Tuileries. Whereas genteel Londoners and Parisians, ladies as well as gentlemen, could stroll without danger of being offended by crude or vulgar people, American streets belonged to everyone, rich and poor alike; so did parks like Boston's Common, New York's Battery Park, and Philadelphia's squares.

The "commonness" of such public places in the city flew in the face of refinement, however. "Neither the Park nor the Battery is very much resorted to by the fashionable citizens of New York," sniffed a visitor, "as they have become too common." Tocqueville, too, was struck by the presence of a vociferous urban lower class, which he described as consisting of freed black slaves ("condemned by law and opinion to a hereditary state of degradation and wretchedness"), and poor immigrants, whom he described as motivated by self-interest rather than good citizenship. The urban rabble was a common feature of European cities. It should hardly have surprised Tocqueville. What Tocqueville did foresee (more or less correctly) was that the large size of American cities and the volatile nature of the urban underclass (although he did not call it that) would eventually threaten personal liberties. Today, a combination of official lethargy and community resignation permits the decay of public behavior, when such simple pleasures as going for an evening stroll in the park or sitting on a public bench are no longer to be taken for granted by many citizens.*

Tocqueville also predicted that the government would be obliged to create an armed force to suppress the excesses of the mob, which had already instigated serious riots in both New York and Philadelphia. He was right about that, too; in 1833 Philadelphia formed its first regular police force, and eleven years later, New York followed suit. As towns became cities and as cities grew in size, social control would have to become explicit. The informal familial and personal mechanisms for exercising authority over miscreants no longer sufficed.

Even before Tocqueville's American trip, it had become obvious that the unruly city population was not amenable to refinement. According to Richard L. Bushman, a historian at Columbia University, "Toward the end of the [eighteenth] century the standards of genteel delicacy rose ever higher, and polite society isolated itself more and more from the coarseness of ordinary city life." The urban bourgeoisie withdrew to what Bushman calls "resorts of gentility"—that is, to selected taverns and assembly rooms, and later, to the "public" rooms of hotels and "public" parlors (there were also women's parlors and family parlors), which were reserved for

*This may be changing. Recently, a few cities (San Francisco, Seattle) have passed laws against loitering, panhandling, public urination, and vagrancy, in a belated attempt to restore order to public places.

the middle class. Carriages became increasingly popular in cities, as they shielded their passengers from the life of the street—much as automobiles would a hundred years later. But the chief resorts of gentility were those constituents of American towns that had distinguished them since the colonial period: genteel people retreated to the private comforts and refinement of their individual houses. "Individualism is a calm and considered feeling which disposes each citizen to isolate himself from the mass of his fellows and withdraw into the circle of family and friends; with this little society formed to his taste, he gladly leaves the greater society to look after itself," wrote Tocqueville.* He was pointing out another unique characteristic of the New World city: it was a setting for individual pursuits rather than communal activities.

When Tocqueville went to the American frontier, he was taken aback to find that the boomtowns and backwoods hamlets were not being settled by European immigrants, as he had expected, but by native-born Americans. "An American . . . changes his residence ceaselessly," he marveled. Here is another explanation for the general lack of refinement in American cities of the nineteenth century—the absence of long-lasting attachment to a place. People moved about: from house to house, from neighborhood to neighborhood, from town to town, from the East to the new frontier. The city—especially the newly built city—was chiefly seen as an anonymous, practical contrivance (hence the frequency with which numbers were used instead of street names). Cities could be started from scratch, built up, and as quickly abandoned, or at least altered. Americans were attached to their homes, to their families, and to their political institutions, but as Tocqueville so astutely observed, they carelessly left cities to their own devices.

*Tocqueville did not coin the word "*individualisme*," but its first appearance in English was in a translation of *De la démocratie en Amérique*, in 1835.

FIVE

In the Land of the Dollar

THERE IS A FAMOUS CURRIER & IVES LITHOGRAPH OF A bird's-eye view of Chicago in 1892. In the foreground is Lake Michigan, and behind it a giant has unrolled an enormous quilt of streets and buildings. The quilt stretches almost all the way to the horizon, where beyond the distant suburbs, there is a glimpse of virgin prairie. The center of the city is defined by the lakefront, the Chicago River, and its South Branch. The first steel-framed skyscraper, the Masonic Temple Building, is plainly visible; so is Louis Sullivan's recently completed Auditorium Building, whose office tower is the world's tallest building. The surrounding city is chockablock with apartment houses, factories, and warehouses; the roofscape is punctuated by a few church steeples and many belching smokestacks. Commercial vessels—steam and sail—cram the river; railway trains chug along the lakeside, and rail lines radiate out from the city into the prairie. Everything appears in motion; intentionally or not, the illustrator has portrayed Chicago as a horizontal anthill.

In 1892 Chicago had more than 1.5 million inhabitants. It was the second-largest city in the United States after New York, which had grown to a staggering 3.4 million; Philadelphia, which had long since surpassed Penn's original grid, now stood at about 1.3 million people. These three enormous cities signaled an important demographic shift: four out of ten Americans now lived in a city or town. Sixty-one years earlier, in 1831, when Tocqueville and Beaumont visited the United States, only about one in ten of the population was classified as urban.

Such measures of urbanization indicate where people live, but don't necessarily describe how they live. Generally speaking, a national urbanization level of 10 percent—the level of present-day Ethiopia, for example—denotes a society whose population, despite the presence of a small number of towns and even large cities (Ethiopia's capital, Addis Ababa, contains 1.5 million inhabitants), is overwhelmingly rural. Typically, in such a society, sharp contrasts exist between the urban minorities and the rest of the population whose way of life is culturally traditional, socially conservative, and technologically backward. America, however, was different.

The difference was already apparent by the time Tocqueville came to America. He had read James Fenimore Cooper's novels set in the wilderness, and he anticipated that a nation that included pioneering settlers as well as urban patricians would display cultural extremes even more striking than those between the rustic French provinces and the sophisticated *capitale*. A travel essay he published in a French magazine describes how a visit to the frontier (present-day Michigan) confounded his expectations. "When you leave the main roads you force your way down barely trodden paths. Finally, you see a field cleared, a cabin made from half-shaped tree trunks admitting the light through one narrow window only. You think that you have at last reached the home of the American peasant. Mistake. You make your way into this cabin that seems the asylum of all wretchedness but the owner of the place is dressed in the same clothes as yours and he speaks the language of towns. On his rough table are books and newspapers; he himself is anxious to know exactly what is happening in old Europe and asks you to tell him what has most struck you in his country." Tocqueville continued: "One might think one was meeting a rich landowner who had come to spend just a few nights in a hunting lodge."

Long before the universal ownership of televisions and videocassette recorders, long before the spread of regional malls, nationwide franchises, mail-order catalogs, the Home Shopping Network, and the Internet, long before the decentralizing impact of the private automobile, American culture already demonstrated a startling tendency toward a far-flung homogeneity. Tocqueville's sketch confirms that consumer goods were widely distributed, as were books and newspapers and ideas; elsewhere, Tocqueville observes with wonder that anything that can be bought in New York City is also on the shelves in small-town stores. "The spirit of equality has stamped a peculiarly uniform pattern on the habits of private life," he writes.

It is significant that the uniform pattern Tocqueville describes was neither countrified nor peasantlike; Americans were rural but that did not mean that they were rustic. Rather, they were, at least culturally speaking, urban. The roots of this urbanity were deep: they were present in the civic ambitions of Annapolis and Williamsburg, in the rapid spread of gentility and middle-class comforts from the main cities to country towns, and in the sophisticated architecture of colonial villages and towns. The British custom of building country houses migrated to colonial America in the form of the riverside plantation mansion, and such prominent republicans as Washington, Jefferson, Monroe, and Madison continued to build country houses that would become famous and acquire the status of shrines. Washington's Mount Vernon, Madison's Montpelier, and George Mason's Gunston Hall, with their formal gardens, well-stocked cellars and libraries, and refined domestic comforts, were distinctly urbane, not provincial. When Jefferson undertook a radical redesign of Monticello in 1794, he based his ideas on a stylish contemporary Parisian city residence, the Hôtel de Salm, and much of his furniture came from France. Jefferson may have lived on an isolated mountaintop—behavior that would have branded him an eccentric in Europe—but he was in many ways a man defined by urban culture.

Lewis Mumford defined the city as a "point of maximum concentration for the power and culture of a community." This was undoubtedly true of the historic centers of Europe and Asia, whose royal courts and centralized cultural institutions were isolated from the traditional agricultural society of the surrounding countryside. But in nineteenth-century America, as Tocqueville observed, culture was much more diffuse. The early American urbanization process did not mirror the social evolution of peasant to townsman that had occurred earlier in Europe. (The only people who could properly be described as constituting a tradition-bound rural society in America were Indians and black slaves.) In the New World it wasn't the town air that made you free—as the medieval German saying went—it was American air, unless you were an Indian or a slave. Because many new settlers were themselves former townspeople and because Americans were inclined to move from place to place, the line between town and country—rural and urban—blurred. Life on plantations and country estates, especially in the South, could be as mannerly as life in the city, and life in small country towns and on prosperous farms was only slightly less refined. As a result, the United States is the first example of a society in which the process of urbanization began, paradoxically, not by building towns, but by spreading an urban culture.

Here is an important distinction, and perhaps also another reason for the ambivalence that marks American attitudes toward the city: there never was a sense of cities as precious repositories of civilization. Because urban culture spread so rapidly, it lost its tie to the city, at least in the public's perception. Institutions and customs that elsewhere would have been considered marks of urbanity, here were simply thought of as national traits. Because of this uniformity, there was, as Tocqueville observed, a less dramatic difference than in Europe between the countryman and the townsman. In America, to say that someone is a farmer merely gives an occupation; in most of Europe, it describes a set of cultural values. A mythical regional distinction between town and country did develop as the American West was settled, with life in the wide open spaces contrasted to that in the crowded eastern cities.

The implantation of an urban culture greatly accelerated the actual building of towns. Braudel, writing about the historic process of urbanization, speculates that about 10 percent of the total population living in towns was the threshold at which urbanization began to attain a minimum degree of efficiency. He suggests that this provided a sufficient concentration of townspeople and a sufficient number of towns to form a network of interdependent urban economies. This may have been true in Europe, but in the United States the threshold appears to have been lower, for urbanization increased at a constant rate, starting at a level of only 5 percent, which was recorded in 1790, the year of the first census. Forty years later urbanization stood at 10 percent, and by 1850 it had grown to 15 percent.

In 1850 there were seven American cities with more than 100,000 inhabitants: New York, Baltimore, which had jumped to number two, Philadelphia, Boston, New Orleans, which had become the main southern port, and ever-growing Cincinnati. The other city close in size was the old French outpost of Saint Louis, which thanks to the opening up of the Mississippi to steamboats had grown in only a decade from a town of about 17,000 to a city of more than 77,000. Over the next fifty years, immigration swelled the total population of the United States from 23 million to 76 million. By 1900, in addition to the three great metropolises—New York, Chicago, and Philadelphia—three other cities had grown to about half a million inhabitants: Boston, Baltimore, and the booming Saint Louis, the fourth-largest city in the nation. Cities with more than a quarter of a million people now included not only Cincinnati and New Orleans but Cleveland, Buffalo, Pittsburgh, Detroit, and Milwaukee, as well as the recent gold-rush mecca of San Francisco; Washington, D.C., with 279,000 people, was finally starting to fill out according to L'Enfant's expectations.

During the last decade of the nineteenth century, the fastest-growing city in the United States, probably in the world, was Chicago. The evolution of Chicago bears closer examination, for in many ways twentieth-century American urbanism got its start here. This is where the skyscraper was invented and given its definitive architectural form, this is where the idea of the American commercial downtown took root, and this is also where the issue of urban design, after a hiatus of almost two centuries, emerged as a topic fit for public and political discussion.

Chicago was a latecomer among American cities. When Tocqueville visited the Northwest Territory he didn't mention

Chicago, which was then a village and was described by another traveler as consisting of "little more than a dozen or so log cabins, a store, two taverns, and Fort Dearborn." The village prospered, and by 1850, the population reached 20,000. Life must have been hard in the muddy town, with its unpaved streets and flimsy wood buildings, but if one believed the claims of Chicagoans, this was the "Gem of the Prairies" and the "Queen of the Lake." Such boosterism was typical of the civic spirit that would distinguish Chicago, which aspired to be more than just another frontier outpost. As early as 1839 there were signs of civic ambition when the city council purchased two acres for a park and also set aside land for what would one day be Grant Park.

Just as Amsterdam was shaped by the Dutch Golden Age or Manchester by the British Industrial Revolution, Chicago was formed by the great commercial and industrial expansion of the late nineteenth century. After the construction of the railroads and a business boom during the Civil War, the city took off like a rocket. Indeed, as far as popular legend is concerned, Chicago was born in a shower of sparks. On October 8, 1871, the preeminent city of the western half of the nation, bursting at the seams with 300,000 people, suffered a calamitous fire that devastated the business center and much of the surrounding area. Catastrophic urban fires were commonplace throughout the nineteenth century and laid waste great portions of New York (1835), Pittsburgh (1845), San Francisco (1851), Saint Louis (1851), Washington, D.C. (1851), Troy, New York (1862), Portland, Maine (1866), Boston (1872), and Seattle (1889). Dense, fast-growing cities like Chicago were particularly vulnerable to fire because most of the buildings were of wood; people used wood- and coal-burning stoves; and the water supply and fire protection were inadequate. When urban fires started, they were hard to put out. The three-day Chicago fire of 1871 destroyed more than 2,000 acres, razed

18,000 buildings, and left 90,000 people homeless. Perhaps as much as a third of the city was burnt to the ground.

The resilience of Chicagoans was extraordinary. The disaster was widely perceived to be a great opportunity. A report published within two months of the fire had chapter titles such as "Good out of Evil" and "The New Chicago." Politicians and businessmen rallied together. Chicago was being tested, and it would rise to the challenge. Partly this was civic propaganda, an optimism made possible because the industrial and manufacturing districts and the grain- and livestock-handling facilities, the foundation of Chicago's prosperity, were not damaged by the fire. So there was plenty of private money available for rebuilding; a year after the fire, almost $40 million worth of new construction was complete. But Chicago's faith in the future was also an expression of a widespread popular belief that it was a new kind of city—different, that is, from the old, established eastern centers like New York, Philadelphia, and Boston. These places represented the past—a decadent past, Chicagoans would have said; Chicago was the future.

The Chicago fire provided a tabula rasa for land developers, builders, and architects. Not guided by any new planning theories, they kept the same street layout. Nevertheless, the new city emerged dramatically different from the old. This was due to a wide range of new urban technologies. Chicagoans thought of themselves as different, but they were not opposed to adopting urban technologies that had been developed chiefly in eastern cities. In 1878, New Haven introduced the country's first telephone switchboard; Chicago got its own the same year. Thomas Edison invented the electric lamp in 1879; two years later electric lights were installed in a railroad-car factory on Chicago's Far South Side, and the following year in a Prairie Avenue mansion. San Francisco introduced cable cars in 1873; Chicago followed suit in

1881. The first electric streetcar ran in Richmond, Virginia, in 1888; four years later Chicago streetcar companies began switching from horse-drawn and cable cars to electric trolleys.

Electric trolley cars and railroads allowed the city to expand horizontally into the surrounding prairie; at the same time the center of Chicago began to grow in an unexpected direction. Of all the technologies that fashioned the new city, few were more influential than the elevator. Passenger elevators originated in mines, but for a long time they were considered too dangerous for the general public and only freight elevators were installed in buildings. It was during the 1853 Crystal Palace Exhibition in New York City that Elisha G. Otis unveiled the first "safety elevator." In a dramatic demonstration, he had the lifting rope severed as he himself stood in the elevator cab; to the astonishment of the public, the cab didn't fall, held in place by a system of pawls and ratchets. Four years later Otis installed the first regular operating passenger elevator in a New York office building, and the device quickly spread. The earliest elevators were powered by steam; after 1889, when the first electric elevator was installed in a New York building, electricity became the chief motive power.

Before the advent of the elevator, the height of buildings had been limited by human endurance in stair-climbing.* Urban buildings were four to six stories, with the occasional church steeple or dome protruding above this height—this was no less true in Victorian London than in ancient Rome—but with the introduction of elevators, buildings could be made as tall as construction techniques and engineering would allow. At first, that was not very high. Buildings with solid masonry walls could be built higher

*The height of commercial buildings was also limitd by the need for easy communication; tall office buildings would not have met with such rapid success had the telephone not been invented.

only by making the walls thicker and thicker at the base to resist toppling over; the practical height limit was about twelve stories. This limit was pushed to sixteen stories in Chicago's Monadnock Building, whose massive walls were six feet thick at the bottom, but by the time the Monadnock opened in 1891, it was already obsolete. There was now a cheaper and more efficient building material: lightweight structural steel.

Rolled steel had been widely used in Europe and in America for railroad tracks and bridge construction, but not for buildings. Steel-frame construction was pioneered in Chicago, where it was first used in 1884, in the upper floors of an iron-framed building, and where the first complete steel frame was erected in 1890. The steel frame had many advantages: not only was it cheaper and more efficient, it also enabled architects to build higher. In 1892 the steel-framed Masonic Temple Building, designed by Daniel Burnham and John Root, the architects of the Monadnock, rose to 302 feet (twenty-two stories). For a short time it was the world's tallest building, soon exceeded by the office tower of Louis Sullivan's Auditorium Building.

The skyscraper, almost always an office building, changed more than the skyline of Chicago; it greatly increased the value of real estate, which in turn altered the character of the center of the city. When buildings were lower and land was cheaper, the center of all American cities since Williamsburg had been a mixture of commercial, residential, and industrial uses. Inevitably, once the price of land was based on renting sixteen to twenty floors of office space, only sixteen- to twenty-story office buildings could and would be built. The low-rise rooming houses, private residences, workshops, industrial lofts, small manufacturing plants, and factories that had previously stood side by side with commercial offices had to move elsewhere.

Where did people live? The greatly increased price of land in and around the Loop, as well as new fire codes prohibiting inexpensive wood-frame construction, guaranteed that most people would live outside the center of the city. Low-paid factory workers lived in tenements in industrial neighborhoods close to their places of employment, but skilled craftsmen and white-collar workers had another option. They could afford to move to new residential neighborhoods where the new fire codes did not apply; the land was cheap, and so was the cost of traveling by railroad and trolley car.* These neighborhoods consisted largely of owner-occupied dwellings, for the most part detached houses with gardens. Although the streets were usually laid out on grids, these new districts did not have a mixture of uses—they were almost exclusively residential.

The character of these outer neighborhoods was initially countrylike, but as the city continued its precipitous growth, they filled up, houses and building lots were subdivided, the density rose, and the hemmed-in streets became less bucolic in appearance. Workingmen's cottages replaced villas, duplexes replaced cottages and, eventually, apartment buildings replaced duplexes. Still, with their broad, tree-lined streets and low buildings, these outlying neighborhoods could not be confused with downtown. No longer rural, but not quite urban either, they presaged the suburban communities that would grow up in the early 1900s on the edges of all large cities.

Thus was the modern American city born. It was different from its European counterpart not just because the buildings were so tall, but also because what people now called "downtown" (the word, too, is of American origin) was a homogeneous, commer-

*In some cases, these new, outlying residential neighborhoods were actually closer to their places of work, since the fire had forced many business to move to peripheral locations.

cial concentration of offices, hotels, and department stores, with a sprinkling of cultural institutions. People worked and shopped and played downtown, but lived elsewhere.

One chief engine of urban growth was immigration. Between 1860 and 1890 ten million immigrants, chiefly from Europe, came to the United States. Then—as today—immigrants settled first in the large cities: New York, Boston, Cleveland, Pittsburgh, and especially Chicago. By 1880, nearly nine out of ten Chicagoans were first- or second-generation immigrants, a larger proportion than in any other American city. Between 1870 and 1880, the decade after the Great Fire, the population of Chicago almost doubled, and by 1900 the city was a full-fledged metropolis.

As the fastest-growing city in the world, Chicago was an unprecedented urban phenomenon that would not be duplicated until the explosive growth of Third World cities in the second half of the twentieth century. What attracted people to Chicago was the promise of employment in the stores, offices, factories, warehouses, slaughterhouses, breweries, and railroad yards that filled the city. The image of a place so unrelentingly devoted to work struck foreign visitors as quintessentially American. "Chicago is conscious that there is something in the world, some sense of form, of elegance of refinement, that with all her corn and railways, her hogs and by-products and dollars, she lacks," observed an English writer, G. W. Steevens, who passed through the city in the 1890s. Steevens went on to record his impressions of the United States in the now forgotten but wonderfully titled travel book, *In the Land of the Dollar.*

One could easily slip into condescension when writing about Chicago; it was so new and so raw compared with European cities. No doubt, American cities were unabashedly places for doing business and for making money, and Steevens's opinion is mirrored in Lewis Mumford's description of nineteenth-century American urbanization: "That a city had any other purpose than to attract trade, to increase land values and to grow is something that, if it uneasily entered the mind of an occasional Whitman, never exercised any hold upon the minds of the majority of our countrymen. For them, the place where the great city stands *is* the place of stretched wharves, and markets, and ships bringing goods from the ends of the earth; that and nothing else." This is unfair. European cities like Paris had started as cities of wharves and markets and trade, too, although by the 1890s Parisian industrial and manufacturing activities were being pushed to the periphery, and the center was being graced by boulevards and public monuments (beautifications that, not coincidentally, increased land values).

The city in the Currier & Ives lithograph may have resembled an anthill, but Chicago was trying to put itself on the cultural map, too. Daniel Bluestone, an architectural historian, suggests that a desire for civility and culture, as well as a celebration of profit-making, characterized the aspirations of the nineteenth-century politicians and businessmen who built Chicago. Many commercial buildings, such as William Le Baron Jenney's Home Insurance Company Building and Burnham & Root's exquisite Rookery Building, transcended their utilitarian nature by, as Bluestone puts it, "self-consciously setting out to ennoble commerce with monumental forms, using rich materials, traditional architectural motifs, and expressions of white-collar cultivation."

To say that the architecture of these buildings is grand is to put it mildly. The composition of the facades generally follows that of Italian Renaissance palazzi: there is a solid-looking base, then the main body of the building (much higher, of course, than a palazzo), and an often richly ornamented roof cornice to top things off. The impressive entrance on the street usually leads to an extraordinary lobby, often several stories high. These public spaces are invariably finished in luxurious materials: stained glass, mosaics, hardwoods, bronze, and marble. The durability of construction is attested to by the fact that many of these commercial buildings, after almost a century, continue to exist and to give service. They incorporated a level of craftsmanship and interior refinement unmatched in any contemporary buildings except perhaps the mansions of the extremely wealthy. The atmosphere consciously evoked a cross between a first-class hotel and an exclusive club. This was "an aesthetic that created a necessary connection between commerce and culture, denying their incompatibility and suggesting instead that refinement might emanate from tasteful workplaces," writes Bluestone.

Refinements were not limited to architecture or decor. The skyscrapers provided their tenants with electric lighting, central heating and ventilation, and hot and cold running water—amenities by no means widespread at the time. The latest comforts also included washrooms on every floor and large expanses of glass for light and view. The first skyscrapers were not simple loft buildings. They offered a host of in-house facilities from restaurants, coffee shops, and newspaper stands to barbershops and rooftop observatories, as well as the services of doormen, cleaning staff, and messenger boys. These buildings were small cities in their own right.

A building like Louis Sullivan's renowned Schlesinger & Mayer (today Carson Pirie Scott) department store is often cited as an example of functionalism because of its undecorated upper facade. For the passerby, however, the impression is different: the richly modeled cast-iron ornament covering the walls and surrounding the display windows along the sidewalk creates a sense of lavish commercial celebration. The contrast between the plain upper floors and the flamboyantly decorated base suggests that Sullivan was reacting to the necessity of making a department store attractive to middle- and upper-middle-class shoppers without spending a lot of money on the less visible upper floors.

It was a sign of how downtown had changed that many of these shoppers were women. Previously, it would have been considered unseemly (and probably unsafe) for respectable women to venture downtown alone. Now there were places for them to go, not only department stores but also office buildings, fashionable retail shops, and high-class hotels. The construction of such civic amenities as arts clubs, Sullivan's Auditorium Building, the imposing new public library, and the Art Institute also contributed to the changed atmosphere of downtown. Middle-class tastes were transforming the center of the city from a raucous, unfettered, and rough place to something more genteel.

Chicago's motto is *Urbs in horto* (City in a garden), which originally referred to the surrounding fertile plains, but starting in 1869, "garden" might just as well have described the green spaces within the city itself. Following the example of New York City, whose Central Park was begun in 1858, Chicago, like Brooklyn, Buffalo, Boston, Louisville, Philadelphia, and San Francisco, undertook the construction of large urban parks. Most of the parks were planned by the same man, Frederick Law Olmsted, who exerted a powerful influence on the beautification of cities throughout North America. (In 1873, he was engaged to design an urban park in Montreal.)

Olmsted's original inspiration was European. The English architect and horticulturalist Sir Joseph Paxton, who later designed the Crystal Palace, is credited with creating the first public urban park, the "People's Garden," in Liverpool, in the early 1840s. Similar parks were established in other British cities, as well as in

France and Germany. These were not merely fashionable promenades, as had been the case with eighteenth-century fenced urban gardens used exclusively by the upper class; they were specifically intended for the general public. Olmsted visited Liverpool and thought that Paxton's park was a concept ideally suited to American democracy. Moreover, in his opinion, cities like New York and Chicago, bursting at the seams of their tight, practical grids and increasingly disease-ridden, overcrowded, and noisy, needed healthy green open spaces. It is worth recalling that the nineteenth-century city was an *industrial* city, and industry then was extremely dirty. Coal-burning factories and electrical generating plants, polluting stockyards and slaughterhouses, stood side by side with the homes of working people. Hundreds of horse-drawn vehicles, including horsecars, polluted the narrow, crowded streets. To Olmsted and his collaborator on many projects, Calvert Vaux, green spaces were not a mere ornament but a crucial antidote to the nervous, inhospitable city; these parks are not conceived of as urban gardens but rather as large chunks of healthy natural landscape.

The largest European parks, like Paris's Bois de Boulogne or London's Hampstead Heath, were outside the city; central urban parks were limited by the cost of acquiring land. London's Victoria Park, for example, which was laid out in 1842, is about 200 acres, and the older Hyde Park is smaller than that; the Tuileries gardens is only 56 acres. Since the construction of urban parks in America coincided with the early stages of cities' growth, it was easier and cheaper to appropriate empty land for park building, and Olmsted was able to achieve an unprecedented scale in many of his parks: Mount Royal Park in Montreal, one of his smallest parks, covers 450 acres. Brooklyn's Prospect Park is more than 500 acres; Central Park spreads over 840 acres; San Francisco's Golden Gate Park is more than 1,000 acres, and Philadelphia's

Fairmount Park, the largest urban park in the country, encompasses about 3,800 acres.

At one time, Chicago had intended to build a great linear park—a sort of giant greenbelt, a quarter of a mile wide and fourteen miles long—roughly following the city limits. This would have girdled the city on three sides, leaving the lake to border the fourth. This ambitious plan was ultimately scaled down by Olmsted and Vaux from 2,240 to 1,800 acres, and from a continuous greenbelt to eight individual parks, many named for presidents: Washington, Jefferson, Lincoln, Grant. The parks are large—200 to 600 acres each—and intended for full-day excursions. They include lakes, canals, sports fields, band shells, conservatories, arbors, zoos, bicycle and pedestrian paths, and broad carriage roads. There were originally no commercial distractions, however—no amusement parks, penny arcades, or beer gardens. This was a conscious effort to provide a civilizing public setting for an urban population with a growing amount of leisure time. The parks are linked by parkways, a favorite Olmsted device. Parkways were not simply big streets, but were really linear parks that achieved several ends: they brought parklike space closer to more people, they further reduced urban congestion, and they could be a tool in directing urban growth, providing an attractive setting for new residential developments.

The Chicago park and parkway system was successful, but its advocates had seen it chiefly as a counterbalance to the congestion of the city—a green refuge—and so had paid less attention to the character of its urban surroundings. The little grid of the 1830s had multiplied and was now filled with fancy skyscrapers and public parks, but this did not really amount to a beautiful city. The laissez-faire attitude to construction was producing some beautiful buildings, but architecture alone is never enough. What was missing was an urban vision grand enough to encompass Chicago's growing and justifiable sense of importance. City planning is not merely about practicalities, it also reflects human ambitions and desires. That is what drove Louis XIV to transform Paris from a medieval town into a modern city. It is the same urge, albeit on a small scale, that impels us to redecorate the kitchen or to move the furniture around in the living room or to repaint the family room. The old rooms don't suit us anymore, they don't feel right; maybe they are starting to look a bit dowdy or old-fashioned. Perhaps it's just time for a change.

Ultimately, the change in Chicago was accelerated by the World's Columbian Exposition, which took place during the summer of 1893. The master plan of the fair was devised by Olmsted and his associate, Henry Sargent Codman, working with Chicago's most prominent architects, Daniel Burnham and John Root. The fair was located beside Lake Michigan on the site of Jackson Park—originally planned by Olmsted and Vaux, but never built. Olmsted produced a spectacular new plan incorporating his concept of the fusion of town and country. He transformed what had been a 600-acre marsh into an entirely man-made landscape, including a system of canals as well as a great, naturalistic lagoon. Root is generally credited with the idea of the Court of Honor, a formal urban grouping of buildings arranged around a 1,100-foot-long water basin. A 600-foot-wide parkway (part of the original Olmsted and Vaux plan) extended almost a mile inland and contained an amusement park, the Midway Plaisance, and the world's first Ferris wheel, 250 feet in diameter and carrying aloft 1,500 passengers at a time.

Burnham was appointed chief of construction, and after Root's untimely death he assumed the leadership role in planning the exposition. He invited several celebrated architects to design the individual pavilions: Richard Morris Hunt, America's premier society architect, was awarded the choice commission, an imposing 250-foot-high domed building standing at the head of the water basin; Charles Follen McKim of McKim, Mead, and White from New York City designed the Agriculture Building, which he modeled on a Renaissance palazzo; Louis Sullivan built the beautiful Transportation Building; George B. Post was responsible for the largest of the exhibition halls, the Manufacturers Building; Charles B. Atwood designed the train station as well as the Palace of Fine Arts. Peabody & Stearns from Boston, Chicago's William Le Baron Jenney, as well as Henry Ives Cobb, who had just built the new Rockefeller-financed University of Chicago, were also involved.

The Columbian Exposition was a spectacular combination of naturalistic and formal landscaping combined with grand public buildings. (As many of these buildings were painted white, the exposition became popularly known as the White City.) The architect Robert A. M. Stern has called the Columbian Exposition "the first effectively planned complex of public buildings built in America since the Jeffersonian era," and, indeed, the Court of Honor does recall an enlarged version of Thomas Jefferson's University of Virginia, with Hunt's tall dome at the head of a water basin occupying the place of Jefferson's library. The planners conceived of the fair as an explicit exercise in forward-looking urbanism; moreover, they saw it as an opportunity to demonstrate the application of classical design principles to public buildings. Burnham, Hunt, Atwood, and McKim were all confirmed classicists, as was the fair's chief adviser on sculpture, the artist Augustus Saint-Gaudens. The classical approach, as practiced by these American designers, demanded not only the use of the classical architectural vocabulary—fluted columns, capitals, and entablatures—and buildings sited along formal axes, but also restraint. The buildings grouped around the basin, for example, all respected a uniform height for their cornice lines, and all incorporated porticoes, providing an almost continuous colonnade.

As for the public, the experience of the Exposition was an eye opener. Only seven miles from the Loop's undisciplined commercial downtown choked with traffic, they could walk around enjoying water pools, the lake view, landscaping, and public art. It was like going to Europe, which is to say that for most people it was their first experience of the pleasures of ordered urbanism. The implication was there: our cities *could* be like that.

Because most of the fair buildings were in the classical style, nativist architecture critics have derided the Columbian Exposition as a foreign import, merely an imitation of European architectural and planning ideas. It is true that classicism originated in Europe, but by 1893 it had deep American roots, not only in colonial architecture, the Federal style, and the Classic Revival, but also in the 1820s Greek Revival of New England. The Colonial Revival had dominated American residential architecture since the 1876 centennial. Thus, to the 27 million visitors who attended the Columbian Exposition, although the grand urban arrangement would have appeared foreign, the architecture would have been familiar. Moreover, the monumental buildings and spaces were in keeping with the burgeoning American cities, as well as in scale with the American landscape. The shore of Lake Michigan is not the bank of the Seine, and the massive white constructions of the Chicago fair were to be appreciated against the backdrop of the vast inland sea. Altogether, the fair was a potent and realistic vision of a new direction for the American city.

The historian James Marston Fitch, who considered the architecture of the Columbian Exposition an impediment to modernism, described the White City as reactionary and subversive, but he did admit that "from contemporary accounts it is clear that the Fair left Americans dazzled by a totally new concept of urban order." There was, for example, what has been called the "sanitary wonder" of the fair—the public areas that were swept and cleaned nightly, the neatly maintained public toilets and drinking fountains, and the segregated delivery vehicles, all suggesting the possibility of how real cities could be made to function more effectively. Public transportation included a rail link to the Loop, an elevated railway that traversed the fair site, and a moving sidewalk.

The most dramatic and novel urban technology demonstrated at the Chicago fair was electricity. The General Electric company built a Tower of Light with ten thousand Edison bulbs, and the Ferris wheel, as well as the pavilions around the basin, were outlined in incandescent bulbs. At night, the White City must have appeared magical. Electricity also powered the elevated railway as well as a fleet of fifty gondolas that cruised the canals and lake. Lake steamers that carried passengers between the fair and the Loop followed a string of electrical buoys; electrically powered communications included telegrams, telephones, and fire alarms. There was, in addition, an entire pavilion devoted solely to the wonders of electricity.

The technological feats fired the public imagination. But the technologies and ideas that the fair espoused were intended not merely for a utopian city of the distant future. It's true that the buildings surrounding the Court of Honor, because they were temporary, were built of steel frames covered with a kind of plaster, but the fountains, the public sculpture, the landscaping, and the urban spaces were real, as was the electric lighting and the sanitation system. This was a tangible demonstration of the collaborative, can-do spirit that turned 600 acres of marshland into the White City. The demonstration could not have come at a more opportune time. There were hundreds of thousands of acres of marshland and forestland and prairie across the continent waiting to be turned into fairyland cities.

SIX

Civic Art

HENRY ADAMS, WHO VISITED THE WHITE CITY, WROTE: "Chicago was the first expression of American thought as a unity; one must start there." The White City offered Americans a new urban model just when one was needed. By the end of the nineteenth century most cities were in the middle of a period of vigorous growth, and it was apparent that while laissez-faire planning might work in small towns, it had severe drawbacks in large cities. A small grid, like that of Alexandria, could be charming, but when it went on for miles, as it did in Chicago, the effect was oppressive. Moreover, the very people who had prospered in the American cities now felt that rough-and-ready planning no longer suited their increasingly genteel way of life. Movers and shakers acquired a taste for the planned avenues and squares of London, Paris, and Rome.

Chicago's Columbian Exposition provided a real and well-publicized demonstration of how the unruly American downtown could be tamed though a partnership of classical architecture, urban landscaping, and heroic public art. Equally important, the planning of the White City brought together an extraordinary group of talented and like-minded creative individuals: the landscape architect Frederick Law Olmsted, the architects Daniel Burnham, Charles McKim, and Richard Morris Hunt, and the artist Augustus Saint-Gaudens. Although their ideas were revolutionary, these were not young firebrands but experienced professionals of social standing with influence among businessmen and politicians. They were followed by a younger generation that included the New York architect John Carrère (codesigner of the New York Public Library), the Philadelphia planner John Nolen, and Olmsted's son, Frederick Law, Jr., and stepson, John Charles, who together carried on the family business. (The senior Olmsted died in 1903, but his active professional life ceased shortly after the Columbian Exposition.)

These men had an ambitious goal. As Werner Hegemann and Elbert Peets, the authors of *The American Vitruvius*, an influential handbook of urban design originally published in 1922, wrote: "Against chaos and anarchy in architecture, emphasis must be placed upon the ideal of civic art and the civilized city." The first chapter of their book was entitled "The Modern Revival of Civic Art," which underlined the common thread that bound together architects like Burnham, McKim, and their followers: a belief in the value of learning from the great urban achievements of the past. Their aim was nothing less than to transplant to the New World the ideals that had underpinned European city building since the sixteenth century—that is, to build classical cities in America. "Classical," in this sense, refers to an architecture derived from the ancient Greeks and Romans, and given its full form by the Renaissance. Classical composition involved a repetition of standardized elements according to predetermined rules, and exemplified, in J. B. Jackson's words, "a devotion to clarity and order." In terms of urban planning, it meant adopting an orderly framework of streets and public spaces within which the work of individual architects could take its place, and introducing such devices as axial views, expansive public squares, and formal groupings of buildings. Although the inspiration was European, the results were distinctive and original. They mirrored the particular conditions of the American city at the turn of the century: available space, rapid urban growth, new urban technologies, and a need for grand civic symbols.

That the public at large was prepared to accept such a reform in urban design was due in no small part to the earlier proselytizing work of Frederick Law Olmsted. By 1900, the prolific landscape architect's parks and parkways were flourishing in almost every major city, and the idea of large-scale urban interventions was commonplace. Not that Olmsted's ideas were accepted wholesale by the younger planners. They considered parks not merely as antidotes to crowded living conditions but as integral parts of the metropolis, and they had more ambitious aims than merely greening the city. Their classically inspired designs were usually more formal than Olmsted's picturesque and naturalistic landscapes, and Olmsted himself remained unreconciled to classicism. Despite his involvement in the Columbian Exposition, he never warmed to classical architecture and was ambivalent about large cities in general. Yet it's difficult to imagine the achievements of the civic art movement and its environmental sensitivity without Olmsted's all-important influence.

One of Olmsted's practical legacies was the knowledge of how to organize a large consulting practice. Olmsted's busy office was a training ground for a whole generation of landscape architects and city planners. He was the first American urban designer to work on a national scale, and thanks to him, it became accepted practice for towns and cities to turn to nationally recognized experts such as Burnham, McKim, Nolen, and the Olmsted brothers for advice. This explains how their ideas spread so quickly from major centers like Chicago to smaller cities like Denver and Dallas.

Idealists they might have been, but the proponents of classicism were not utopians, and they achieved some remarkable successes. The most prominent of these was undoubtedly Washington, D.C., where under the leadership of McKim, and with the active involvement of Burnham, Frederick Law Olmsted, Jr., and Saint-Gaudens, the final realization of L'Enfant's 1791 plan was undertaken. In terms of civic art, the state of the national capital in 1900 left a lot to be desired. The area between the Capitol and the Potomac was unfinished; the Washington Monument, designed by Robert Mills and completed in 1884, had been built slightly off L'Enfant's planned axis, lining up with neither the White House nor the Capital; a mere eighty years after the city's founding, permission had been granted to the Baltimore and Potomac Railroad to lay tracks right across the mall and to build a marshaling yard along with a large terminal blocking the vista from the Capitol to the Washington Monument.

Beginning in 1901, McKim and the members of the Senate Park Commission (also known as the McMillan Commission) visited various European capitals and in less than a year produced a master plan for Washington that included a realigned mall, the placement of the Lincoln and Jefferson memorials, as well as a new railroad terminal with relocated railroad tracks—in a tunnel underground. Some contemporary critics pointed out that the enlarged mall—L'Enfant's "Grand Avenue" was now 1,000-feet wide—had become inhuman, and that replacing the residential scale and atmosphere of Lafayette Square with government offices isolated the White House from the rest of the city. Others were uncomfortable with what they perceived to be imperial grandeur in a republican capital. On the whole, however, the new plan, widely covered by the press, was well received by the public, and implementation of it began right away.

This time the national capital did become a model for the rest of the country, and it encouraged other cities to undertake similar civic improvements. In 1904 Burnham was invited to prepare a master plan for the rapidly expanding city of San Francisco. He spent more than a year on the work and produced a detailed study that would have completely reorganized the major streets according to the lessons of Washington, D.C., with broad diagonal boulevards intersecting at plazas and public building sites. A month before the report was to be made public, San Francisco was struck by the great earthquake and the ensuing fire that destroyed a large part of the city. There was now not enough time to develop a consensus around Burnham's new plan, and in the rush to rebuild, the old street layout was repeated and an important opportunity lost.

There were many other occasions, however, for wholesale redesign. In 1903 John C. Olmsted began work on a new master plan for Seattle, and in 1912 Frederick Law Olmsted, Jr., was retained by the city of Denver to develop plans for a system of parks and parkways. Kansas City and Dallas also undertook to install parkways and boulevards. In 1908 Philadelphia started to plan Fairmount Parkway (later renamed the Benjamin Franklin Parkway), a great boulevard cutting diagonally through Penn's grid and linking the new city hall with Olmsted's park. The parkway sliced through one of Penn's original squares (now Logan Circle), which was redesigned to resemble a Parisian square, complete with two buildings patterned after the *hôtels* that the eighteenth-century architect Jacques-Ange Gabriel had built on the Place de la Concorde.

Such ambitious projects were possible because the advocates of civic art had an extraordinarily broad base of support, exemplified by the popular movement known as the City Beautiful. According to the architectural historian William H. Wilson, the term "City Beautiful" emerged in 1900 as a slogan for an urban improvement campaign in Harrisburg, Pennsylvania. It became a rallying cry that brought together civic reformers, community volunteers, businessmen, and municipal politicians, with crusading architects and landscape architects. This makes the City Beautiful movement the equivalent of, say, the historic preservation movement today, although it was shorter-lived, lasting only until about 1910.* Local chapters of the American Institute of Architects, the American Park and Outdoor Art Association, and the American League for Civic Improvement spread the word. The last two merged, in 1903, into the American Civic Association under the leadership of J. Horace McFarland, a businessman turned activist who became a national spokesman. The public learned about urban beautification through books such as Charles Mulford Robinson's *The Improvement of Towns and Cities* and *Modern Civic Art*, through essays in *The Atlantic Monthly* and *Harper's*, as well as through articles in such popular women's publications as *Home and Flowers* and the *Ladies' Home Journal*.

Thanks to City Beautiful activists, American cities started to look at themselves critically. One way to improve a typical gridded downtown was to introduce a formal civic center. This group of public buildings usually included the city hall, a public library, and an auditorium placed around a square or landscaped mall. In 1902 a commission made up of Burnham, Carrère, and the architect Arnold Brunner prepared a plan for a civic center for Cleveland that was consciously modeled on the concept of the Court of

*In his 1909 *Plan of Chicago*, which I will discuss later, Daniel Burnham never uses the term "City Beautiful"; nor did Werner Hegemann and Elbert Peets in *The American Vitruvius*.

Honor of the White City. In 1912, Brunner and Olmsted, Jr., collaborated on a design for a civic center for Denver that arranged municipal buildings, a library, and an art building along a landscaped mall facing the state capitol. The design for Saint Louis's civic center likewise used a mall as the focus. New York City acquired a vertical civic center in the Municipal Building, designed by McKim's firm of McKim, Mead, and White. There were also civic centers built in Springfield, Massachusetts, Rochester, New York, and other smaller cities. The civic center introduced noncommercial buildings into downtown in a prominent way that was intended to give people a sense of civic pride. The most famous existing example of a grand civic center is in San Francisco, built in 1912 following the 1906 earthquake and fire. Although it did not follow Burnham's original proposal, the more modest and compact plan developed by the architects John Galen Howard, Frederick H. Meyer, and John Reid, Jr., has proved to be adaptable over the years. It began with City Hall (modeled after Saint Peter's in Rome!); in 1936 an opera house and the Veterans Building were added; in 1980 a symphony hall; and in 1986 a new state office building completed the ensemble.

Civic beautification also produced the grand American railroad stations. The urban railroad terminal was a peculiarly characteristic building of the first quarter of the twentieth century when railroads were the preeminent means of transportation. Central terminals served a vital role in the life of cities and were used by both long-distance travelers and commuters. As one historian put it, urban railroad stations were also focal points for the expression of civic values. The symbolic role of the terminal, like the ceremonial gateways of medieval towns, was to signal arrival in the city. Terminal Station at Chicago's World's Columbian Exposition, whose design Peirce Anderson of Burnham's firm adapted in Washington, D.C.'s Union Station, became the architectural model. It was followed by the two New York City terminals: McKim's Pennsylvania Station, modeled on the Baths of Caracalla of ancient Rome, and Grand Central Terminal. Jarvis Hunt, the nephew of Richard Morris Hunt, who had designed the main building of the White City, was chosen to design the new Union Station in Kansas City, which had just completed an extensive park and boulevard system. Kansas City's station was one of the largest in the United States, with a ninety-foot-high lobby almost as big as a football field.

Two outstanding later examples, both designed by Peirce Anderson after Burnham's death, were Chicago's Union Station and the Cleveland terminal. The Cleveland station was part of a nine-building group that included a fifty-two-story Terminal Tower, a hotel, a department store, and offices. (This group of buildings replaced Burnham's civic center plan, which was not carried out.) In 1927, Anderson's firm, Graham, Anderson, Probst, & White, started work on one of the last great terminals, Philadelphia's beautiful Thirtieth Street Station, whose details are influenced by Art Deco but still recall their classical antecedents, as do the seventy-one-foot-high Corinthian columns that form a colonnade at the entrance. The consistent success of these architects in turning what was essentially a transportation interchange into a civic symbol is all the more admirable when one considers the fate of the modern airport, which despite the best efforts of modernist architects has failed to transcend its utilitarian role except in very few cases, such as Dulles International Airport in Washington, D.C., whose large departure hall with its column-free space is in some ways a reworked classical railroad terminal.

Civic art concerned itself with two other types of buildings: expositions and university campuses. As a result of Chicago's Columbian Exposition of 1893, major fairs were held in a series of cities: Buffalo (the Pan-American Exposition, 1901); Saint

Louis (the Louisiana Purchase Exposition, 1904), which introduced Americans to the work of German and Austrian architects such as Peter Behrens, Joseph Maria Olbrich, and Josef Hoffmann; and Seattle (the Alaska-Yukon-Pacific Exposition, 1910). All these popular fairs drew upon classical principles such as axiality and formal symmetry for their planning. In 1915 two large fairs were held in California: San Francisco's Panama-Pacific International Exposition and San Diego's Panama-California International Exposition. In the San Diego fair, whose overall design was coordinated by the architect Bertram Grosvenor Goodhue, the use of the Spanish colonial style demonstrated that the classicism that had first taken root in Chicago and Washington, D.C., could be adapted successfully to Southern California.

The beginning of the twentieth century witnessed the construction of many new large universities. The planned college campus was a well-established tradition in America (going all the way back to Jefferson's University of Virginia), especially in New England, where the numerous private colleges included such architectural gems as Williams, Amherst, and Smith (whose parklike plan was devised by the elder Olmsted). The new campuses were larger, and many, including the Massachusetts Institute of Technology, and Columbia University and New York University, both designed by McKim, Mead, and White, were urban. All three were classically inspired in layout and appearance, with columned porticoes, domed rotundas, and pedimented porches. Classicism became a hallmark of urban universities the same way that Victorian Gothic had characterized many of the small colleges, but there were other styles, too. The layout of Johns Hopkins University in Baltimore followed the best classical precepts, with a central lawn and a symmetrical layout, but the architecture was colonial. Houston's Rice University, planned by Goodhue and his partners, Ralph Adams Cram and Frank W. Ferguson, exhibited an exotic sort of classicism with Byzantine motifs and multicolored Saracenic arches. The University of California at Berkeley held an international competition for its campus; the winner was a Beaux Arts–educated Parisian, but the buildings—many designed by John Galen Howard, a San Franciscan—were in the Spanish colonial style.

The original parts of these campuses, where buildings, landscaping, and public plazas complement each other, remain the most fully realized examples of the civic art ideal and probably its most tangible legacy. These academic enclaves, many of which were built from scratch, gave architects the opportunity to design what were in effect small, self-contained towns. With the advantage of a private (and rich) patron and without the constraints imposed by zoning, commercial interests, multiple landowners, and municipal politics, architects could build large, comprehensively planned environments on a scale and with a consistency impossible in the city itself. Here was proof, if proof was required, that Americans could build beautiful urban places.

Jane Jacobs has called the City Beautiful movement an "architectural design cult" rather than a "cult of social reform." This is only partly true. The advocates of civic art did believe in the value of design, both architectural and urban, but they did not think of parks and boulevards as merely civic adornments; these were to be places for leisure and public recreation, and improvements to the very fabric of cities. The focus on railroad stations and on urban transportation likewise reflected a concern for the broad public good. On the other hand, it's true that building grand railroad stations did not address housing issues at precisely the time—the early decades of this century—when the living conditions of most working people were abysmal. But the chief handicap of the practitioners of civic art was not a lack of social concern, nor, even less, their partiality to classicism. It was an inability to face up to the reality of the American city.

This inability is best exemplified by what the urban historian John Reps has described as "one of the great accomplishments of American planning," the Burnham plan for Chicago. In 1906, more than a decade after the Columbian Exposition, Burnham and his associate, Edward H. Bennett, were commissioned by the Merchant's Club, a Chicago businessmen's association, to produce a visionary plan for the city. The project took three years to complete and is estimated to have cost almost $70,000—a vast sum that did not include Burnham's own time, which he volunteered free of charge. The result was a 164-page report, published in 1,650 copies, with a text by Burnham and many illustrations—photographs, diagrams, plans, and sketches, as well as a beautiful series of colored views of the city-to-be drawn by the New York painter, illustrator, and set designer Jules Guerin.

Burnham and Bennett's extraordinary plan covered an area enclosed by a circle drawn with a sixty-mile radius around the Loop. It was in effect a proposal for the entire metropolitan region of Chicago. It showed how the city should be linked to surrounding suburban towns by highways and railroads, and analyzed the movement of passengers and freight throughout the region. It proposed forest reserves and greenbelts, and within the city, parkways and urban parks, including a long lakefront park built on reclaimed land and forming a series of inland lagoons. Diagonal avenues were cut through the traditional grid, and a thirty-mile circular parkway that recalled Olmsted and Vaux's earlier plan for a linear park provided a "grand circuit" linking half a dozen of the city's major parks. Another dramatic innovation was the creation of a brand-new civic center, not in the Loop but inland, east of the Chicago River. Here, at the exact geometrical center of the entire plan, Burnham and Bennett placed a huge domed municipal administration building facing a great plaza flanked by county and federal offices.

Burnham and Bennett held public hearings and political consultations, and their report included material prepared by numerous committees charged with studying railroads, freight movements, ports, road traffic, and recreation. The comprehensive nature of the plan belies the proposition that the concerns of City Beautiful advocates were solely aesthetic. Burnham's original draft incorporated reforms to public utilities, hospitals, daycare centers, and schools. This was hardly the work of a "design cult." Nor was the plan intended to be a theoretical exercise; a postscript entitled "Legal Aspects of the Plan of Chicago," written by Walter L. Fisher of the Chicago Bar, set out the legislative basis for instituting the proposed changes, and was endorsed by county and municipal governments.

"We have found that those cities which retain their dominion over the imaginations of mankind achieve that result through the harmony and beauty of their civic works," wrote Burnham, who imagined that the "Metropolis of the Middle West" would be a city along the lines of London, Paris, Vienna, or Berlin. To him, "civic works" meant impressive squares and stately public buildings—features which, in Burnham's view, would provide the chief urban and architectural identity of the city, and which therefore should be given physical preeminence. Guerin's panoramic watercolor views of the new Chicago showed the tall dome of the civic center rising from a city composed entirely of buildings seven to twelve stories high. This low-profile city bore an undeniable resemblance to Paris; not coincidentally, both Guerin, an American, and Bennett, an Englishman, had studied at the Ecole des Beaux-Arts.

Despite its practicality, the Chicago plan had one utopian feature: Burnham and his colleagues, who scrupulously delineated existing streets, public parks, and even railroad rights-of-way, chose to ignore the tall buildings (many built by Burnham's own firm) that were downtown Chicago's most distinctive feature. This rejection of the skyscraper was certainly not an implied criticism of commercial development—the conservative Burnham was not antibusiness—nor was he suggesting that dozens of existing Chicago skyscrapers be demolished. Presumably, Guerin was portraying an ideal future, not merely making pretty pictures. But in that case, how were the heights of buildings to be controlled? The legal section of the report does mention easements that might be applied to lots abutting parks or boulevards, but there is no mention of restricting building height. This is a curious omission, since Washington, D.C., with which Burnham had extensive experience, did have rigorous height limits: 90 feet for residential streets, and 130 feet on wider avenues. But these limits were imposed by Congress in 1899, two years before Burnham was involved, and since there was no pressure to build tall buildings in Washington anyway until the late 1930s, the significance of height controls may have passed unnoticed.

It is possible that Burnham and Bennett simply wanted to avoid the thorny issue of architectural controls altogether, since such prohibitions flew in the face of the American tradition of allowing property owners to build with a minimum of restrictions. It was one thing to have height restrictions in the national capital, quite another to propose them in commercial cities. While large cities were beginning to enact building regulations, especially with regard to fire safety and public health (zoning ordinances were introduced for the first time in Los Angeles in 1907, and in New York City in 1916), aesthetic regulations such as standardized building height, uniform frontage, and a common cornice line were felt to be intrusive.

It is also possible that the two men could not reconcile their urban theories—which assumed that public buildings would take precedence over commercial and residential structures—with the actual state of affairs in the American downtown. Tall buildings like New York's Municipal Building or Cleveland's Terminal Tower were intended to act as civic symbols, but there was no place in Burnham's vision for downtowns made up of commercial skyscrapers. Yet it was precisely the tall office buildings that impressed the European visitor to Chicago and New York City, and set American cities apart from Europe. In Europe the most impressive urban monuments were public structures like the Eiffel Tower, or religious buildings like the dome of Saint Paul's Cathedral in London, or freestanding campaniles; in Chicago and New York the tallest buildings were privately built and privately owned, and they towered over the cathedral, the city hall, and the public library. It is true that in medieval Lucca, Bologna, and San Gimignano, wealthy merchant families had also built competing towers that rose as high as three hundred feet. Eventually many of these towers were demolished or reduced in height as communal or princely authority affirmed its power over private interests. The American skyscraper found no such opposition.

Commercial towers were symbols of the entrepreneurial American city. The tall office building not only made money for its corporate owner but also celebrated and symbolized the making of money. They were also a source of wonderment for the general public, a dramatic index of technological achievement. Having "the tallest building west of the Mississippi" or "the tallest building in the British Empire" marked a city in much the same way as a pennant-winning baseball team does today.

The clash between horizontal ideals and vertical aspirations is dramatically illustrated in the evolution of North Michigan Avenue in Chicago. As early as 1896, Burnham had proposed linking the Loop with the area north of the Chicago River—the so-called Gold Coast—by building a tunnel under the river at Michigan Avenue and broadening the existing street. The 1909 *Plan of Chicago* elaborated this idea, replacing the tunnel with a bridge and extending Michigan Avenue northward as an elevated boulevard in the mold of the Champs-Elysées. Guerin's bird's-eye view shows a broad avenue lined with trees and flanked by uniform seven-story buildings with distinctly Parisian mansard roofs. The median strips are marked by heroic sculptures; a sort of traffic island contains a large fountain. There are crowds of promenaders, including many women with parasols, both on the sidewalks as well as in the street itself; the pedestrians seem oblivious to the carriages, horse-drawn omnibuses, and automobiles.* The chief impression of this charming drawing is a kind of ease and a sense of spaciousness that were in marked contrast to the busy congested streets of the Loop.

There was a great deal of interest in implementing this proposal, not the least because of the impact such an important street would have on adjacent property values. The mayor formed a planning commission to oversee its execution. Four years later the city council passed an ordinance for the construction of the new bridge and widening the avenue north of the river. The project incorporated many, though not all, of the original designers' ideas (after Burnham's death, Bennett continued to serve as a consultant to the planning commission). The idea of an elevated boulevard was scrapped, but the overall architectural concept was preserved. The North Central Business District Association, which had been

*Although Burnham's plan did not anticipate the mass ownership of cars and the effect that this would have on the downtown—production of Henry Ford's Model T was started in 1908, but low prices did not come into effect until about 1914—he did accurately foresee that the automobile would accelerate the growth of the suburbs.

formed to rule on details of the project, recommended that all buildings on the avenue maintain a uniform cornice line, just as in Guerin's drawings, and be ten stories (about 120 feet) high, the maximum allowed by the Chicago building code in that area. It's true that a ten-story limit was higher than the original cap of seven stories, but this would still have produced the desired result: buildings whose heights were proportional to the width of the avenue. It seems that the association, at least, realized that uniformity and height controls were an integral part of Burnham and Bennett's plan.

Chicago would finally get its Champs-Elysées. But just as work on the avenue was beginning, the building code was revised to permit a maximum building height of two hundred feet, and the first building constructed on North Michigan Avenue rose sixteen stories, or almost exactly two hundred feet. The North Central Business District Association appears to have been silent on this point—hardly surprising, as the association was composed of property owners who stood to profit by the new height limit. In 1919 the maximum building height was again revised: now protruding towers were allowed to soar to four hundred feet. On North Michigan Avenue, the celebrated Wrigley Building took full advantage of the new code: the top of its central clock tower is 398 feet above the street.

This is not the end of the story. In 1923 the building code was again rewritten, with the result that the maximum height of towers was almost unrestricted; so was the height of buildings that did not cover the entire block but left at least three-quarters of their site open. The sky was the limit. During the 1920s, North Michigan Avenue became the site of some of the city's tallest and most spectacular buildings: John Mead Howell and Raymond Hood's 450-foot-high Tribune Tower (winner of a famous international competition) and the exuberant 42-story Medinah Club, which was built for the Shriners and is topped by a minaret and pear-shaped dome. The last tall building erected in the 1920s was the Union Carbide & Carbon Corporation Building that rose 40 stories straight up from the sidewalk. A poignant footnote: its architects were Burnham Brothers, Inc., a firm founded by Hubert and Daniel H., Jr., the old man's sons.

"North Michigan's transformation would see the construction of some of Chicago's most significant individual works of architecture," writes John W. Stamper, who teaches architecture at the University of Notre Dame, "yet at the same time this would result in a highly inconsistent pattern of urban design." Or rather, all too consistent. Each building squeezed the economic possibilities of its site to the utmost and simultaneously celebrated and asserted the individuality and achievement of its owners and designers. As Stamper notes, the fate of North Michigan Avenue illustrates one of the persistent dilemmas of urban design in American cities: where land values were high, control over development was essentially impossible. And if Burnham's ideals were compromised even in his native Chicago, what chance did they have elsewhere? For a public caught up in the excitement and glamour of seeing taller and taller skyscrapers, a primarily horizontal downtown must have appeared increasingly staid and old-fashioned. In the Land of the Dollar, Burnham's genteel vision of civic harmony was given short shrift; the city profitable replaced the city beautiful. A profitable city was to be as little regulated as possible. It meant a city in which the no-nonsense street grid was reasserted without any urban frills such as diagonal boulevards or public squares.

According to William H. Wilson, the newly established associations of professional city planners, a new generation that replaced the old guard architect-planners like Burnham, never really warmed to the idea of civic art. These self-styled specialists did not appreciate the interference of architects, laypeople, and politicians, whom they perceived as meddlesome intruders, into their field. As city planning increasingly became the responsibility of municipal governments (therefore more bureaucratized and technical), it became increasingly common to denigrate the calls for urban beautification as the untutored opinions of misguided amateurs. At the First National Conference on City Planning, held in 1909, attempts to beautify cities were decried as exercises in "civic vanity" and "external adornment." The bureaucrats and engineers felt that city planning should be concerned with engineering, economic efficiency, and social reform, not with aesthetics. They asserted that whatever functioned well would automatically produce a beautiful, or at least an acceptable, urban environment.

Our cities would not be "like that" after all. Perhaps the demise of civic art and the City Beautiful was inevitable, or at least foreordained. John Lukacs has characterized the fifty years after 1895 as "the bourgeois interlude: the half-century when American civilization was urban and urbane." The ideal of civic art was in large part a reflection of the tastes and aspirations of an urbane bourgeoisie. Lukacs distinguishes between bourgeois and middle class, and maintains that the values of American urban culture, in particular, were bourgeois, "with a tinge of the patrician." The desire for aesthetic rules, for polite urbanity, and for architectural decorum, as well as for sublimating private display for the sake of the public good, might be described as an attempt to translate bourgeois values into physical urban form. But the "civilized city" that Hegemann and Peets had called for in *The American Virtruvius* was not to be. The decline of the bourgeoisie and its replacement by a catch-all Middle America would take the American city in a very different direction.

SEVEN

High Hopes

EVERY HISTORICAL PERIOD HAS ITS URBAN BELLwethers—that is, cities that command attention because they embody the values of their particular epoch. These cities are appreciated for their culture, envied for their prosperity, and admired for their dynamism; frequently, they are also the cities whose architecture and urban design is imitated. The Rome of Pope Sixtus V (1521–90) was such a place; its imposing civic monuments and Baroque planning influenced town planning across Europe. In the eighteenth century, London, a comfortable, rambling city of townhouses, private residential squares, and public pleasure gardens, became the model to emulate. During the 1850s, attention shifted to Paris. The transformation of that city from the sixteenth-century city created by Henri IV to a modern industrial metropolis occurred during the Second Empire (1852–1870), and was due chiefly to the enterprise of Napoléon

III and to Baron Georges-Eugène Haussmann, the man he appointed as prefect of the Seine. Haussmann's powerful post combined the roles of mayor, minister of public works, and chief city planner. Paris got new railroad stations, hospitals, markets, and numerous civic buildings; Haussmann himself built new aqueducts and sewers, introduced public gas lighting to the streets, and created almost 5,000 acres of parkland, including the Bois de Boulogne. But he is best remembered for relentlessly pushing wide boulevards through old residential quarters, a strategy that combined a concern for sanitation with traffic engineering, as well as an interest in facilitating rapid troop deployment in a city prone to public disturbances.

It was during this period that Paris acquired its modern persona, the image of a city with an atmosphere of urban gaiety, a preoccupation with fashion and food, and a taste for grand architectural gestures. The composer Jacques Offenbach provided the gaiety. Napoléon's wife, the Empress Eugénie, popularized the crinoline skirt and the plunging neckline, and Charles Frederick Worth, a transplanted Englishman, was the first of a long line of couturiers who made Paris the world's fashion center. Brillat-Savarin and Carême had established *la grande cuisine* earlier in the century, and fashionable restaurants such as the Petit Moulin Rouge (where Auguste Escoffier was employed) lined the boulevards of a city also renowned for its elegant hotels. Architects provided the grandeur. Charles Garnier, the magnificent new opera house; Henri Labrouste, the cavernous reading room of the Bibliothèque Nationale; and J. I. Hittorff, the cathedral-like Gare du Nord; even the central market (Les Halles, designed by Victor Baltard) was impressive. The architectural heritage that we admire today depended on material prosperity, of course. Industrialization, land speculation, and profitable colonial ventures had made some Parisians rich, and this had produced a society dominated by the making and spending of money, just like Chicago's, although with different results.

Paris was the destination not only of the fashionable upper classes but of a broad range of people, for starting in mid-century, the city became the world's leading locale for international exhibitions. Eleven million people visited Napoléon III's Great Universal Exhibition in 1867; sixteen million came in 1878 and saw the Trocadero palace (a Moorish confection that stood on the present site of the Palais de Chaillot); an extraordinary thirty-two million came in 1889 and saw the city from a completely new vantage point—the top of the Eiffel Tower; and even more attended the Universal Exhibition of 1900.

Visitors admired the technological marvels and exotic exhibits that were—and still are—the staple of international fairs. But since the French exhibitions, unlike the relatively concentrated Columbian Exposition of Chicago, were spread over a large part of Paris, the city itself was on display. There was much to see: architectural novelties such as the multistoried department stores (the world's first electrical arc lights were installed in a Parisian department store in 1877); monumental railroad stations, topped by the lavish Gare d'Orsay, built in 1900; aboveground, omnibuses, and underground, the new subway with its striking Art Nouveau station entrances designed by Hector Guimard; and boulevards illuminated by electricity, giving rise to the sobriquet City of Light. Soon versions of these Parisian innovations appeared as far afield as Cairo and Mexico City. Along the newly widened streets, like the Avenue de l'Opéra and the Boulevard de Sébastopol, were luxurious apartment buildings and hotels built by property developers. It was these apartment houses, designed according to strict height, setback, and projection regulations established by Haussmann, that so impressed architects like Charles McKim and Edward Bennett, who as young men came to Paris to study at the Ecole des Beaux-Arts, and who later tried to introduce the lessons of Paris to American cities.*

World's fairs were obviously an important part of nineteenth-century urbanism, not only because of the civic monuments and the public works they left behind, but also because the fairs themselves served as highly visible laboratories for innovation in urban design. For example, the Crystal Palace erected in London's Hyde Park for the Great Exposition of 1851 spurred the construction of large glass-roofed shopping arcades in many European cities. The Paris exhibition of 1889 introduced the world to large-scale electrical street lighting. Ideas spread quickly. The French, impressed by Chicago's Columbian Exposition, incorporated grand neoclassical buildings—the Grand Palais and the Petit Palais—into their Universal Exhibition of 1900.

The Columbian Exposition marks the moment when Europeans first took notice of urbanism in the New World. The French were influenced by American railway stations when they built the Gare d'Orsay. The British were also aware of American town planning. A City Beautiful conference was held in Liverpool in 1907; three years later, at the Town Planning Exhibition and Conference in London, Daniel Burnham was an invited speaker, and the impressive drawings of the Washington, D.C., plan were prominently displayed. The latter did not necessarily influence

*Regulations were not the only reason for the agreeable architectural homogeneity of the Second Empire apartment houses. As Anthony Sutcliffe argues in *Paris: An Architectural History*, building permits were reviewed by municipal architectural overseers, who exercised a harmonizing influence on individual buildings; in some cases, Haussmann built model apartment blocks that served as prototypes; and the widespread use of dressed limestone also helped. So did the fact that virtually all architects favored the classical style, which proved remarkably adaptable to the needs of standardized, repetitive building. "Flexibility rather than creativity was the theme," Sutcliffe writes, "and the result was a classical architecture for the industrial era rather than an industrial architecture."

British urban design, however. Opportunities for large urban projects were rare, nor did the monumental scale of the American work suit most architects, who were more interested in exploring the indigenous vernacular of British towns and villages. One exception was the talented Edwin Lutyens, probably the greatest English architect since Wren. Lutyens loved grand gestures and classical design, and he did eventually get a chance to implement a Burnhamesque urban plan in the imperial capital of New Delhi.

When American urbanism took center stage, after the 1920s, it was precisely the nemesis of the City Beautiful movement, the skyscraper, that captured the world's imagination. Like so many later American inventions—blue jeans, fast food, rock and roll—the skyscraper had mass appeal, and for the rest of the century, the American skyline of tall towers epitomized the modern metropolis, just as Parisian boulevards had earlier.

Although the skyscraper originated in Chicago, it was New York that became the exemplary skyscraper city. The first true New York skyscraper was the Flatiron Building, designed by Chicago's Daniel Burnham in 1902. At twenty-two stories, the Flatiron was the tallest building in the city, and it was also the most dramatic. Its site is a narrow triangle facing Madison Square Park, which meant that unlike previous skyscrapers, which were simply taller versions of conventional street-frontage buildings, the Flatiron really did look like a slender freestanding tower (an image captured successfully in the famous photograph by Alfred Stieglitz). Some Chicago skyscrapers were taller, but none as striking. The public loved the Flatiron, and businessmen and their architects took notice.

The vertical growth of New York was partly a result of immigration that swelled the population of the entire city, partly caused by the limited space of Manhattan Island, and partly a function of geology. Hard rock is the most economical base for extremely tall buildings and eliminates the need for expensive foundations, and Manhattan has shallow bedrock chiefly in two areas: at the southern tip of the island around Wall Street, and in Midtown south of Central Park. The following decade saw many more corporate stalagmites in both locations, and notable skyscrapers included the 600-foot neoclassical Singer Tower and the Woolworth Building, with its cathedral-like lobby and Gothic-revival exterior, which soared up 792 feet, making it the tallest building in the world. On the Upper East Side, verticality was evident in the form of apartment buildings, a Parisian import that had become extremely popular with fashionable New Yorkers.*

Never before had American civilization been so resolutely urban. By 1920, more Americans were living in cities than ever before, and most of the people who could be classified as urban lived in the largest cities. But America also had become urban in another sense: cities like New York (after World War I the biggest city in the world), Chicago, and Philadelphia, as well as Detroit, Pittsburgh, San Francisco, and many smaller cities, were home to a new, dynamic, metropolitan way of life. The hallmarks of this way of life were above all architectural: great railroad stations and department stores, nightclubs and musical theaters, impressive public libraries and concert halls, grand hotels and luxurious apartment houses.

Although many of the most prominent manifestations of this urban civilization were associated with the upper-middle class, there was also a parallel urban culture with broader appeal: mass-circulation newspapers (including such innovations as comics, color supplements, and women's pages), amusement parks, professional spectator sports, and movie palaces. While not all of these were American inventions—popular movies, for example,

*The first New York City apartment buildings, which were built in the 1870s, were called "French flats."

were pioneered in Germany and France—the prosperity of American cities ensured enthusiastic application and acceptance of such innovations. Amusement parks like New York's Coney Island and Chicago's White City (the successor of the Midway Plaisance) were more extravagant than elsewhere; movie palaces, even those in small cities, were grander; and downtown streets were more crowded—with pedestrians, pushcarts, horse-drawn wagons, streetcars, omnibuses, and automobiles.

As far as architecture was concerned, the period leading up to the Depression was marked by eclecticism. Beaux Arts classicism, neo-Gothic, and Art Deco competed for attention. Atop the Chrysler Building were eagle gargoyles that mimicked the hood ornaments on the company's cars; the twin towers of the San Remo apartments were capped by finialed Roman temples; the 1,250-foot Empire State Building was crowned by a tall mast, intended for mooring airships. It was an epoch that remains unrivaled for the sheer exuberance of its architecture, its technological inventiveness, and its structural accomplishments. The result was hardly the polite and carefully orchestrated urbanism of Burnham's dream, however. It was brash, pragmatic, and often vulgar. Bright lights, skylines, activity, excitement—there was little intellectual underpinning to the vertical city, whose appeal was visual and visceral. Jazz had originated in the South, but during the twenties it blossomed in the cities of the North: Chicago, Kansas City, Philadelphia, and especially New York. Like jazz, the vertical city was marked by improvisation—like the colonial builders of Woodstock, Vermont, who modified their plans to suit changing circumstances, the builders of New York made it up as they went along.

The advocates of the profitable city had been correct: unleashing commercial forces had produced a dynamic urbanism that was the envy of the rest of the world—certainly, after 1918, of war-weary Europe, whose own cities seemed tame and old-fashioned by comparison.* One European who visited the United States was a Parisian architect, Swiss-born Charles-Edouard Jeanneret, or Le Corbusier, as he preferred to be called. He arrived in 1935. Like Tocqueville a century earlier, Le Corbusier traveled by ship, but his vessel, the *Normandie*, was not detoured, and he was greeted not by the sight of the little houses of Newport but by the towers of New York. "We saw the mystic city of the new world appear far away, rising up from Manhattan," he recounted. "It passed us at close range: a spectacle of brutality and savagery. In contrast to our hopes the skyscrapers were not made of glass, but of tiara-crowned masses of stone. They carry up a thousand feet in the sky, a completely new and prodigious architectural event; with one stroke Europe is thrust aside."

Where Tocqueville came to America to learn, Le Corbusier came to instruct. He was already well known as a leading practitioner of the new International Style that had been sanctioned by the Museum of Modern Art in a prominent exhibition three years earlier. It was the museum that invited Le Corbusier and, together with the Rockefeller Foundation, organized a speaking tour that took the French architect to twenty cities, including Chicago, Philadelphia, Detroit, Pittsburgh, and Boston. He also visited college towns, lecturing at Princeton, Yale, and Vassar.

Le Corbusier spent two and a half months in the United States. He recorded his impressions in a short travel memoir published in France immediately on his return. He wrote quickly, and his book, titled *When the Cathedrals Were White*, is an uneven collec-

*Other forces were unleashed, too. Prohibition produced urban gangsterism on an unprecedented scale, and resulted in the corruption of public officials that lingers still.

tion of architectural bombast, self-serving anecdotes, and canny insights. Like Tocqueville, Le Corbusier admired American practicality, and he enjoyed the informality of American social life; he also deplored and commented on the treatment of black Americans. Like Tocqueville, he was condescending toward American high culture, especially when it imitated Europe—although he loved jazz—and he too was impressed by the cleanliness of American cities. After a visit to Pennsylvania Station and Grand Central Terminal, for example, ignoring the grand classical architecture, he observed that "the beautiful stone slabs of the floor are shining and spotless at all times. Papers never lie about on it."

New York fascinated him; "the City of Incredible Towers," he called it. Although Manhattan was Le Corbusier's first experience of skyscrapers, he had been thinking of a vertical city for more than a decade. In 1922, undaunted by his lack of experience in city planning, he prepared an exhibit for a "contemporary city for three million inhabitants." The plan was an unremarkable grid, but its downtown was composed uniquely of huge freestanding office towers. Three years later he suggested razing a 600-acre section of Paris around Les Halles, the rue de Rivoli, and the Faubourg St-Honoré, and building eighteen sixty-story skyscrapers and a crosstown expressway. Although his so-called Voisin Plan preserved the Louvre and Notre-Dame Cathedral, the medieval street pattern was totally obliterated. These projects and other concepts were included in two books: *The City of Tomorrow*, published in 1925, and *The Radiant City*, which appeared just before his American trip.

Radical urban surgery—one might describe it as a lobotomy—like the Voisin Plan gave Le Corbusier notoriety. Looking back, it is difficult to understand how someone who could make such absurd—not to say despotic and inhumane—proposals might be taken seriously. But he was, at least by intellectuals; to Le Corbusier's continued chagrin, his projects never garnered much political or popular support. Perhaps politicians saw through the mask he presented to the world; although he dressed in sober, dark suits, and wore thick, circular eyeglasses that gave him the air of an accountant, Le Corbusier was really a bohemian. He had received his only formal professional education as an engraver in a school of applied arts, and by temperament and inclination he was an individualist and an artist. He was about as prepared to be a town planner as, say, Andy Warhol.

Nevertheless, by dint of his formidable ego and a Warholian gift for self-promotion, Le Corbusier made himself into an urban expert. His architecture was certainly original—in the spare, progressive fashion of the time—and his vaguely socialist theories appealed to New Deal liberals (he himself seems to have been a political chameleon). Le Corbusier is now best remembered for his architectural work, but he devoted a great deal of time to town planning. He was one of the founders of the Congrès Internationaux d'Architecture Moderne (CIAM), a series of international conferences whose intent was to introduce modern urbanism to Europe. He made a tour of South America. As he plane-hopped from city to city, he sketched unsolicited proposals for the radical reconstruction of São Paulo, Rio de Janeiro, Montevideo, and Buenos Aires; he also had plans for Algiers, Barcelona, Geneva, Stockholm, and Antwerp.

Journalists gave Le Corbusier much free publicity because he was the source of colorful quotes. The day after his arrival in New York, the *Herald Tribune* carried the following headline over an article featuring an interview with the French architect: FINDS AMERICAN SKYSCRAPERS MUCH TOO SMALL. Although he admired Manhattan, Le Corbusier thought there was room for improvement. In an article he wrote for the *American Architect* he unveiled a version of his Voisin Plan for Manhattan: he replaced the clusters of office towers with giant skyscrapers set far apart. (Le Corbusier had already proposed a huge office building for Algiers that could accommodate 10,000 workers, which was more even than the recently completed Empire State Building.) Between the skyscrapers, a park extended over the entire island; instead of sidewalks there were winding footpaths, and instead of streets, high-speed expressways.

Le Corbusier realized that most New Yorkers lived in brownstone rowhouses, walk-ups, and low-rise tenements. "Between the present skyscrapers there are masses of large and small buildings. Most of them small," he noted. "What are these small houses doing in dramatic Manhattan? I haven't the slightest idea. It is incomprehensible. It is a fact, nothing more, as the debris after an earthquake or bombardment is a fact." The convoluted language aside, the message was clear: the debris had to be done away with. Le Corbusier had the answer to that, too. He proposed apartment blocks—lower than the office buildings, about sixteen stories—organized in long slabs that each could house three thousand people. Instead of streets and sidewalks, there were elevators and corridors, or "interior streets," as he called them. It was all very rational—"Cartesian" was a favorite Le Corbusier term—cars over there, living over here, work above, play below. Voilà! The city of the future.

But the city of the future would have to wait. When Le Corbusier visited America in 1935, the country was in the midst of what one historian has called a period of arrested urban development. Thanks to the Depression and World War II, the years between 1930 and 1945 saw relatively little building activity. The Public Works Administration did undertake urban beautification projects, civic buildings, and some public housing. But with a few notable exceptions—Rockefeller Center in New York—there was no downtown construction, and with massive unemployment and factory closings, the suburban home-building industry all but disappeared.

Not until the postwar decade were long-delayed investments made in buildings and urban infrastructure. It was high time. In addition to fifteen years of neglect, cities like New York and Chicago had a nineteenth-century heritage of hurriedly built tenements with truly awful living conditions. One of the consequences of the war and returning veterans was an enormous need for new housing. The favorite solution was to start afresh. Old buildings were demolished to give way to new; downtown blocks were razed; and new versions of the City Beautiful civic centers were built, this time including convention halls, hotels, and performing arts centers. Billions of dollars poured into cities in what was probably the largest burst of construction since the boom period of the late nineteenth century.

Urban renewal, as this initiative was optimistically termed, was not only the result of private investment; for the first time, cities became recipients of massive government spending. The 1949 Housing Act called for "a decent home and a suitable housing environment for every American family," and mandated the use of federal money for the acquisition and demolition of slums, providing funds for the construction of more than 800,000 units of public housing. This by itself was an enormous urban intervention (most of the public housing was in cities), but shortly it was followed by an even bigger government program: the Federal-Aid Highway Act, passed by Congress in 1956. Interstate highway construction was not originally intended to affect cities, since federal planners wanted to avoid building in congested urban areas, but with the active lobbying of big-city mayors, the 41,000-mile interstate highway system was altered to include 6,100 miles of expensive urban freeways, and more than half of the entire proposed budget of $50 billion was diverted to urban construction. Highway construction represented a massive injection of capital into the urban economy but proved a Pyrrhic victory. There was temporary creation of construction jobs, to be sure, but the highways (usually elevated) wrought physical havoc in the established urban fabric, reducing the older housing stock, creating physical barriers between neighborhoods, and often cutting cities off from their waterfronts. Urban highways also ultimately accelerated central city decline by providing ready access to the suburbs from downtown.

The removal and replacement of deteriorated parts of the city is always a painful process. (Haussmann's beautification of Paris had been bought at great human cost, as had Sixtus V's reconstruction of Rome.) It is never easy to identify "the slums," since physical deterioration of neighborhoods is never consistent. In any case, what appears an eyesore to some is home to others. Inevitably, people are displaced, everyday life is disrupted, and neighborhoods are thrown into disarray. Inevitably, too, greed corrupts the political process and the wrecker's ball—a crude instrument under the best of circumstances—is swung with casual recklessness. Such a destructive process finds its only excuse—if any excuse is possible—in the quality of the results. Only an extremely successful end justifies the means.

The tragedy of the urban renewal projects of the fifties and sixties is not just that money was often squandered in unfinished projects or that many people were adversely affected (in total, more housing was demolished than constructed). That was bad enough, but what was worse was that all this was done in the name of a misbegotten ideal. The postwar notion of progress and technological improvement suggested that cities should be modernized, a notion that in itself was not the problem. The problem was that this period coincided with a time when urbanism and architecture were in the grips of planning theories that, in hindsight, were profoundly mistaken about the nature of cities and of urban life. The core of this misunderstanding was the assumption that old ways of building cities should be supplanted by twentieth-century so-called modern urbanism. Modern urbanism meant abandoning the traditional street layout wherever possible, and in the name of separating drivers and walkers, replacing sidewalks with pedestrian malls and underground or elevated walkways. Buildings no longer lined streets in the time-tested manner, but stood free in plazas. Streets were merely for transportation—the faster the traffic moved, the better. Above all, these modern improvements defined themselves by their isolation from the rest of the city, not only by the style of their architecture, which was aggressively and uncompromisingly modern, but also by their size, which was huge.

The process of piecemeal urban growth—plot by plot, building by building—had always provided variety and scale to the city, adding new buildings side by side with old ones. Even the ambitious projects of the City Beautiful movement, like the renewal of North Michigan Avenue, were based on progressive addition: Burnham, like Haussmann before him, made big plans for streets and avenues, but assumed that these would be filled in with relatively small buildings. The advocates of urban renewal, on the other hand, were impatient with such a process. In the rush to garner the economic benefits of new construction, city administrations helped developers assemble huge parcels of land. Now urban redevelopment schemes encompassing entire blocks, and even multiple blocks, were being built by a single developer and designed by a single architect. The long-term effect of ponderous, inward-looking complexes such as Philadelphia's Penn Center and Montreal's Place Bonaventure on the surrounding street life was deadening. Even bigger were the so-called megastructures. Architects such as Paul Rudolph and Buckminster Fuller proposed different designs for projects that were in effect enormous beehives, large enough to encompass entire urban districts. Fortunately, these single-minded urban visions remained unbuilt.

There is no better way to understand the failure of the urban renewal episode in American urban history than by looking at one of its most ambitious endeavors: housing for the poor. Although the first federally funded urban public housing was the result of the relatively modest Housing Act of 1937, with the 1949 act the Truman administration embarked on a policy that aimed to build more than 800,000 new public housing units across the country. For a number of reasons, including an earlier federal court decision that struck down the right of the federal government to use its powers of eminent domain to build publicly owned housing, and the tying of public housing provision to slum clearance, most public housing ended up in inner-city locations. The size of this undertaking, combined with the large scale preferred by most urban planners, produced the great public housing projects of the 1950s.

Modern planning advocated the separation of different functions within the city. The tendency of American cities to become functionally specialized has already been noted—people lived in one part of the city and worked in another—but in the 1950s this separation was not complete. Only suburbs were exclusively residential; in the city, working-class homes within walking distance of factories were common. In the downtown area, shops, bars, movie houses, and apartment houses were within a few blocks of each other, and shopping streets ran through the center of the older neighborhoods. This mixture ensured the sort of animated street life that Jane Jacobs tried to describe in *The Death and Life of Great American Cities*. Modern planners replaced the mixture of stores, theaters, and office buildings with large, exclusive shopping zones, entertainment zones, and commercial zones. Even culture was zoned: New York acquired Lincoln Center; Montreal, Place des Arts.

The earliest and most extreme cases of single-use zoning were the new public housing projects. Large areas of land—usually cleared slums—the size of small towns were to be set aside exclusively for housing. No stores, no businesses—no uses at all other than housing (and no housing other than public housing)—were to be allowed.* Instead of a grid of streets, there would be large so-called superblocks, for pedestrians only; instead of small buildings, there would be mammoth widely spaced apartment buildings; instead of being subdivided into private gardens, the spaces between the buildings would be public parks. These were essentially the design rules Le Corbusier had set down in his *American Architect* article. The acceptance of modernist architecture and planning, at least by the authorities and the architectural and planning professions, ensured that what had appeared outlandish twenty years before now seemed like a sensible idea.

One of the first large public housing projects was Cabrini-Green on Chicago's Near North Side. It is not the biggest housing project in the city—not as big as Robert Taylor Homes, which is said to be the largest housing project in the world—but it is big enough. Cabrini-Green, which was begun in 1955, houses 10,000 people and extends over seventy acres, about the area of the entire Loop. Cabrini-Green followed the Chicago prototype: between 1957 and 1968, the Chicago Housing Authority built about 16,000 public housing apartment units, almost all of them in

*The only nonresidential uses permitted in the public housing projects were schools and community centers.

high-rise buildings. The decision to house low-income families in high-rise buildings is sometimes explained by the need to reduce land-costs. In fact the net density of a project like Cabrini-Green, about 70 dwelling units per acre of residential land, could easily have been reached by building traditional walk-up houses.* But that would have required conventional streets and sidewalks, which did not accord with the modernist vision of freestanding buildings in a parklike setting.

In the name of housing the poor, the social reformers of the 1950s adopted the urbanism of postwar, rebuilt Europe and introduced a new type of planning, quite foreign to any previous American ideal. (Curiously, the same architectural historians who railed against the foreign influences in the City Beautiful movement had no objection to this latest import.) The architecture, too, was unfamiliar. The Cabrini-Green apartment slabs, which ranged from ten to nineteen stories high, resembled high-rise factories with exposed concrete frames filled in with glass and brick. They followed the architectural style pioneered by Mies van der Rohe, who had built his first concrete-frame commercial apartment building in Chicago in 1949, after arriving from Germany eleven years earlier. Public agencies were probably attracted to this kind of architecture for the same reason that many real-estate developers are partial to modernist design: repetitive, stripped-down, and undecorated buildings can be erected quickly and inexpensively.

However, it's one thing to build apartment towers for the upper-middle class—as Mies usually did—and quite another to em-

*Jane Jacobs cites a number of residential neighborhoods that achieve high density with predominantly three- to five-story buildings: San Francisco's North Beach–Telegraph Hill (80 to 140 units per acre), Philadelphia's Rittenhouse Square district (80 to 100), Brooklyn Heights (125 to 174), and Manhattan's Greenwich Village (124 to 174).

brace them as solutions for housing the poor. The well-off have doormen, janitors, repairmen, baby-sitters, and gardeners; the poor have no hired help. Without restricted access, the lobbies and corridors are vandalized; without proper maintenance, broken elevators do not get fixed, staircases become garbage dumps, and broken windows remain unreplaced; without baby-sitters, single mothers are stranded in their apartments, and adolescents roam, unsupervised, sixteen floors below; without gardeners, the exterior landscaping deteriorates, and is replaced by beaten dirt and asphalt parking lots. Aesthetics aside, these open pedestrian areas are problematic: windblown, unconducive to walking, and less safe than conventional streets and sidewalks overlooked by individual homes. There are also problems with the design of the buildings at Cabrini-Green: to save money, no private balconies or terraces were provided, access galleries and elevator lobbies were left open to the elements (in frigid Chicago!), and the unshaded windows of the tall buildings face east and west, with no air-conditioning.

Among housing experts, Cabrini-Green has had a bad reputation for some time, but it attracted national attention in October 1992, when one of its residents, Dantrell Davis, a seven-year-old boy, was murdered. He was walking to school and was shot (for no apparent reason) by an unknown sniper in one of the empty high-rise buildings. (At the time, one-third of the apartments at Cabrini-Green had deteriorated so badly that they were abandoned; two of the worst buildings were completely closed.) Television journalists drew parallels with violence-ridden Sarajevo. This sounds far-fetched, but I was struck by how much the bleak background behind the television reporters did indeed resemble a war zone. The littered expanse of bare earth, the abandoned cars and broken windows, the battered apartment blocks with walls covered in graffiti and piles of garbage in the corridors. This place had been beaten into the ground, but it had obviously not been loved for a long time.*

In 1993, the centenary of the World's Columbian Exposition, the *Chicago Tribune* held an architectural competition whose subject was Cabrini-Green. Entrants were asked to reconfigure the housing project "to provide a model for decent and humane public housing." They were free to suggest demolishing or retaining existing buildings, and were not obliged to follow existing zoning and building regulations. There was no cost limitation, but it was pointed out that "the Chicago Housing Authority is a cash-strapped public agency," and although the program was hypothetical, the emphasis was clearly on practicality rather than utopianism.

I was interested in the competition and visited the Chicago Athenaeum, where a selection of the roughly three hundred entries was on display. The proposed solutions were a mixed bag. They ranged from the touching entry of two girls who lived in Cabrini-Green, whose recommendations included new stop signs at a dangerous corner and demolishing "a very bad drug building," to the sort of intellectual posturing that characterizes so much of contemporary architecture. One entry, for example, mysteriously linked Cabrini-Green to the tidal cycles of Lake Michigan; another archly incorporated an amusement park into the public housing project; yet another nastily suggested "circling the wagons for safety" by creating fortresslike housing structures surrounded by

*Architecture and urbanism were not entirely to blame. In the beginning, public housing projects were a success. Applicants were carefully screened, which ensured a balance between working families and welfare recipients, say, and between two-parent and single-parent families. But by the 1960s, bureaucratic inefficiency and lawsuits launched by the American Civil Liberties Union virtually eliminated the screening process, and public housing became de facto welfare housing, with all the attendant problems such specialization brings.

masts with batteries of high-intensity spotlights. One technically inclined designer, apparently a devotee of Buckminster Fuller, produced a solution based on prefabricated concrete spheres—the houses resembled light bulbs. Thomas Beeby, a well-known Chicago architect, and his wife, Kirsten, suggested abandoning Cabrini-Green altogether and building small, unassuming single-family houses, to be owned by their low-income occupants, on sites scattered throughout the city. There would be not more than a hundred of any one particular design, and not more than three houses would be located in a given square mile. It is an attractive notion, but one that raises difficult administrative problems for a municipal body such as the Chicago Housing Authority.

The Beebys' modest solution underscores the fact that scale is an important issue in public housing. Despite the argument of one of the Cabrini-Green competition entrants that "Architecture is not the solution, architecture is not the problem," it's obvious that large islands of standardized high-rise apartment blocks that contribute to social isolation *are* a problem, not only because they are inhuman in scale but also because they stigmatize their occupants. "One must avoid the danger of building for the poor under regulations or in a style very different from that to which the middle class is accustomed," wrote Nathan Glazer more than twenty-five years ago. The winning project in the Chicago competition, the work of two assistant professors of urban design at North Dakota State University in Fargo, North Dakota, Jim Nelson and Don Faulkner, addressed this issue by proposing that the Chicago Housing Authority demolish many of the dysfunctional high-rise buildings and sell off a good part of Cabrini-Green to private developers, who would build residential, commercial, and retail buildings; almost two-thirds of the 8,000 dwellings in the final scheme would be privately owned. The public and private housing would be indistinguishable, which holds out the hope that public housing might finally be socially and economically—as well as architecturally—integrated into the city.

Nelson and Faulkner's urban design brims with midwestern good sense. Rebuild the old street grid, the designers suggest, and fill in the open spaces with traditional rowhouses oriented to the streets. Save as many of the existing apartment blocks as possible and mix in commercial buildings; introduce small parks and squares as well as civic buildings like police and fire stations, churches, and daycare centers. Create avenues linking two large neighborhood squares. Instead of the two large schools, build several small schools.

Although the *Chicago Tribune* competition was held only to elicit ideas, it seems likely that some of Nelson and Faulkner's proposals will be implemented. Less than a year later, Vincent Lane, the activist chairman of the Chicago Housing Authority, announced plans to demolish three buildings at Cabrini-Green and to lease the cleared land to private developers, who would be required to reserve one-quarter of the housing for low-income tenants; the remaining public housing was to be renovated. Chicago is not alone in rethinking its approach to public housing. In Newark, where most of the 10,000 public housing units are in high-rise towers, there are 3,000 empty apartments, all in buildings that the city considers unlivable. Plans have been announced to raze eleven towers and substitute townhouses with their own lawns and front doors. In other words, the vertical Radiant City is being replaced with its opposite, something approximating turn-of-the-century American urbanism. The urban renewal movement of the fifties and sixties is being laid to rest.

The occupants of the first public housing on the Cabrini-Green site, built in 1941–43, were white. But the tenants of Cabrini-

Green today are predominately African Americans, as are the majority of the 150,000 people living in Chicago's public housing. This is a reminder that the period of urban renewal coincided with an event that would leave an indelible stamp on the American city: the black urban migration. Although southern blacks were moving to northern cities in significant numbers as early as 1917, the bulk of the migration took place between the mid-1940s and about 1970. During this relatively short period, five million people abandoned the rural South and moved to the urban North. Nicholas Lemann, author of *The Promised Land*, has called this "one of the largest and most rapid mass internal movements of people in history—perhaps the greatest not caused by the immediate threat of execution or starvation." It changed the nature of black America. In 1940, three-quarters lived in the South, and about half were rural; by 1970, only half were Southerners and less than a quarter were rural. It also had a profound effect on American cities; after 1940, urban problems increasingly revolved around the question of black poverty and flawed race relations.

There were many reasons for the migration, among them the attraction of better-paying industrial jobs in the booming northern cities, as well as escape from southern racism. Another immediate cause, Lemann writes, was the successful introduction of the mechanical cotton picker in 1944. At one stroke, this machine, which did the work of fifty people at about one-eighth the cost, eliminated sharecropping, the occupation of most of the descendants of slaves. Seeking work, the unemployed sharecroppers headed for the largest industrial cities: New York, Chicago, Philadelphia, Baltimore, Detroit, Cleveland, and Los Angeles. In many cities, the black population doubled between 1940 and 1970; in some, it tripled. Chicago's black population grew from 278,000 in 1940 to more than 800,000 in 1960; in 1950, only one-sixth of the populations of Cleveland, Detroit, and Saint

Louis was black, but by 1960, all three cities were almost one-third black. Under the best of circumstances, the integration of so many poor and predominantly uneducated people would have been extremely difficult. But the circumstances could hardly have been worse. These were rural folk who had uprooted themselves from an especially backward environment (a backwardness that was not, obviously, of their own making), they were desperately poor, and although they were hard-working (the experience of sharecropping saw to that), they were ill prepared for life in a modern, industrial society. And of course they also faced segregation—often institutionalized—discrimination, and intolerance.

The artificial stimulus of wartime production was followed by a postwar boom, but by the early 1960s, the urban manufacturing that had provided well-paid jobs for workers with low skills was in decline. Some industries left the country altogether, but many merely left the old cities and moved to new locations—to the suburbs and to newly developing urban areas in the South and the West. Urban manufacturing closed down. Many southern blacks, who had entered the job market at the very bottom of the ladder, were the first to be let go. Poorly educated, with few technical skills, with weak social networks and fragile family structures, and with extremely limited economic resources, they were hard hit. Although many eventually followed the jobs to new locations and did begin a climb to middle-class status, a significant number remained in the old inner cities. Black workers had migrated thousands of miles in search of productive employment only a decade or two earlier, so what stopped them this time? The new ingredient, as many social critics have pointed out, was the Great Society, with its social agencies, welfare programs, and cash benefits. Since many of these benefits were not portable, people stayed put. It was the beginning of the urban underclass.

The old manufacturing cities of the Northeast and the Midwest began to feel the severe effects of what came to be called deindustrialization. They were doubly affected. At the same time as they were losing manufacturing and industrial jobs and the associated tax revenue, they were bearing the costs associated with increasing demands on the new social programs. As if that were not enough, the black urban riots of the sixties caused many middle-class citizens, black as well as white, to leave the city for the surrounding suburbs, causing tax revenues to fall still further. That most cities were ineffectively administered by bloated and entrenched bureaucracies didn't help. Their efforts to deal with their fiscal malaise by crudely reducing services, raising property taxes, and optimistically—or Pollyannaishly—instituting income taxes and business privilege taxes only drove away even more residents and businesses. All this eventually led to bankruptcy, or near bankruptcy, for New York, Cleveland, Detroit, Baltimore, Cincinnati, and Philadelphia.

The end of the sixties saw the once great American cities, battered and torn apart by the well-meaning but clumsy advocates of urban renewal, beaten down by economic forces outside their control, their cores scorched by the fires of black frustration, and increasingly abandoned by the middle class. It is hard to believe that less than thirty-five years had passed since the high hopes exemplified by the City of Incredible Towers. Part of the problem was that no one, least of all city officials, could believe that the big cities were no longer the economic—and cultural—magnets they had been in the past. That was why city governments perversely increased taxes and reduced services. They assumed that the slowdown in urban growth was temporary, and that it was only a matter of time before people tired of suburban life and returned to the city. After all, they reasoned, the suburbs could hardly compete with the attractions of city life.

EIGHT

Country Homes for City People

DURING HIS VISIT TO NEW YORK, LE CORBUSIER FOUND it strange that many of the academics, professionals, and businesspeople he met did not live in the city but in the suburbs. This was unheard of in Paris, where most people who worked in the city lived in the city. There were outlying towns such as Auteuil, Boulogne-sur-Seine, and Neuilly where some rich Parisians built villas, including some designed by Le Corbusier himself, but in the 1930s not many middle-class people owned the cars necessary to commute to such far-flung locations. To most Parisians, then, *les banlieues* (the suburbs) referred chiefly to the dreary industrial districts that ringed the city like a sooty pall. Only workers who manned the factories lived there.

Suburbs in the New World were different—not industrial but residential, and not proletarian but professional and managerial—and one senses grudging admiration as Le Corbusier describes the American suburban landscape with its generous unfenced lots and its green amplitude. Always attracted to technology, he was impressed by the comfortable trains that linked Connecticut to Manhattan, and made the leisurely suburban way of life possible. But there is an underlying sarcasm in his description of the suburban commute: "After a stimulating cocktail they [the commuters] pass through the golden portals of Grand Central Terminal into a Pullman which takes them to their car; after a ride along charming country roads they enter the quiet and delightful living rooms of their colonial style houses." The notion of a decentralized city ran counter to all Le Corbusier's urban theories and he would have none of it. In *When the Cathedrals Were White*, the chronicle of his American visit, he vociferously condemned the concept of suburban living, convinced that the city of tomorrow would be a concentrated vertical city, not exactly Manhattan, perhaps, but a version of Manhattan, nevertheless.

He was wrong. Fernand Braudel once wryly observed that the French visitors to nineteenth-century northern England, horrified at the ugly, jerry-built factories and crowded mill towns, could not have dreamed that it was precisely Manchester and Glasgow, not London, that were the harbingers of the new Industrial Age cities soon to spring up in France and all over Europe. In 1935, when Le Corbusier saw the houses of the American suburbs he could not imagine that it was they, not the towers of Manhattan, that were the precursor of the postindustrial urban future.

Le Corbusier was too caught up in his own urban theories to stop and ask, "Why are *their* cities like that?" Had he asked, he might have found that the different form of American cities represented a long-standing desire on the part of their inhabitants for a different way of life. Unlike Parisian workers, Americans lived in suburbs by choice and had been doing so for a long time, more than a hundred years. The architectural historians Christopher Tunnard and Henry Hope Reed date the earliest New York suburbs at 1814, when a ferry service for commuters was started between Manhattan and Brooklyn, and New Yorkers who could not afford a house in the good parts of Manhattan settled in suburban Brooklyn Heights. Soon the commuters ventured farther. The Harvard historian John Stilgoe quotes Nathaniel Parker Willis, complaining in 1840 that "There is a suburban look and character about all the villages on the Hudson which seem out of place among such scenery. They are suburbs; in fact, steam [Willis was referring to the steamboats that linked the villages to Manhattan] has destroyed the distance between them and the city." Similar patterns were unfolding in other cities: Henry Binford of Northwestern University traces the origin of the first suburban communities around Boston to 1820; and Rutgers historian Robert Fishman dates the first West Philadelphia suburbs, which were reached by horse-drawn omnibus, at the 1840s.

By the time of Le Corbusier's visit, suburban living was a well-established fact of American life; one out of six Americans lived in the suburbs. This number was increasing rapidly: of the six million new homes built between 1922 and 1929, more than half were single-family houses, and most of these were in the suburbs. More significantly, suburbs were growing faster than cities. Between 1860 and 1920, the number of people living in urban areas had increased from only 20 percent of the population to more than half, but by the thirties and forties, the rate of urban growth slowed to almost zero. The use of streetcars and buses, a good indicator of urbanization, peaked in the mid-1920s and fell thereafter. One of the most urbane cities in America, Boston, started losing population as early as 1930. The entry on "Chicago" in the

1949 edition of the *Encyclopaedia Britannica* notes that the decade 1930–40 had seen the smallest increase in population in the city's history, and adds: "The rate of regional growth about the city seems to be increasing as the rate of strictly urban growth declines." By 1950, New York City, Chicago, and Philadelphia and many smaller cities had all stopped growing. Not that the metropolitan regions surrounding these cities were not vigorous, but 1950 is probably as good a date as any to mark the end—or, more accurately, the beginning of the end—of traditional, concentrated cities.

One reason that it's not easy to clearly identify what has happened and is happening to cities is that urban terminology is very inaccurate. Terms such as "city" and "suburb" are used as if they represent two distinct polarities. In fact they are often only polemical categories: depending on your point of view, either bad (dangerous, polluted, concrete) cities and good (safe, healthy, green) suburbs, or good (diverse, dense, stimulating) cities and bad (homogeneous, sprawling, dull) suburbs. The reality is more complicated.

Like "bourgeois" or "capitalist," "suburb" is one of those words that is difficult to use in a precise discussion because it describes something that has become a stereotype. And like most stereotypes, it is composed of clichés. For example, compared with urban housing, suburban housing is held to be monotonous, although urban tenements and industrial-era rowhouses are equally standardized and repetitive. Another cliché holds that suburban areas are rich, white, and white-collar. While this was true of the first suburbs, suburban areas have grown to include a diversity of incomes, classes, and, increasingly, ethnic and racial groups. (A manifestation of this growing diversity is the appearance of ethnic restaurants and food stores in suburban malls.) Indeed, it is the cities that are more likely to be homogeneous with more than their representative share of the poor, of blacks, and of Hispanics.

Only in a legal sense is the difference between urban and suburban clear: everything inside the city limits is urban, and everything outside is suburban. On the ground, there is often little distinction between the physical appearance of urban and suburban neighborhoods or the life they contain. Of course, there is a marked contrast between crowded inner-city neighborhoods and the outer suburbs, where large houses stand on one-acre lots, but these are the two extremes. In most cities—especially those newer cities that grew in the postwar period—urbanites live in houses, mow lawns, drive cars, and shop at malls, just like their suburban neighbors. Even a city like New York, once one leaves Manhattan, is composed of many neighborhoods in which houses with front gardens and backyards line the streets.

American cities grew—and grow, at least in the West and Southwest—by annexing surrounding towns and villages, hence producing urban areas that include neighborhoods that are suburban, even rural, in character. Houston and Minneapolis annexed entire counties and created an apparently anomalous hybrid: bucolic outer suburbs inside the city limits. Some annexed suburbs, like Queens or Staten Island, maintained a suburban atmosphere; others were physically transformed and grew denser, and are now indistinguishable from the rest of the city. Suburbs were not always integrated into the adjacent central city. Academic enclaves like Cambridge, Massachusetts, and Berkeley, California, started as suburban villages, and developed into small, independent cities without losing their small-town, suburban character. Brooklyn, on the other hand, had become the third-largest city in the United States when it was annexed by New York City in 1898.

The Connecticut suburbs that Le Corbusier described were the offspring of what John Stilgoe has characterized as "borderlands": nineteenth-century residential enclaves typically one or two hours outside the city that were cherished for their semirural character and their sylvan surroundings. Stilgoe makes the point that the "women and men who established these communities understood more by *commuting* and *country* than train schedules and pastures," and what drove them was a search for better, healthier, more restorative surroundings than were available in the city. They were not simply leaving the city for the country, but rather creating a new way of life that contained elements of both.

But trains were expensive, and less wealthy commuters relied on horse railcars, which were pulled on tracks and were later replaced by electrified streetcars. Stilgoe deplores the kind of dense inner suburbs that sprouted along streetcar lines, where people lived "without the joys of genuine city life and without the pleasures of borderland residence." This judgment may be too bleak. Another Harvard historian, Alexander von Hoffman, argues in a recent book, *Local Attachments*, that the evolution of Jamaica Plain in Boston demonstrates that streetcar suburbs could provide some of the advantages of city life. By 1850, this farming community had grown large enough to incorporate itself as a separate town of about 2,700 people. Over the next two decades, the town grew, chiefly as a result of the arrival of middle- and upper-class commuters, who traveled by horse railcar from Boston. In 1873 the townspeople voted for annexation to the City of Boston, which promised jobs, development, and growth. Growth did come, fueled by inexpensive electric streetcars and later by the railroad, and at the turn of the century the population had mushroomed to almost 33,000, the equivalent of a small city. Was Jamaica Plain merely a residential appendage to Boston? Von Hoffman presents compelling evidence to the contrary. The railroad did bring upper-middle-class commuters, but it also brought factories; people commuted out of Jamaica Plain, but also into it (much as they do in contemporary suburban cities). "During the second half of the nineteenth century, Jamaica Plain matured from a fringe district to a heterogeneous city neighborhood, a type of urban area that heretofore has not been generally recognized," he writes. "It evolved into a local urban community, not as an isolated or segmented district, but as part of the larger growth patterns of Boston." Such outer-city neighborhoods, unknown in Europe, were physically different from their inner-city counterparts—instead of tenements there were small houses, and the density of buildings was generally lower—and while their location and character was suburban, the way of life they contained was urban.

The presence of suburban elements in cities like Berkeley or in urban neighborhoods like Jamaica Plain is a reminder, as Robert A. M. Stern, has pointed out, that the suburb is defined neither by location or legalities alone. "The suburb is . . . a state of mind based on imagery and symbolism," he writes. "Suburbia's curving roads and tended lawns, its houses with pitched roofs, shuttered windows, and colonial or otherwise elaborated doorways all speak of communities which value the tradition of the family, pride of ownership and rural life." Stern also suggests that as long as the image—not necessarily the reality—of a freestanding house on a tree-lined street is maintained, the suburban ideal can be applied in a wide variety of situations, which explains the surprisingly rich diversity of suburbs.

Suburban growth in America was the result of coincidences. First, there was the availability of land. Then there was the pressure of the growth of the commercial downtown, which engulfed the traditional downtown residential neighborhoods of the rich and the middle class. There was transportation—the railroad (which in many cases was already in place) and the streetcar. Above all, there were businessmen who had the resources and the vision to undertake the task of creating new communities. The first comprehensively designed suburban residential development was Llewellyn Park in West Orange, New Jersey, begun in 1853 by a young, successful Manhattan merchant, Llewellyn S. Haskell. Haskell intended his project, which he called a "villa park," to be a healthy and picturesque alternative for New Yorkers who wanted ready access to the city. Llewellyn Park is about twelve miles from New York City and connected by train, although there is a two-mile drive to the station, a journey originally made by carriage. Llewellyn Park attracted enterprising individuals; its most famous resident was probably Thomas Alva Edison, who lived there for more than forty years and established his laboratory nearby. For ordinary folks, however, the high cost of commuting to New York and the price of the generous lots were prohibitive; buyers in Llewellyn Park were well-to-do. Llewellyn Park was exclusively residential; no industrial, commercial, or retail uses were allowed. Deed restrictions included rules about architecture and landscaping—fences, for example, were banned. This became the pattern for many of the early suburbs; moreover, developers used their own discretion to ensure that the new home owners were socially acceptable.*

Haskell's architect, Alexander Davis, did not simply subdivide the 400-acre parcel of mountainous terrain on Eagle Ridge into building lots. He carefully manipulated the landscape to produce a natural experience. He heightened the impression of being in a virgin forest by leaving a heavily planted fifty-acre nature preserve, cleft by a ravine, in the center of the development. Today, the visitor to Llewellyn Park is impressed not only by the terrain

*Haskell did not screen buyers at Llewellyn Park, but such openness was unusual. Explicit racial zoning ordinances were common in cities and suburbs, not struck down by a Supreme Court ruling until 1917. Race-restrictive covenants continued to be attached to private deeds (especially in new suburban housing) until as late as 1948.

and the planting—Haskell spent more than a hundred thousand dollars on landscaping—but also by the romantic appearance of the houses themselves. Their Gothic, Swiss chalet, and Italianate styles were not chosen for their cultural connotations, but simply to please the eye.

Davis was a skillful architect and the author of *Rural Residences*, a popular book of house patterns for architects and builders. His ideas were influenced by his friend and frequent collaborator, Andrew Jackson Downing, whose *Cottage Residences* and *The Architecture of Country Houses* were the most widely read books on domestic design of the period. Downing recommended that houses should be designed in an irregular, picturesque manner; the rambling architecture was to be augmented by naturalistic landscaping and informal street layouts. This became the hallmark of all early American suburban developments, although the actual architectural styles varied. The preferred style at Garden City, one of the first Long Island suburbs, founded in 1869, was Italianate; at Short Hills, another New Jersey development, the society architects McKim, Mead, and White were commissioned to design a model home in the English cottage style.

The entire development of Llewellyn Park, including the nature preserve and the streets, was treated as private property; public access was restricted by a peripheral fence and a gatehouse. This, too, became common practice. This type of exclusive enclave represents one branch of the suburban tradition. In its contemporary guise the exclusive enclave has become a new kind of town, composed uniquely of private homes, socially homogeneous, and privately governed. The chief legal vehicle of the enclave is the homeowners' association (also pioneered at Llewellyn Park), which enforces the rules established by the original property developer and administers the commonly owned landscaped areas. Over time, the amenities of such enclaves have come to include not only gardens but recreation areas like golf courses, tennis courts, riding paths, and swimming pools. The homeowners' associations administer common services such as garbage collection, road maintenance, and policing; in other words, many if not all of the functions normally carried out by municipal governments.* These types of communities, called Common Interest Developments, have proven very popular with developers and buyers alike; according to Evan McKenzie of the University of Illinois at Chicago, there are currently some 130,000 such developments in the United States, housing about 30 million people—12 percent of the population—and he has estimated that by the year 2000, as many as 30 percent of Americans will be living in some form of community association!

If McKenzie is correct in suggesting that Common Interest Developments "are not only the present but the future of American housing," the further development of enclaves is likely to accentuate the existing inequalities between rich and poor communities. That would be a shame, because the exclusive enclave is not the only model for suburban developers. The Anglo-American garden suburb represents a different ideal. In America, its antecedents were developments like Riverside, on the outskirts of Chicago, planned by Frederick Law Olmsted and Calvert Vaux in 1869. Nine miles from the Loop on the Burlington and Quincy Railroad, sixteen hundred acres of farmland was transformed by Olmsted into a beautiful parklike setting. The landscape approach is similar to Llewellyn Park (Olmsted, too, planted thousands of

*Interestingly, some of the features of Common Interest Developments are appearing in urban areas in the form of Business Improvement Districts, private associations of merchants and home owners that provide services such as policing and garbage removal.

trees), but Riverside was not gated, and its scale was truly urban; there was also a commercial town center. Today, the graceful streets display the soundness of Olmsted's vision. Chicago was ideal for suburban development since it had a ready-made commuter system in place—the railroad. The 1880s saw many similar upper- and upper-middle-class suburbs—Winnetka, Highland Park, Lake Forest—stretching as far as thirty miles from the Loop.

The British branch of the garden suburb tradition originated in an urban movement that was analogous to but different from the City Beautiful. In 1898 Ebenezer Howard, an English court stenographer inspired by the American Edward Bellamy's best-selling futuristic novel, *Looking Backward*, himself published a book containing a working blueprint for a new kind of city. In *Tomorrow: A Peaceful Path to Real Reform* (later retitled *Garden Cities of Tomorrow*) Howard elaborated in detail how to build completely new, economically self-sufficient communities. These "garden cities" would be planned at a relatively low density to avoid the overcrowding and squalor of Victorian industrial cities; they would be surrounded by greenbelts to preserve the countryside, and would include industry and commerce to provide employment to their inhabitants. Howard acquired a wide popular following. In 1899, a group of British industrialists, businessmen, and social reformers formed the Garden City Association, and in relatively short order marshaled the resources to start building the first garden city.

Founded in 1904, in Hertfordshire, some thirty miles from London, Letchworth Garden City was an ambitious undertaking that encompassed almost 4,000 acres and was intended to house 30,000 people. Howard had written nothing about the actual design of the proposed city, but the plan devised by Raymond Unwin and Barry Parker, two young architects who were members of the association, became a model for all later garden suburbs. Unwin and Parker came up with a loose, village-like layout, and for the buildings, they adopted an informal domestic style loosely based on the traditional architecture of British country towns. Although Letchworth incorporated Howard's novel ideas about urbanism, to most people it looked comfortably familiar.

Letchworth was followed by a second garden city: Hampstead Garden Suburb. As the name suggests, it was not a true city, but a suburb, a short subway ride from London. The developer of Hampstead was Henrietta Barnett, a friend of the famous housing reformer Octavia Hill and a social activist herself. Barnett saw the new suburb as an opportunity to offer working-class Londoners an alternative to the crowded inner city. Therefore Hampstead incorporated housing for people in various income brackets, and included rental cottages and flats affordable to clerks and artisans (although Barnett's dream of rehousing slum dwellers never materialized). Hampstead Garden Suburb was laid out in 1906 by Unwin (with the later collaboration of Edwin Lutyens). With Letchworth under his belt, Unwin, one of the most talented urban designers of the period, produced in Hampstead a plan of great sophistication and subtlety. It incorporated a picturesque street layout, extensive landscaping in the residential areas, a range of innovative housing types, and a compact town center. The site covered more than three hundred acres, and at an average density of eight houses to the acre—about half the density of a typical inner-city neighborhood—there was plenty of parkland and other open spaces. Nevertheless, compared to many later suburbs, Hampstead was densely occupied. The Long Island suburban communities built by William Levitt in the 1950s, for example, usually had a density of about four houses per acre, and many contemporary suburb developments average less than that.

Unwin's plan was neither a simple grid nor a Beaux Arts diagram, but rather a complex (Lynch would call it organic) composition that took advantage of topography and natural features. There was variety in the road system: avenues, side streets, cul-de-sacs, and service lanes were all integrated into the plan. "It was not deemed enough that a road should serve as a means of communication from one place to another," said Unwin, "it was also desired that it should offer some dignity of approach to important buildings, and be a pleasant way for the passer-by." This comprehensive planning was based on the visual and spatial experience of a place. It was similar to Olmsted's approach but distinctly more urban; Hampstead was a conscious attempt on Unwin's part to capture some of the charm of the traditional country towns he so loved. The housing groups, designed by Unwin and Parker and by the notable Arts and Crafts practitioner M. H. Baillie Scott, were based on English vernacular architecture. Lutyens planned the town center in a more formal manner, with a large rectangular green flanked by two churches and a Wren-inspired housing terrace, all designed in masterful fashion by him.

Hampstead has been called "the jewel in the suburban crown." It is one of the most beautifully designed suburbs of the period—indeed, of any period—and influenced suburban developers everywhere, especially in the United States. One of these developers was George Woodward of Chestnut Hill, an outlying neighborhood of Philadelphia. Once a summer retreat for wealthy Philadelphians, twelve miles from downtown, Chestnut Hill was annexed by the city in 1854. Unlike Jamaica Plain, Chestnut Hill was merely a small part of what was then the largest annexation in American history. Philadelphia, which occupied only about two square miles, added to itself an entire county, and overnight became a metropolis of 129 square miles.

In 1873 Woodward's father-in-law, Henry Howard Houston, a successful Philadelphia businessman, had acquired more than 3,000 acres along the picturesque Wissahickon Creek, in and around Chestnut Hill. Eleven years later, Houston persuaded the Pennsylvania Railroad (of which he was a director) to build a spur line through his property, linking Chestnut Hill to the city. He began an ambitious effort to create a new suburban community by constructing a large hotel; for recreation, he created a lake for canoeing, and an arboretum for promenading; for worship, a church. He also deeded land to the Philadelphia Cricket Club (which moved from downtown), and convinced the annual Philadelphia Horse Show to relocate to Chestnut Hill. These last two moves were not motivated by philanthropy but by business. Houston wanted to attract Philadelphia socialites to his real estate venture and he succeeded; he built about a hundred houses for predominantly upper-class families.

When Houston died in 1895, Woodward took over the direction of the family business. He displayed a not-uncommon characteristic of turn-of-the-century suburban developers: a curious blend of entrepreneurship and idealism. A physician by training, Woodward was a progressive reformer, politician, and state senator, and also president of Philadelphia's Octavia Hill Association. Following the example of the British reformer, the association was engaged in building and rehabilitating low-rent housing and model tenements for workers. Hence, although he was a businessman, Woodward regarded Chestnut Hill as more than merely a real-estate venture. His ideas about architecture were inspired by both John Ruskin (Octavia Hill's mentor) and William Morris. Many of the Woodward houses are in the Arts and Crafts style; all are characterized by solid, honest construction and good craftsmanship. Woodward was also familiar with the Garden City movement and with projects like Hampstead Garden Suburb, which he heard about in meetings of the National Housing Conference and during frequent visits to Britain.

One of the design issues that Unwin had addressed in Hampstead was forming a town composed uniquely of small, detached houses. "So long as we are confined to the endless multiplication of careful fenced-in villas, and rows of cottages toeing the same building line, each with its little garden securely railed, reminding one of a cattle-pen, the result is bound to be monotonous and devoid of beauty," he had written. Unwin's solution was to group individual houses into terraces, picturesque clusters, and large quadrangles or courts. This created larger, common spaces, as well as a variety of house types and building forms along the street. A small group of houses served by a narrow driveway instead of a wide road also saved money and land. The houses Woodward built in Chestnut Hill included terraces of rowhouses surrounding landscaped courts, clusters of houses whose freestanding character is disguised by connecting stone walls and outbuildings, and interesting groups of attached cottages that produce the visual effect of larger houses. There is also a Woodward innovation: quadriplexes consisting of four dwellings arranged in a cruciform plan, sharing a central core.* Between 1910 and 1930 Woodward commissioned about 180 houses. He sent his young architects—H. Louis Duhring, Robert Rodes McGoodwin, and Edmund Gilchrist—to England and France to study traditional architecture, and as a result, Chestnut Hill acquired several picturesque streets composed of Cotswold-style cottages as well as a group of eight houses designed by McGoodwin in the Norman style, known locally as the French Village. On one wall is a *Loi de 1881, Défense d'afficher* sign, to complete the French theme.

The houses built by Woodward, including smaller dwellings for young families as well as large houses, were not sold but rented. (He

*The quadriplex design is usually associated with Frank Lloyd Wright, but the Chestnut Hill quads were designed by H. Louis Duhring in 1910, and according to historian John Sergeant, Wright first proposed this idea in 1913.

did sell individual lots to people wishing to build their own houses.) This assured a high degree of conformity with Woodward's architectural ideals. But no effort was made to physically separate the development from the surrounding neighborhood. There were no gates—this was not an exclusive enclave. Access to the parks was unrestricted, and the streets were all public thoroughfares; in fact, it was not easy to tell exactly which parts of Chestnut Hill the Woodwards owned. Moreover, Chestnut Hill encompassed various income groups, including a large North Italian community of masons who had been attracted to the area by the Woodward construction projects (which were all built of local stone), as well as other artisans, domestic servants, and local shopkeepers. Woodward himself did not build retail spaces; he did not have to, since Germantown Avenue, a commercialized country road, traversed the entire neighborhood. Although most of Woodward's tenants were upper- and upper-middle-class families, and despite its semirural character, which was accentuated by the adjacent forested tract of Fairmount Park, Chestnut Hill resembled Hampstead Garden Suburb: that is, it was more like a small town than a villa park.

Houston and Woodward were unable to innovate in the street planning of Chestnut Hill. They had to adhere to the layout established earlier by the city of Philadelphia, a continuation of Penn's downtown grid. The regularity was somewhat relieved by the rising and falling topography of Chestnut Hill and by the ragged edge of Fairmount Park, as well as by the several angled, colonial-period roads, but it was not the sort of plan that the builders of garden suburbs preferred. Woodward did introduce an Unwinesque, crescent-shaped group of houses that flanked a public green, and he created a public park, but his design for a formal approach road was never implemented.

For a fully realized planned garden suburb in the United States, we must turn to the village of Mariemont, built in the 1920s on the outskirts of Cincinnati, overlooking the Ohio River. Like Chestnut Hill, it was the work of an enlightened developer, Mary M. Emery, who wanted to create a model community that would demonstrate the value of modern (that is, Garden City) planning ideas. In 1914 she engaged John Nolen, a Philadelphia native and an experienced planner and architect who had been active in the City Beautiful movement. Starting from scratch on 420 acres, Nolen created a formal town center focused on a village green and bisected by a boulevarded avenue, with streets radiating out into the village. The plan is an extraordinarily subtle exercise in axial formalism combined with a very relaxed form of grid planning, which is all the more impressive when one appreciates that this is among the first suburbs planned expressly for the automobile. Nolen provided space for on-street parking, and rear lanes giving access to garages. (The British garden suburbs did not have to contend with the automobile; private car ownership was so low.) Emery intended Mariemont to be an affordable community, and it included a variety of lot sizes, as well as low-rise apartment buildings and commercial buildings with flats above stores. The housing was designed by several architects of national stature, including Grosvenor Atterbury of New York, and Wilson Eyre and Paul Philippe Cret of Philadelphia; McGoodwin and Gilchrist, who had worked for Woodward, also designed interesting housing groups at Mariemont.

The development of Chestnut Hill and Mariemont coincides with a general increase in suburban construction that lasted from about 1910 to 1930. There were garden suburbs in all parts of the continent: Country Club District in Kansas City, Missouri, which was founded in 1907, grew over the next three decades and finally encompassed over 4,000 acres; Shaker Heights in Cleveland developed into one of the most beautiful garden suburbs; Forest Hills Gardens, fifteen minutes by rail from Manhattan, was the American suburb that most resembled Hampstead, planned and designed by Atterbury, with landscaping by the Olmsted brothers; Lake Forest, north of Chicago, included an exemplary market square, forerunner of the regional shopping center; in Montreal, the Canadian National Railway commissioned Frederick Todd in 1910 to plan the Town of Mount Royal, a garden suburb linked to downtown by CNR tracks; a few years later, Todd was hired by the Canadian Pacific Railway to design the town of Leaside, just outside Toronto. This suburban boom was caused by the increased congestion of traditional urban neighborhoods, encouraging people who could afford it to seek alternatives, and by the advent of automobile ownership that, especially after 1920, made outlying areas accessible and freed developers from dependence on railroad companies. Above all, there was the attraction of the garden suburbs themselves.

Whereas most people today equate suburban development with negligent planning and incompetent design, the earliest garden suburbs were distinguished precisely by the sophistication of their layouts and the quality of their architecture. What is impressive is the consistency of this quality. This was as true in North America as it was in Britain. A small group of exceptional planners—Elbert Peets, the Olmsted brothers, Nolen, Todd—set the example, and others followed. It is also striking how many talented architects—Atterbury, Cret, Eyre, Howard Van Doren Shaw, Bertram Goodhue, Myron Hunt—worked in the garden suburbs. Good planning and imaginative architecture made the garden suburbs popular with the buying public, but more important, they also assured their longevity. Like Chestnut Hill and Mariemont, *all* the garden suburbs of the teens and twenties have remained attractive places to live; some, like River Oaks in Houston, Beverly Hills and Palos Verdes outside Los Angeles, and Coral Gables outside Miami, have become synonymous with wealth.

The architectural and urbanistic qualities of the garden suburbs made them particularly attractive—and hence in the long run drove up real-estate values—but as the example of Chestnut Hill shows, they were by no means elitist. Nor were they always middle class. In 1918 before the end of World War I, the New York Shipbuilding Company of Camden, New Jersey, built Yorkship Village, a community of about 1,000 dwellings intended for its workers. (At the end of the war the houses were sold to their tenants.) The plan of Yorkship, designed by Electus D. Litchfield, a New York City architect, bears some resemblance to Mariemont: there is a square green in the center, flanked by shops with flats above. Two diagonal avenues lead from the green to a boulevard, where a streetcar line connected Yorkship with Camden. Most of the dwellings are tiny rowhouses arranged in small terraces. The plan, which includes a system of rear service lanes, is carefully designed to avoid long, unobstructed vistas and to create a sense of intimacy through pleasant, closed spaces. Yorkship Village (now known as Fairview) has survived intact. It continues to be a solid community, not far from its blue-collar roots; the small houses are well taken care of; shops still surround the shaded village green; and there is an active community association. It's hard not to credit Litchfield's careful planning, whose human qualities are still in evidence, with the vitality of this community, a community in the city of Camden, itself a sad model of urban decay and devastation.

Garden-suburb planning was even used in public housing. Mark Alden Branch, a contemporary architectural journalist, writes about two public housing projects in Bridgeport, Connecticut, both originally built to house defense workers. Seaside Village, constructed in 1918, is a small (257 dwellings) version of Yorkship: the street layout is village-like and includes a small green; the houses are similarly arranged in small groups; as in Yorkship, the architecture is simplified colonial. Marina Village, directly across the street, was built in 1940; its 408 apartments and flats are similar in size and quality of construction to those at Seaside. The urban design, however, is very different. The uniform blocks are lined up side by side like barracks, fronting pedestrian walkways rather than streets. This is planning done strictly by the CIAM (Congrès Internationaux d'Architecture Moderne) and the Le Corbusier book. Although the construction is brick like Seaside Village, the roofs are flat, and the undecorated houses are devoid of domestic imagery. Seaside and Marina were both built as "model" projects, according to Branch, but they have turned out very differently. Seaside Village, which became a cooperative in 1954, is solid working-class, well maintained, with a low crime rate. In fact the main problem for the residents appears to be neighboring Marina Village, which since the 1960s has had a history of vandalism, crime, and drugs (and failed attempts at co-op conversion). As in Yorkship Village, it is hard not to credit garden-suburb planning for some of the success of Seaside, just as it is difficult not to blame the cheerless, Corbusier-inspired urbanism of Marina for its dismal performance.

The period 1900–1930 is a largely forgotten chapter in the history of the American suburb, and merits closer study. The early garden suburbs of this era display none of the clichés of later suburban planning. The garden suburbs were clearly intended to offer a green alternative to the city, but their developers understood that town planning was an important tool in achieving their aims. Compared with contemporary suburban developments, the garden suburbs were paragons of urban design. Instead of confusing layouts of cul-de-sacs, there were carefully planned hierarchies of avenues and streets interspersed with parks and squares. Instead of the ubiquitous bungalow, there was variety: rowhouse terraces, clusters, twins, and courts, as well as freestanding cottages and villas. By the 1920s, the automobile had to be accounted for, and it was integrated in subtle ways: instead of lines of garage doors on the street, there were service lanes (shades of old Savannah) and garages at the back of the garden; to avoid high-speed traffic, secondary roads were kept relatively narrow. Above all, the garden suburbs were less spread out. Instead of one-story ranch houses, homes were planned on two and three floors; instead of being set back behind large front lawns, houses were often close to the street. This meant that lots were small, producing compact neighborhoods in which, despite the automobile, one could walk to the store, to school, or to the park.

Jane Jacobs has written critically of Ebenezer Howard and the Garden City movement, which she describes as profoundly anti-urban; presumably she would extend this criticism to include the garden suburbs as well, but to people like Woodward and Unwin, she would be wrong. In 1909 Unwin published *Town Planning in Practice*, a combination manifesto and field manual that outlines in great detail his ideas about town planning. Several conclusions can be drawn from this illuminating work. First of all, the garden suburb planners had no antipathy to the traditional city. In a chapter entitled "Of the Individuality of Towns," Unwin discusses a variety of historic examples, including Edinburgh, Cologne, and Philadelphia. Throughout the book he uses large European cities to illustrate the proper way to lay out squares and plazas, to dimension streets, and to establish pleasing relationships between buildings and urban spaces. It becomes clear that what Unwin does reject is the nineteenth-century *industrial* city. "We have become so used to living among surroundings in which beauty has little or no place that we do not realise what a remarkable and unique feature the ugliness of modern life is," he writes, and adds: "We are apt to forget that this ugliness may be said to belong almost exclusively to the period covered by the industrial development of the last century. We do not find evidence of it before that period, in our towns or in those of a character to be compared with our own in other countries." The aim of *Town Planning in Practice* is to explain what it is that makes towns and cities of the preindustrial period pleasing, and to formulate specific principles of urban design that can be adapted to the modern period.

Unwin subtitled his book *An Introduction to the Art of Designing Cities and Suburbs*, but in the organization of his material he did not distinguish between the two. He illustrated a chapter on the design of public spaces with big-city squares like the Place Vendôme in Paris; small-city squares like Marienplatz in Munich; marketplaces in country towns; and Lutyens's Central Square in Hampstead Garden Suburb. One gets the impression that although he obviously recognized the differences in scale between these examples, Unwin considered them intimately related. In the same way, Unwin and the other designers of garden suburbs did not think of their work as an alternative to the city—still less as anti-urban—but rather as a part of the long tradition of city-building.

Suburban construction slowed down during the Depression and did not resume until after World War II. The postwar suburbs were different from their predecessors, however. They came to be called subdivisions—aptly so, for there was little artistry in the way they were planned. It's almost as if a sort of amnesia had set in and the garden suburb was forgotten. There were several reasons for this. The postwar suburbs were marketed chiefly on the basis of low prices. The selling price of houses was kept affordable by reducing overhead costs. Developers quickly realized they could dispense with the niceties of architectural design and urban planning without harming sales.

Scale also differentiated the postwar suburban developments—they were huge. Railroad and streetcar suburbs had to be compact since people still walked a great deal; automobile suburbs could spread out—and, starting in the late 1940s, they did. One of the most famous, Levittown on Long Island, eventually housed about 80,000 people; the second Levittown, outside Philadelphia, had 60,000 residents. Compared with the garden suburbs, these were really small cities: the second Levittown also included light industry, office buildings, ten elementary schools, two high schools, recreation areas, swimming pools, and about eighteen churches. Size was an important ingredient in the economic success of these subdivisions, since it was by mass-producing the houses (on the site, not in factories) that the Levitt brothers in 1949 were able to market a four-room Cape Cod cottage for $7,990. (Thanks to the GI Bill of Rights there was no down payment, and the low monthly charges were actually cheaper than the rent for a comparable city apartment.) Although it was small—750 square feet—the two-bedroom house included an unfinished attic and such amenities as underfloor radiant heating, a fireplace, and a Bendix washing machine.

This achievement was the result of standardizing the way in which the houses were built. What is less obvious is that the urban planning was also standardized. The basis for the standardization was the individual lot for a detached house (the only kind of housing available in the postwar suburb) and the need to handle car traffic. High-speed arterial roads cut the developments into large blocks, which were further subdivided by feeder roads, usually culminating in cul-de-sacs around which the lots were clustered. There was nothing resembling a public center. Schools, recreation facilities, and shopping centers were scattered throughout the development—large buildings surrounded by parking lots. It was assumed that people would drive from place to place, and indeed, the low density of the postwar suburb (with predominantly one-story houses on large lots) made walking impractical. Standardization also meant that subdivisions largely ignored local topography and landscape features.

Unlike the builders of garden suburbs, the subdivision developers did not seek out prominent architects and planners. In order to save money, they preferred to use either stock plans or in-house architects. In any case, by 1945 people like Unwin, Nolen, Goodhue, Atterbury, and McGoodwin were either dead or retired, and the succeeding generation of architects had no interest in suburban housing. These architects were caught up in international modernism, and when they did design housing, it was more likely to be publicly funded housing for low-income people, which produced results like Marina Village and Cabrini-Green. As for city planners, they had moved away from physical design altogether, preferring to concern themselves with statistical and policy analysis. The undiscriminating buyers have to carry some of the blame for the bland subdivision as well, but the turning away of the architectural profession and of professional schools from the design of suburbs and suburban housing after 1930 contributed greatly to their decline in quality.*

The failure of the postwar subdivisions was, paradoxically, a result of their great commercial success. The making of suburbs, which had been an honorable branch of town planning, became simply a way of marketing individual houses. By concentrating entirely on making houses affordable, the developers overlooked the chief lesson of the 1920s garden suburbs: subdivisions should not be composed solely of private dwellings but also need shared public spaces where citizens can feel that they are part of a larger community. Suburbs are located outside the traditional city, but that does not mean that they cannot be urban, too. Civic art belongs in the suburbs just as much as in the cities.

*Tragically, this remains largely true today. "The appalling fact is that most recent [architecture] graduates know very little about the organization of housing production, the technology of home building, and the kinds of housing requirements that are important to consumers," writes the sociologist Robert Gutman.

NINE

The New Downtown

DOWNTOWN PLATTSBURGH IN UPSTATE NEW YORK, where I used to go for lunch until the Metropole bar closed its dining room, has seen better days. It's not so much that things have been allowed to run down, although here and there boarded-up windows deface the staid Victorian storefronts. It is the general air of patient but unmistakable retreat. This is visible in the types of stores that line the main street—the secondhand bookshops, a thrift store, an outlet for used restaurant equipment—the sort of businesses whose survival depends on low overheads. There are no snappy or fashionable establishments; the signs tend to be home-made, the window displays unchanging and dusty. Merkel's, a department store that is descended from a tobacconist established by Isaac Merkel more than a hundred years ago, appears to be barely hanging on. A snack bar across the street keeps changing owners and menus; now it's an ice cream parlor, but next month, who knows? Down the street, the site of a fire remains an empty lot; there is not enough demand for commercial space. The movie theater, a proper one with a marquee, is still operating, although it doesn't show the kinds of movies that people line up for—my wife, Shirley, and I have sometimes been the only patrons. On the street there is evidence of sporadic attempts at civic beautification—benches and planters—and there is an attractively landscaped promenade alongside the Saranac River. But these improvements haven't had their desired effect. The streets are more or less empty; there is simply none of the bustle or activity normally associated with downtown life. The unbroken facades of the three-story brick buildings along the main street—stores below, offices and rooms above—remind me of an Edward Hopper painting, *Early Sunday Morning*, in which the artist portrays a row of small-town storefronts. The blank stares of the vacant windows and the still emptiness of the Plattsburgh street are Hopperesque, too.

Empty it may be today, but Plattsburgh had a proper little downtown once. The old Customs House is gone, as is the imposing Weed Building, a thousand-seat theater for drama and opera opened in 1893, as well as the Witherill, the biggest of five downtown hotels in operation at the turn of the century. Enough of the architectural heritage remains, however, to remind the visitor of what a handsome town this must have been. Still in operation is the Clinton County Courthouse, a grand building in stone and brick, surrounded by a bevy of lawyers' offices; not far away is an elegant obelisk designed by John Russell Pope, the architect of the National Gallery in Washington, D.C. The monument commemorates a naval victory in the War of 1812. Further along the shore of Lake Champlain is the railroad depot, built in the Richardsonian Romanesque style in 1886, when Plattsburgh became an important stop on the Delaware & Hudson line between Montreal and New York City. The depot functioned as a transfer point to stagecoaches and to the paddle steamers that linked Plattsburgh to Burlington, Vermont, across the lake.

Plattsburgh's main street is called Margaret Street—the founders had a charming habit of naming streets after their wives and daughters. In a photograph of Margaret Street taken in 1918 one of the stores displays a telephone sign. Plattsburgh had had a telephone system as early as 1880, and an electric power company since 1889. There is a trolley car running down the center of the street. The Plattsburgh Traction Company operated six and a half miles of trolley line linking downtown to the residential neighborhoods, the fairgrounds, the baseball park, and the army barracks; a spur ran out to the Hotel Champlain, a rather magnificent 500-room resort hotel south of the city. The trolley car in the photograph is an open-air model, suggesting it is summer. There are also a horse-drawn buggy and several automobiles on the tidy, brick-paved street. On the sidewalk, a number of well-dressed men and women window-shop under striped canvas awnings. It is a distinctly urban scene.

What happened to this urbanity? To answer the question, one should note, first, what did *not* happen. Plattsburgh did not suffer the devastating loss of employment of many nineteenth-century mill towns in upstate New York and New England. True, the power supplied by the falls of the Saranac, which is what drew the founder Zephaniah Platt here in 1784, is no longer an industrial asset, and firms like the Williams Manufacturing Company (maker of the Helpmate sewing machine) and the Lozier Motor Company (of the Lozier touring car) no longer exist, but other industries have replaced them. The grand Hotel Champlain has been converted into a community college. The tourists still come, not by train and steamer, but by car and camper to nearby Adirondack State Park. Plattsburgh has a state college campus, and the army barracks have grown into a giant air force base, part of the Strategic Air Command. All in all, Plattsburgh has prospered.

The decline of downtown Plattsburgh has nothing to do with deindustrialization or with crime or with white reactions to black migration. Nor is it due to a drop in population. Since the middle of the nineteenth century, population growth has been steady, if unspectacular: in 1918 the population of the city of Plattsburgh was about 12,000 people; today it is nearly twice that size. The county has also grown and made the city an important regional center for shopping and entertainment. Plattsburghians did not move to the suburbs, and most of them still live in large comfortable houses on quiet, tree-lined streets in the residential neighborhoods that surround the downtown, much as they did one hundred years ago. What caused the downtown to change was neither urban decay nor suburban flight.

The first indication that change was in the air occurred on November 11, 1929, when the Plattsburgh Traction Company folded.* This was less than two weeks after the stock market collapsed on Wall Street, but that was not the reason—the company had been losing money consistently for the previous nine years. Rising operating costs were part of the explanation, but the real problem was that fewer and fewer people were riding the trolley; they were driving cars. In 1900 there were only 8,000 private automobiles registered in the United States, but in the following decade this number grew to almost half a million, thanks in no small part to the introduction of the Ford Model T. By 1920, car ownership stood at eight million. Car ownership started in the large cities, but it spread quickly to smaller towns, judging from a

*The trolleys were replaced by buses, but these did not prosper. By the 1960s only a summer service to the beach had survived, and that ceased operation in 1969.

report in the Plattsburgh *Daily Press*, which in 1928 reported traffic congestion on Margaret Street.

Downtown Plattsburgh was formed by the same forces as big cities: the railroad, hotels, and a concentration of stores and businesses. The railroad brought travelers, who in turn sustained the hotels, which offered civic amenities like dining rooms, bars, ballrooms, and evening entertainment. The stores and other businesses (including manufacturing) brought more people downtown, both shoppers and employees. But cars (and later planes) changed the way people traveled; when measured in terms of passenger miles, patronage of non-commuter passenger trains in the United States dropped 84 percent between 1945 and 1964. Local train service in Plattsburgh ceased in 1971 (the converted depot contains rental offices and a restaurant). Now only the New York–Montreal train stops twice a day to take on and discharge passengers, and in 1994, Amtrak announced that this train, too, would cease operation.

By the 1960s the Witherill was the only remaining first-class hotel in downtown Plattsburgh, and before the end of the decade it too had closed, unable to compete with the tourist cabins and motor courts that had sprung up along the main roads leading into the city. This also became the location for automotive needs: garages, car washes, showrooms, and used-car lots. This strip development did not affect other Plattsburgh downtown businesses until the shopping center showed up. By the 1960s, Plattsburgh had three shopping centers, all built next to highways, on the west, south, and north sides of the city: North Country Plaza, Plattsburgh Plaza, and the Skyway Shopping Center. Downtown was finished.

The success of shopping centers, in Plattsburgh and elsewhere, was predicated above all on the existence of the supermarket. In combination with the refrigerator and the automobile, the supermarket changed shopping habits. Since they could store food in refrigerators—and later freezers—housewives didn't have to shop every day; weekly shopping meant having to transport many bags of heavy groceries, which is where the car came in. In fact, the first supermarket pre-dated widespread car ownership and originated in an urban area. Piggly Wiggly, started in Memphis in 1916, was the first self-service grocery-store chain and the model for large supermarkets like King Kullen, which opened its first store in Queens in 1930. But large supermarkets were not really suited to downtown. Unlike department stores, supermarkets are spread out on one floor and, especially when parking is taken into account, require large building lots, which are more affordable on the edge of town.

Personal mobility was responsible for the shift from downtown to the strip, and personal mobility molded American cities and towns in a way that was impossible to imagine in Europe. Not only was automobile ownership higher, but American physical mobility was combined with a high degree of social mobility and the space to exploit the advantages of rapid, easy movement. Only in Canada, New Zealand, and Australia were these conditions duplicated, and it is no accident that urbanism in those countries took a similar course. (Eventually, private automobile ownership did increase in many European countries, and postwar European cities started to incorporate some of the features—strip development, shopping centers—previously seen only in North America and Australia.)

A key feature of this new American mobility was not only individual freedom, but also the freedom to move goods and services. Large long-distance trucks replaced the railroad. Since trucks arrived in the city on highways, the edge of town was the ideal location for distribution warehouses, the new railroad depots. Small industry and workshops, the kind that earlier would have been downtown, near the railroad tracks, also relocated; small trucking companies distributed services as well as goods around the city. They, too, settled beside the convenient highway. As the landscape historian J. B. Jackson wrote, "The automobile—especially the commercial automobile, the truck, the pickup, the van and mini-van and jeep—has been most effective in introducing a different spatial order. For what those vehicles contain (and distribute) is not only new attitudes toward work, new uses of time and space, new and more direct contacts with customers and consumers, but new techniques of problem solving." Jackson's valuable observation underlines the fact that the "automobile city" was also the "truck city," and that personal mobility affected not only *where* people worked, but also *how* they worked.

The strip spawned drive-in establishments like diners, dairy bars, and juke joints. By the 1960s, when teenagers could afford to buy cars, the strip also became a hangout and place for cruising. Despite the disappearance of the railroad and hotels—as well as grocery stores—downtown continued as a home for many traditional businesses; it was still where you bought a record album, a bouquet of flowers, or a hat, and it was where you went to a movie, got a prescription filled, or opened a bank account. Soon that changed, too. You could do all these things and more without setting foot in downtown because the shopping centers had arrived. The chief attraction of the early shopping centers, which usually included a supermarket, was the concentration of commercial establishments in one spot. This meant that shoppers could park their cars and walk from store to store, instead of driving up and down the strip.

From 1960 to 1970, more than 8,000 new centers opened in the United States, but the first shopping centers, sometimes referred to as "shopping villages," emerged much earlier, in the first decade of the century. The shopping village had three identifiable features: it consisted of a number of stores built and leased by a single developer; it provided plenty of free off-street parking; and it was usually located near the center of a planned suburb. According to the *Guinness Book of World Records*, the first shopping center opened at the turn of the century in Roland Park, an exclusive suburban enclave planned by the Olmsted brothers and George Kessler about five miles north of downtown Baltimore. With only six establishments, however, Roland Park barely qualifies as a shopping center.

A more impressive early example is Market Square, designed by Howard Van Doren Shaw in 1916 for the Chicago garden suburb of Lake Forest. Now on the National Register of Historic Places, the exquisite Arts and Crafts–style buildings house a combination of small stores and a Marshall Field department store. The buildings sit on three sides of a landscaped plaza across from the railroad station, and include two charming clock towers. These, as well as the intimate scale of the arcaded stores and the integration of apartments on the second floor, make Market Square not merely a shopping center but a true town center. Country Club Plaza, which opened in 1925, was the town center for Jesse Clyde Nichols's Country Club District outside Kansas City. Like Market Square, it is broken up into several buildings containing retail and commercial spaces—including a movie theater—and incorporating professional offices on the second stories. Shoppers can park in small lots discreetly concealed by low brick walls and walk through landscaped squares interspersed between the buildings. There is nothing discreet about the architecture, however, which is a flamboyant Spanish-Moorish concoction that includes a copy of Sevilla's Giralda tower. Nichols, the founder of the Urban Land Institute, a developers' trade association, was a tireless proselytizer for planned suburbs, and thanks to him, Country Club Plaza became well known.

Market Square and Country Club Plaza consciously recalled small-town shopping districts in the intimate, almost domestic scale of their architecture and in their layouts—the stores faced the street and the parking lots were in the rear. This was not accidental. The developers of the shopping village were also the developers of the surrounding residential areas, and retail areas were designed to fit into the overall master plan. One of the most attractive shopping complexes of this period was developed by the architect Addison Mizner in Palm Beach in 1924–25. Two picturesque pedestrian alleys lined with small shops—Via Mizner and Via Parigi—cut through the block; an arcade along Worth Avenue provided additional retail space. The pedestrian had the impression of walking through an old Spanish town, with crooked walls, wrought-iron balconies, worn steps, and clouds of falling bougainvillea, all artfully arranged by the architect. Mizner, whose scenographic approach to architecture is insufficiently appreciated, intended the complex to resemble a converted medieval castle. As he colorfully described it to a reporter, he wanted the shopping complex to appear as if "with the advent of more civilized times the armies were dismissed and commercially minded people converted the cellar-like rooms into small shops."

Not all the early shopping centers were part of planned suburbs. Farmers Markets, a California chain, were the 1930s equivalents of today's discount warehouses. The stores faced an inner, completely private pedestrian walkway, which presaged the inward-looking shopping centers of the future. To keep overheads low, Farmers Markets were built on cheap land on the edges of cities, and the peripheral location was no longer an inconvenience because most people drove to go shopping. This did not escape the attention of developers, who understood that with almost universal car ownership the pool of potential customers for any single shopping center—those who lived within a ten-minute drive, say, rather than within a ten-minute walk—had grown very large.

The spread of shopping centers was slowed by the Depression and World War II, and in 1946 there were still only eight large shopping centers. The postwar period saw much new suburban construction, but just as the subdivision replaced the garden suburb, the shopping village was replaced by the regional shopping center. Probably the first such center was Northgate, which opened on the outskirts of Seattle on May 1, 1950. The architect John Graham, Jr., devised a long, open-air pedestrian way that was a sort of carless street lined with a department store and a number of smaller stores. The idea was that the department store—called Bon Marché—would attract people, who would then walk and shop along the way. In addition to stores and a supermarket, Northgate eventually acquired a gas station, a drive-in bank, a movie theater, and a bowling alley. Like all future suburban shopping centers, Northgate was built next to a highway. Unlike the earlier shopping villages, it was developed, literally, as a freestanding project—the inward-oriented building was surrounded on all sides by a 4,000-car parking lot that took up about three-quarters of the sixty-acre site.

During the 1950s the construction of shopping centers, in tandem with the construction of subdivisions, began in earnest; the total went from about 100 centers nationwide in 1950 to about 3,700 only a decade later. Not only were there more centers, but they were growing bigger. One of the largest was Northland in Detroit, which opened in 1954 and included more than a million square feet of rentable space and parking for 7,400 cars. The 250-acre site around the center was planned to accommodate a host of nonretail buildings, including offices, research laboratories, apartments, a hospital, and a hotel.

In 1956 a shopping center that was to become a model for the next three decades opened in Edina, a suburb of Minneapolis.

Southdale (the early centers all seemed to be named after compass points) was not particularly large, just over half a million square feet, and it followed the usual pattern of buildings surrounded by parking lots. It incorporated one striking innovation, however: the public walking areas were indoors, air-conditioned in the summer and heated during the winter. The architect, Victor Gruen, a transplanted Viennese and a prolific designer of shopping centers (he had been the architect of Northland), cited the glass-roofed, nineteenth-century *gallerias* of Milan and Naples as his inspiration, even though the bland, modernistic interior of Southdale held no trace of its supposed Italian antecedents. Indoor shopping streets are attractive anywhere the climate is marked by hot, humid summers or harsh winters or a lot of rain; hence enclosed shopping malls appeared in the cold Midwest and Northeast, in the South and Southwest, in hot Southern California, and in the wet Northwest—that is to say, everywhere.

Starting in the sixties, most new regional shopping centers, following Southdale's success, were indoor shopping malls. To optimize the extra investment, malls were built on two or even three levels (an idea also introduced at Southdale). This made for shorter walking distances and more stores. In 1970, suburban Houston's Galleria, which did recall its Italian namesakes by providing a grand skylit promenade, opened with 1.5 million square feet of retail and commercial space; the following year Woodfield, outside Chicago, enclosed 2 million square feet of shopping under one roof. During the 1980s malls got even larger: the Del Amo Fashion Center in Torrance, California—3 million square feet—and the mother of all malls, the Ghermezian brothers' West Edmonton Mall in Alberta—5.2 million square feet. In all, from 1970 to 1990, about 25,000 new shopping centers were built in the United States: during that period every seven hours, on average, a new center opened its parking lot to the public.

The Galleria in Houston, whose centerpiece is a year-round ice-skating rink, added yet another ingredient. The developer, Gerald Hines, incorporated a variety of nonretail uses within the mall itself. A hotel guest or an office worker could go out of the lobby and straight into the mall, a simple change with a great impact. Malls were no longer merely shopping centers; they were urban places. Although retail functions continued to dominate, mall developers started leasing space to a variety of clients, including health and athletic clubs, banks, brokerage houses, and medical centers. Malls now also house civic functions: with public libraries, in Saint John, New Brunswick, and Tucson, Arizona; a United Services Organizations (USO) outlet in Hampton, Virginia; a city hall branch office in Everett, Washington; and federal and state agencies elsewhere. The Sports Museum of New England, in East Cambridge, Massachusetts, is housed in a mall; so is a children's museum in Ogden, Utah. The Board of Education of Ottawa has been leasing space for a storefront classroom in a local shopping mall since November 1987, and a local high school recently opened a counseling center in the West Edmonton Mall, which also contains a small synagogue. Just as noncommercial spaces are showing up in shopping malls, malls are popping up in unexpected places: York University in suburban Toronto recently added a shopping mall to its campus, and Pittsburgh's new airport includes a mall with more than a hundred outlets, three food courts, and a chiropractor.

The introduction of noncommercial tenants into shopping malls, which made them more like traditional downtowns, raised the issue of public access. Were malls private property, as mall owners maintained, or had they become, as the American Civil Liberties Union argued, public places where principles of free speech applied? Mall owners were not keen on the idea of abortion groups arguing their cases in the food court, or of having their customers witness a violent altercation between the Ku Klux Klan and its opponents, which actually happened in a Connecticut mall in the mid-1980s. On the other hand, if large regional malls wanted to be a part of the community and attract a broad cross section of the population, it was in their interest to allow access to as many people as possible, including various community groups.

In 1976, the United States Supreme Court ruled that there were no rights of free speech at shopping malls. Nevertheless, several state supreme courts, including those of California, Oregon, Massachusetts, Colorado, Washington, and New Jersey, have ruled in favor of allowing a certain degree of free-speech activities such as leafleting and canvassing in malls. Mall owners may eventually even support public access, since it has proved neither troublesome nor expensive. In 1991 the giant Hahn Company, which owns and operates thirty malls in California, signed an agreement with the American Civil Liberties Union that permits leafleting and canvassing in designated locations in most of its malls. Robert L. Sorensen, vice-president of Hahn, told *Shopping Centers Today*, an industry monthly: "We haven't seen expenses rise because of it, and I don't think it's costing us shoppers." In other states, although not legally required to do so, mall owners are beginning to make similar provisions. The Rouse Company provided a booth for community activities in its mall in Columbia, Maryland, and encourages its mall managers to make similar accommodations; so did The Edward J. DeBartolo Corporation of Youngstown, Ohio, the nation's largest shopping center developer and manager.

Legal issues aside, it is disingenuous for mall developers to argue that they are merely merchants. They are the new city builders, and as such should be prepared to take the bad—or at least the awkward—with the good. In fact, many malls have been acting more and more like municipal governments, sometimes banning smoking, for example, even in states where they are not legally obliged to do so. This does not mean that shopping malls will become like downtown streets. I think that what attracts people to malls is that they are perceived as public spaces where rules of personal conduct are enforced. In other words, they are more like public streets used to be before police indifference and overzealous protectors of individual rights effectively ensured that *any* behavior, no matter how antisocial, is tolerated. This is what malls offer: a reasonable (in most eyes) level of public order; the right not to be subjected to outlandish conduct, not to be assaulted and intimidated by boorish adolescents, noisy drunks, and aggressive panhandlers. It does not seem much to ask.

Work and play, shopping and recreation, community service and public protest—more and more of the activities of the traditional downtown have moved to the mall, including that newest of urban industries, tourism. With its skating rink and glass-roofed promenade, Houston's Galleria quickly became a tourist attraction. The builders of the West Edmonton Mall, which includes a resort hotel, also installed a skating rink as well as an aviary, a dolphin pool, an artificial lagoon with a submarine, a floating replica of the *Santa María*, an amusement park, and the world's largest indoor water park, complete with artificial beach and rolling surf.

A large portion of the visitors to the Mall of America, the recently opened 4.2-million-square-foot mall in Bloomington, Minnesota, outside Minneapolis, are tourists. The Mall of America is counting on attracting an average of about 100,000 people a day; this was exceeded during the first three months after its opening in August 1992, when nearly a million people a week visited the mall. Indeed, the owners of the Mall of America expect it to outdraw Walt Disney World and the Grand Canyon.

The Mall of America is extremely large—four department stores, about 360 specialty stores to date, more than forty restaurants and food outlets—but the three-level retail area is not particularly remarkable, only bigger than most. What is unusual is the fact that the stores are grouped around a huge (seven-acre) glass-roofed courtyard containing an amusement park complete with twenty-three rides, two theaters, and dozens of smaller attractions. The courtyard design brings to mind another building that combined shopping and recreation—the eighteenth-century incarnation of the Palais Royal in Paris. The instigator of that project was the Duc de Chartres, whose family home in Paris, beside the Louvre, included an extremely large garden. The duke, chronically short of funds, decided to use the garden as the site for a commercial venture. He engaged the architect Victor Louis to design a building to include commercial spaces and rental apartments, and to make the centerpiece of the project a public pleasure park, following the current English fashion. The so-called Palais Royal opened in 1784 to immediate accolades and dominated Parisian social life for fifty years. Like many developers since, the duke did not reap the profits of his brilliant scheme—financially ruined by the heavy investment, he was forced to sell off most of the project.

The Palais Royal consisted of a large landscaped courtyard about one hundred yards by three hundred yards, surrounded on three sides by a five-story building; the fourth side, which was never completed, was temporarily closed by wooden stalls. Facing the garden was a continuous two-story arcade. Within the arcade were glass-fronted shops and a variety of other establishments: cafés, eating places, social clubs, gambling rooms, music rooms, auction houses, a puppet show, a silhouette show, a waxworks, several hotels, a Turkish bath, and a theater (which later became the home of the Comédie Française). The upper floors contained apartments and rooms, many of which were rented to the *courtisanes* for whom the Palais became famous. The central pleasure garden contained a roofed amphitheater—the Cirque Royal—used for public performances, concerts, and balls.

In today's language, the eighteenth-century Palais Royal might be described as an upscale mall. Most establishments were luxurious and frequented solely by the rich—or by army officers on a spree—but the arcades and the garden were open to all except the lowest orders (invited in only three days a year), and it was where the aristocrat and the bourgeois mingled. The Palais Royal merged shopping, entertainment, and leisure. "Should an American savage come to the Palais Royal," the Russian novelist Nicolai Karamzin wrote, "in half an hour he would be most beautifully attired and would have a richly furnished house, a carriage, many servants, twenty courses on the table, and, if he wished, a blooming Laïs who each moment would die for love of him."

The Palais Royal still exists, although today it's a sedate place that includes antiquarian stores selling books, prints, and military memorabilia. Where does the average Parisian go for his running shoes or his VCR? He or she drives on the *périphérique* to a giant *hypermarché* out in the suburbs. The Paris of vast shopping marts and high-speed highways is not what Danielle was thinking of when she asked me her question, nor is it the Paris of my youthful visits.* But it's worth underlining that the *hypermarché* (the model for the warehouse-type shopping mart) is a French invention and not, like Disney World or Macdos (McDonald's ham-

*Fast food and takeouts are taking their toll of traditional French life; according to *Le Limonadier*, the trade journal of French bistros, whereas in 1960 there were 220,000 bistros, in 1994 there are fewer than 65,000.

burgers), an American import. Perhaps our cities are more alike than we imagine.

Kenneth T. Jackson, the author of *Crabgrass Frontier*, a history of the suburbs, argues that shopping malls represent almost the opposite of downtown areas. "They cater exclusively to middle-class tastes," he writes, "and contain no unsavory bars or pornography shops, no threatening-looking characters, no litter, no rain, and no excessive heat or cold." In fact, large malls do appeal to a variety of tastes—they have to. The Mall of America, for example, has The Gap as well as Bloomingdale's, Sam Goody and Brooks Brothers, Radio Shack and Godiva Chocolatier, video arcades and NordicTrack, a maker of expensive exercise machines. The eating establishments also cater to different tastes and budgets: there is an array of fast-food outlets arranged around two food courts; several family restaurants (with occasional live entertainment); an assortment of inexpensive steakhouses; several mainstream Italian eateries; an upscale restaurant serving California cuisine; and a Wolfgang Puck pizza and pasta emporium, the first one outside California. There is also a nightclub area where a sports bar, a comedy club, and a country-and-western supper club are open until one in the morning. It is true that there are no pornography shops in the Mall of America, although the video stores certainly rent soft-core porn, and as for threatening-looking characters, there are plenty of weird-looking (to me, at least) teenagers.* Yes, malls (like city streets in Canada and many northern European cities) are clean, but the notion that urbanity is somehow repre-

*According to an American friend living in Edmonton, the West Edmonton Mall does have bag people. "There aren't many," she writes, "but there are enough to make a transplanted New Yorker feel at home."

sented by litter is surely a sad comment on the miserable state of American downtowns rather than a serious criticism.

Unquestionably, shopping malls are managed places. They are strictly policed, regularly cleaned, and properly maintained; public washrooms are provided; goods are delivered without disruption; leases are terminated on failing or unprofitable businesses; and as spaces become vacant, new tenants are found to fill them. Mall owners strive to achieve a balanced mix of stores and attract high-profile tenants who will benefit the smaller stores. Special events such as bazaars, concerts, and festivals are organized to attract shoppers; and advertising programs promote the shopping mall as a whole. "In ambiance and retail mix the suburban model of success turned its back on the market-driven chaos of downtown and left little to chance," two MIT professors of urban planning, Bernard Frieden and Lynne Sagalyn, observe. Interestingly, this tactic has proved so popular with the public that it has been emulated by downtown merchants' associations, who realize that the traditional hit-or-miss approach to retailing will no longer do.

And what of the issue of enclosure? Does the fact that shoppers are protected from extremes of heat and cold disqualify malls as urban places? I don't think so. Merchants have been building enclosed shopping spaces for a long time. Glass-roofed arcades, or *passages*, first emerged in the center of Paris in the early 1800s, and were widely imitated across the Continent and in England. Nineteenth-century London and Paris also had shopping bazaars, and Milan, Naples, and other Italian cities had gallerias; these were large, often multilevel shopping arcades with independent stalls, covered by impressive roofs constructed of cast iron and glass. One of the few surviving examples of a shopping-bazaar building is the splendid GUM department store in Moscow, completed in 1893. Compared with the high-flown, extravagant interiors of the Victorian shopping bazaars and department stores, which celebrated shopping and consumerism on a scale unrivaled before or since, the architecture of most contemporary shopping malls is downright modest.

Still, Jackson has a point—the lack of extremes of weather does make malls feel artificial. Downtown shopping areas are traditionally made up of open as well as enclosed public spaces, which is one of the appeals of the early shopping centers like Market Square and Country Club Plaza. Part of this atmosphere is undoubtedly produced by the landscaping, the shaded arcades, and the sunny outdoor squares. Contemporary developers, in their rush to build completely enclosed malls, may have missed an opportunity for greater diversity. In Boston, Baltimore, and New York City, The Rouse Company, a major shopping-mall developer, has built so-called festival marketplaces, which are really shopping malls in a waterfront setting. Since the commercial spaces in Faneuil Hall Marketplace, Harborplace, and South Street Seaport are located in rehabilitated dockside buildings, much of the public space is outdoors; in that sense, these malls resemble Lake Forest's Market Square more than Southdale. Indoor/outdoor malls have proved extremely popular as well as commercially successful, and have spawned imitators, like the shopping area in New York's Battery Park City, which has a glass-roofed space that recalls Crystal Palace, and is visually and physically related to the outdoors. Horton Plaza, an urban mall in downtown San Diego, is a large, multilevel shopping complex that dispenses with enclosed traffic areas altogether in favor of arcades and open-air courtyards. Jon Jerde, the architect of Horton Plaza, also designed Citywalk in Universal City, California. Taking a page from Mizner's Palm Beach work, he has created a picturesque pedestrian mall flanked with small-scale buildings. The architecture is not intended to recall Spain, however, but the Los

Angeles region, including Sunset Strip, Melrose Avenue, and Venice Beach.

The debate about whether shopping malls could or should replace or augment downtown is academic. In places like Plattsburgh, there is little doubt that the shopping mall *is* the new downtown.* The Plattsburgh mall, which was built in the 1970s and greatly enlarged a few years ago, is about two miles from downtown, next to the interstate. It is enclosed, and large enough to qualify as a so-called regional mall—defined as including more than 400,000 square feet of retail space and at least one department store. According to the National Research Bureau, at the end of 1992 there were 38,966 operating shopping centers in the United States, of which 1,835 were regional malls. Although plenty of upscale malls cater to the rich, the mall in Plattsburgh is not an effete oasis of luxury; like most malls it serves Middle America—that is, the broad middle class, which here also includes people from the surrounding farms and small towns.

When I lived in Hemmingford, across the nearby Canadian border, every two or three weeks Shirley and I would drive down the interstate and go to the mall, sometimes to shop, sometimes to go to a movie, sometimes just to stroll. The atmosphere was lively, a marked contrast to the emptiness of downtown's Margaret Street. There were crowds here, excited teenagers swarming to the video arcade, parents trailing children on the way to the movie theater, young couples window-shopping, elderly people walking for exercise or sitting on park benches. On Saturdays, there were

*The New Jersey Supreme Court based its 1994 decision protecting free speech in malls on the fact that "suburban shopping centers . . . have substantially displaced the downtown business districts as the centers of commercial and social activity."

usually booths selling the sort of mass-produced crafts that one finds at country fairs: hand-painted ties, varnished wood carvings, junk jewelry. The chamber of commerce occupied a stall and promoted local tourist attractions. There were even Girl Scouts selling cookies.

Families ate lunch in the food court, a sunny space that almost felt like the outdoors thanks to the fairly large trees and the natural light filtering through the stretched fabric roof. The large open area, which was the convivial focus of the mall, was full of tables and seating; on the periphery were counters whose colorful overhead signs proclaimed a variety of take-away foods: Tex-Mex, Chinese, Italian, Middle Eastern. People carried their trays to the tables. Because there was no physical boundary between the eating area and the surrounding mall, the impression was of a giant sidewalk café.

I suppose that some people would find this an unsophisticated version of urbanity (although you could get a reasonable espresso here), and some of my academic colleagues would refer darkly to "hyperconsumerism" and artificial reality. But I was more encouraged than depressed by the Plattsburgh mall. I saw people rubbing shoulders and meeting their fellow citizens in a noncombative environment—not behind the wheel of a car, but on foot. As for hyperconsumerism, commercial forces have always formed the center of the American city—the old downtown no less than the new—and it is unclear to me why sitting on a bench in the mall should be considered any more artificial than a bench in the park. Admittedly, I still liked to walk down Margaret Street, but it was a nostalgic urge. When I wanted to be part of a crowd, I went to the mall.

TEN

The Best of Both Worlds

"SO, WHERE WOULD YOU LIVE IF YOU COULD CHOOSE anywhere at all?" a friend asked me not long ago. I was stumped for an answer. Everyone has had the experience of visiting a particularly attractive place and thinking, "I wish I could live here someday." Venice had struck me like that, as had Key West, and Victoria, British Columbia. I could see myself living in Woodstock, too. But I don't believe in dream houses, still less in dream places, and I really can't imagine picking a place to live in the way that you might pick a dish from a restaurant menu. It is either too arbitrary or too calculated, I'm not sure which, but it feels wrong.

Still, it wasn't altogether a hypothetical question. At the time, my wife and I were discussing moving from the Boathouse, the country house we had built ourselves and lived in for fourteen years, and where my friend Danielle had asked me, "Why aren't our cities like that?" When the idea of moving had first come up two years earlier, we had talked about it in a vague, uncertain way. It was one of those what-if conversations that start as idle speculation and take weeks and months to coalesce into not exactly certainty, but at least possibility. No single overriding reason prompted this speculation, but there were many small ones. I was getting stale in my university work—after almost twenty years I had accomplished most of the things I had set out to do, and I felt I could benefit from the stimulation of new surroundings. I was fifty years old, and if I was to move, it would have to be soon, or never. There was also the unsettled political situation in French Quebec, whose separation from Canada seemed likely, if not imminent. Although I wished French Canadians well, their passionate quest for political independence seemed to me quixotic at best and foolhardy at worst. In either case, their quest was not my own. Last, while both Shirley and I had adjusted to country life, we had to admit that there were some things about it we didn't like. The isolation, for one thing. The township of Hemmingford, where we lived, was relatively remote—fifty miles from Montreal and the university where I worked—and even going to the Plattsburgh mall meant a forty-minute drive. I don't dislike driving (Shirley does), but I had to agree with her that it would be nice to live in a place where you could walk to a corner store, or where public transport was available to go to work, say, or to the airport. That is, it would be nice to live in more urban surroundings.

Most people have firm ideas about the ideal place to live. When a 1989 Gallup poll asked Americans the same question my friend had asked me—where would you choose to live if you could live anywhere: in a city, suburb, small town, or the country?—34 percent said they would prefer to live in a small town, more than chose any other category. Opinion polls regularly uncover this same bias—Gallup asked a similar question in 1972 and found almost a third in favor of small towns. This partiality should not be surprising, for the concept of "small town" exercises a powerful hold on the American imagination. It's unclear exactly what population constitutes a small town, but it is probably less than 10,000 people. Christopher Alexander, the author of *A Pattern Language*, a primer on architecture and urban design, recommends between 5,000 and 10,000 as the ideal population for small towns; like Aristotle before him, Alexander bases this figure on the number of people that can effectively govern themselves. Whatever the exact size, most people would agree that the small town has to have a main street with stores, a few offices, and a town hall, probably across from a park or square near the center. There should be houses, preferably with porches, facing streets lined with large, overhanging trees. The small town is not a village—there is a denser sense of community, people are living close together—but it isn't a city, either. Perhaps the most important thing about the small town of the public imagination is not its physical attributes but that it is a recognizable community.

The affection Americans have for small towns, remarked on so many years ago by Tocqueville, has since been celebrated on stage, in movies, and on television. A small town was the setting of Thornton Wilder's *Our Town* and Frank Capra's *It's a Wonderful Life*, as well as of innumerable television dramas, including the 1950s classics "Father Knows Best," set in the town of Springfield, and "Leave It to Beaver," set in the town of Mayfield. Canadians, too, share this preference for small towns. The best-loved works of Canadian literature, Lucy Maud Montgomery's *Anne of Green Gables* and Stephen Leacock's *Sunshine Sketches of a Little Town*, are set in small towns; so is Robertson Davies's masterful

Salterton trilogy, beginning with *Fifth Business*. Movies, television, and novels in both countries strengthen the perception of the small town as more authentic than the city, and "Main Street, not Wall Street" continues to raise a cheer in any political speech.

It's worth pointing out that this affection for the idealized joys of small-town life has had its ups and downs. Hadleyville in the Western movie *High Noon* or Maycomb in *To Kill a Mockingbird* are small towns that are shown to be less than perfect; even Capra's fictional Bedford Falls, New York, in *It's a Wonderful Life*, has its darker side. Sherwood Anderson fled a small town and went to Chicago to write *Winesburg, Ohio*. Sinclair Lewis's 1920 novel, *Main Street*, described the complacency and narrow-mindedness of small midwestern towns; its locale, Gopher Prairie, was based on the author's hometown, Sauk Center, Minnesota. For Lewis's generation, the small town was chiefly a place to escape from. But there were, and are, other novelists—Faulkner, Steinbeck, Welty, Updike, Davies—for whom the small-town atmosphere proved congenial. Affection for small towns is distinctly American; although the country village plays the small-town role in English culture, one cannot imagine a Frenchman, say, or an Italian, preferring small towns to large cities.

I had spent about half my life living in large cities, but I had to admit that I liked small towns, too, and given half a chance, I might have moved to one. But things worked out differently. The University of Pennsylvania called me with the generous offer of a newly established chair. Suddenly speculation turned into reality. After due consideration, I accepted. With regret, we put the Boathouse up for sale and started to pack.

Once we had navigated the bureaucratic channels of the U. S. Immigration and Naturalization Service and acquired visas, we had to officially enter the United States, which in our case involved nothing more than driving to the rural border crossing two miles from our house. After the formality of having our passports stamped, I was talking to the American immigration officer, who offhandedly asked me where we would be going.

"Philadelphia," I answered.

"Why?"

The incredulous look on his face suggested that the question was not, "What are you going to do in Philadelphia?" or "Why Philadelphia, in particular?" Really what he was asking was "Why would you want to go to a place like Philadelphia?" or more to the point, "Why on earth would you want to leave these peaceful country surroundings and move to a dirty, crowded, dangerous city?"

Why, indeed. I could understand his puzzlement. Most Americans given a choice would get out of a big city, not move into one. In 1994, *The Wall Street Journal* commissioned a study to identify the fastest-growing, wealthiest, and most educated areas of the country—that is, those areas to which its own younger readers (white-collar executives, corporate managers, and professionals, definitely people with choices) were moving. Among the criteria used by the researchers were that median household incomes be $30,000 or more (the 1990 national median was $29,943; the actual median incomes in the growth areas varied between $35,000 and $55,000); that at least a quarter of the residents be between thirty-five and fifty-four (these were not retirement communities); and that at least a quarter of the adults be university educated. None of what the article called "the power centers of tomorrow" were in big cities or in traditional suburbs or even in metropolitan areas; they were all in rural counties, twenty to fifty miles away from the nearest city. The top three areas were Douglas County, Colorado, lying between Denver and Colorado Springs; Fayette County, Georgia, south of Atlanta; and Fort Bend County, Texas, southwest of Houston. Nor were all these "power centers" in the

South and West—eight of the twenty were in the northeast, and three in Minnesota. What attracted people and companies to these places were better schools, cheaper housing, low crime rates, and the chance to improve what is usually referred to as quality of life, even if this means driving an hour or more to work. One expert quoted in the article observed, "A lot of baby boomers want out of the urban scene at whatever sacrifice."

Hemmingford, in a rural county, hardly qualified as a power center of tomorrow, but in moving to a large city we did seem to be bucking a trend. What I had told the immigration officer, however, was not precise. We were moving to Philadelphia, but not to the center of the city. Our new home is an old stone house in the garden suburb that Henry Houston started to build in 1884 in the northwest corner of the city—Chestnut Hill.

In a way, we were moving to a small town and a city both. The population of Chestnut Hill is that of a small town, about 10,000, spread over less than three square miles, which is more persons per square mile than, say, present-day Charleston or Savannah, but considerably less than most larger cities. Despite its location, Chestnut Hill gives the impression of an only slightly urbanized Arcadia. This is what William Penn must have had in mind when he planned his "green country town." The trees that Houston and Woodward planted are fully grown and throw a broad canopy over the streets; the heavily planted gardens in front of many houses add to the atmosphere of an extended public park. Some things have changed. The lake that Houston built has been drained and his hotel has been converted into a private school, but the Cricket Club is still here, as is the Gothic revival church. Most of the Woodward and Houston houses survive, still owned by descendants of the two families, and long waiting lists attest to their continued popularity with tenants. Chestnut Hill is no longer the upper-class WASP bastion of the early 1900s, when it had more residents in the *Social Register* than any other community in the Philadelphia region.* It has become more socially and economically heterogeneous. There are now apartment buildings, townhouses, and modestly priced rental units. In fact the variety, from studio apartments in high-rises to cavernous mansions, is much greater than in most urban neighborhoods, let alone small towns. The main commercial street, which deteriorated in the 1950s as more and more people shopped at nearby suburban shopping centers, has been revived by an active merchants' association that refurbished buildings, created common parking lots, and turned Germantown Avenue into a successful shopping street, precisely the sort of old-fashioned pedestrian district people find so attractive. The stores are a mix of locally owned businesses and national chains.

Chestnut Hill is legally and emotionally part of the city of Philadelphia, but it is no longer precise to describe Chestnut Hill as "a suburb in the city." In 1990, the same number of working people were commuting *out* to the surrounding suburban counties as were commuting *in* to downtown, or what Philadelphians call Center City. The same dichotomy applies to other activities. From Chestnut Hill one goes to Center City to the Spectrum, the Academy of Music, the Philadelphia Museum of Art, and good restaurants; and in the other direction, into suburban Philadelphia, to visit the Barnes Foundation, to have one's car repainted, to buy lumber, to go to a movie at the mall. Chestnut Hill stands between two different urban worlds.

The Philadelphia metropolitan area encompasses several cities and counties in four different states; three-quarters of its residents

*The term WASP—white Anglo-Saxon Protestant—was originated by sociologist E. Digby Baltzell, born and raised in Chestnut Hill.

live outside the city of Philadelphia. The term metropolitan area was formally adopted by the U.S. Census Bureau in 1949 in order to recognize that urbanization had outstripped traditional city limits and that a new classification was needed. The Latin root of "metropolis" means mother-city, and the metropolitan area was intended to embody this notion. In the United States, a metropolitan area is defined as a large population nucleus—that is, a central city (typically with at least 50,000 people)—and the adjacent communities—that is, suburbs—with which it has a high degree of social and economic integration. The Canadian definition is similar, although no minimum size for the city is stipulated. In both countries metro areas must have at least 100,000 residents to qualify. There are currently more than three hundred metro areas in the United States and twenty-five in Canada, and they are home to about three-quarters of the population of each country.

This definition of a metro area describes the main city as a nucleus and suggests that the surrounding suburban towns and counties represent satellites of a kind. The metaphor is misleading, or at least outdated. For one thing, although metro areas are named after their largest city, most metro areas include not one but several nuclei. Metro San Francisco, for example, includes San Jose, which is actually a more populous city, as well as Oakland; metro Houston includes Galveston and Brazoria; the metro region of Toronto includes no less than eight cities and sixteen towns. Moreover, because metro areas are so large, the so-called nucleus is only a small part of the whole. In the case of metro San Francisco, only about 700,000 people out of more than 6 million live in the city itself; the city of Toronto has about 635,000 residents out of a total metropolitan population of 4 million. The city of Paris—about 2.3 million residents—likewise represents a fraction of metro Paris's 10.5 million; metropolitan growth is not confined to North America.

The nucleus/satellite metaphor is misleading in another way, because it implies that the surrounding suburbs are subservient to the central city. Before 1950 this was largely true: central cities were richer, and offered more employment than their suburbs. Cities were also the most populous part of the metro area: in 1950, seven out of ten Americans living in metropolitan areas lived inside the limits of the main central city. Forty years later the situation has reversed, and now only four out of ten live in central cities. It isn't just that more people are choosing to live outside the city and commute in; employment also has moved to the suburban fringe. The extent of this shift is remarkable: by 1990 only half as many Americans nationwide were making the traditional suburb-to-city trip as were traveling from home to workplace without leaving the suburbs. The relationship between suburb and city has changed radically, from one of simple dependency to uneasy parity.

Most metro areas have grown vigorously, but metropolitan growth has not everywhere been accompanied by city growth. Between 1950 and 1990, old manufacturing cities like Chicago, Philadelphia, and Baltimore lost almost a quarter of their population; in some cases, like Saint Louis, Cleveland, and Detroit, the loss was closer to half. Despite a different political system that encourages metropolitan government, the same thing is taking place in Canada, although slightly delayed. The population of the city of Montreal, for example, which was 1.2 million in 1971, shrank over the next twenty years to about 1 million. Equally engaging cities like Boston and San Francisco have also experienced decline in the last decades. This is not only a question of people deciding to move from city to suburb or from city to city—chiefly from the northeastern cities to the South and West—but also of new arrivals choosing to locate their homes and businesses outside the central city. Thus, as metro Philadelphia gained over a million residents between 1950 and 1990, the city of Philadelphia declined by half a million.

Downsizing need not adversely affect the quality of city life. After all, businesses, institutions, even the military, are obliged to consolidate, so why not cities? Vienna, Venice, and Glasgow are smaller today than in the past, but this has not made them inhospitable places to live. The number of thriving small cities, both here and abroad, suggests that unlimited growth is not the only urban policy. Population shrinkage can be acceptable as long as resources are properly managed. Unfortunately, for many cities, poor management and shrinking resources are precisely the problem. The image of the successful central business district assiduously cultivated by city planners and municipal administrators in the 1970s and 80s, with glamorous skyscrapers and exciting cultural showplaces, has turned out to be a false measure of urban health. Neighborhoods are the lifeblood of any city. The loss of the old industrial jobs together with the middle-class move to the suburbs has turned many urban neighborhoods into dysfunctional communities of chronic unemployment and welfare dependency. Nor are these merely "pockets" of poverty—the average income across entire cities like North Chicago, East Saint Louis, or Camden, New Jersey is now much less than half that of surrounding suburbs. Their traditional tax base reduced, cities have been unable to maintain standards in urban services such as policing, education, transportation, and street cleaning. To make up for lost revenue, local taxes are raised. But reduced services and higher taxes hardly attract financially secure newcomers, and such desperate measures only serve to drive more people away.

David Rusk, the former mayor of Albuquerque and author of *Cities Without Suburbs*, has studied the relationship between central cities and metropolitan areas. According to his analysis, when the average city income drops to less than 70 percent of the average suburban income, the disparity is so great that investment and job creation in the city come to a virtual halt. "The bottom line is that once past the Point of No Return, I have not found a city that has ever made up economic ground on its suburbs by even one percentage point! . . . The situation is not hopeless," he writes, "but the city can no longer 'save' itself through its own efforts and by programs within its own municipal jurisdiction."

The cities that have passed Rusk's point of no return will require external intervention to equalize their increased share of the national burden of poverty-related problems (including a disproportionate share of immigration). Central cities cannot be asked to continue to shoulder these responsibilities without a more equitable distribution of national financial resources. Whatever the nature of this intervention, one thing is certain: if it is to survive, the central city must be better integrated into the metropolitan area, although no longer as *the* center, but as one of *many* centers. Popular media representations to the contrary, New York is not only the towers of Manhattan (it wasn't even when Le Corbusier visited), just as Chicago is not only the Loop or the Gold Coast. These may be the urban images that attract conventioneers and tourists, but for the scores of communities that inhabit it, the metro area consists of different places, each with its own character, its own geography, and its own focus. The traditional downtown is usually still an important business center, and its historical buildings and cultural institutions may make it a destination for tourists, but the airport, which is on the urban fringe, is also a major nucleus, as important as the harbor or railroad terminus of old. Urban neighborhoods, rich and poor, have their own retail centers—as they always have had. The suburbs, no longer strictly residential, have developed town centers around shopping malls and office complexes; some of these suburban centers have grown into dense agglomerations of retail, commercial, office space, and research facilities, which the journalist Joel Garreau has christened "edge cities." With names like Princeton Corridor and Perimeter Center (near Atlanta), the edge cities now boast more prestige office space than the downtown. The strip, especially in smaller cities, represents another kind of focus, linear and dynamic, often a fertile breeding ground for entrepreneurs. And the outer suburbs have acquired their own nuclei, often located in existing country towns. The metro area—that is, the modern city—is *all* of these.

Broadacre City was the imaginary metropolis that Frank Lloyd Wright started designing in the mid-1930s. This was his answer to Le Corbusier: The city of the future would not be vertical, but horizontal. Instead of concentrating people in apartment blocks, Broadacre City dispersed them in individual houses on one-acre lots. This was not a suburb, however, for Wright dispensed with the traditional downtown altogether, and scattered public and commercial buildings throughout the landscape. The citizens of Broadacre City would get about on a network of multilevel highways, in bizarre vehicles that looked like a cross between a tractor and a modern minivan; or they could leapfrog from house to house in their family helicopters, called "aerotors." They would shop at drive-in "wayside markets," strolling among fountains and greenery under glass-roofed galleries; assemble in drive-in civic centers; and worship in drive-in churches set amidst rolling farmland.

Wright tinkered with the design of Broadacre City for the last twenty years of his life, but it remained unrealized, and most architectural critics refused to take it seriously, considering it the embarrassing foible of an aging master. Today, on the whole, much of Broadacre City is surprisingly familiar. Wright was correct in assuming the automobile had drastically altered the way that Americans wanted to live, and our spread-out metro areas vindicate his vision. What he had not foretold, however, was the extent to which the pedestrian pleasures of traditional cities and towns have made a comeback. North Americans, who used to go to Europe to stroll the ancient streets of Venice and Strasbourg, can now enjoy restored British, French, or Spanish colonial towns like Charleston, Quebec, or Saint Augustine, or rebuilt urban historic districts, or re-creations of urban places, like Williamsburg or Disneyland's Main Street. Even shopping malls are starting to be designed to look like traditional streets. Undoubtedly, this is partly nostalgia and partly an interest in history, but it might also be evidence, as the contemporary planner and architect Andres Duany has argued, that Americans have preserved a taste for the experience of old-fashioned pedestrian-based urbanism.

This fondness for a more traditional form of urbanity is apparently what prompted the organizers of 1994's Final Four tournament of college basketball to create a temporary "downtown" in the center of the host city, Charlotte, North Carolina. Charlotte is the third-largest banking center in the United States and a prosperous metro area, but what had been downtown is now no more than a conglomeration of spanking-new high-rise commercial buildings. For the tournament, a four-block area was turned into a so-called entertainment zone complete with sports bars, comedy clubs, and restaurants, located in empty buildings and in tents pitched on vacant lots. For this one weekend at least, downtown Charlotte had a vibrant street life once more, even if, as one journalist observed, it was all as permanent as a movie set. "We're only reacting to the fact that visitors will want to come here to have an urban experience," a local architect was quoted as saying. This is what continues to attract out-of-towners to the centers of New York, Boston, and Philadelphia, where one's two feet are the preferred mode of transportation, and where urban life is still experienced firsthand.

"Firsthand" may not be quite the right word, since people experience cities in cars as well as on foot, but the desire to counterbalance our enervating mobility with something more calming, smaller scale, more old-fashioned, is real enough. Equally real is the craving for a sense of local identity, for sharing experiences at a smaller scale. The desire for community—or at least for a *sense* of community—is undoubtedly responsible for the success of so-called Traditional Neighborhood Development, an approach to planning suburban communities that combines smaller plots, more public spaces, and short walking distances to concentrated town centers with traditional-looking architecture. Such planned developments have proved popular with home buyers and developers in both Canada and the United States. In the suburbs of San Francisco and Portland, Oregon, the planner Peter Calthorpe has designed new neighborhoods focused on transit stops that are combined with commercial centers, much in the way that the builders of Market Square placed shops next to the railroad station in Lake Forest, Illinois. Andres Duany and Elizabeth Plater-Zyberk, the Miami-based couple who invented Traditional Neighborhood Development, are planning a 1,500-acre suburban development in Markham, in metro Toronto, that is designed so that all of the 27,000 residents will be within a five-minute walk of parks and small commercial centers. This type of planning is sometimes described as neotraditional, and indeed, Duany and Plater-Zyberk used Yorkship Village, New Jersey, as a model for the plan of their acclaimed Florida resort community of Seaside, whose small, porch-fronted houses and narrow streets recall a nineteenth-century small town.

Still, a desire for local identity and old-fashioned architecture should not be confused with really wanting to return to the static communities of the past—no matter how profound our nostalgia. It is unlikely that we will ever sacrifice our freedom and mobility (both physical and social) for the constraints implied by life in the small towns we say we admire. The Canadian architect Moshe Safdie is best known for the housing project Habitat, a sort of vertical suburb, with roof terraces replacing private gardens. He has also worked on town designs in the United States and Israel, and has suggested that "Policy for the coming decades cannot rest on the premise of forcing a reversal of the desire to disperse, but rather, on facilitating and shaping our wanderings: creating new centers of concentration within sprawling districts—in other words, designing the best of both worlds." Safdie is right. The popularity of shopping malls and of historic districts shows that people still enjoy meeting face-to-face. On the other hand, the diversity of modern city life can no longer be contained in a single main street or in a small, local neighborhood center. The simple organization and limited choices provided by traditional urbanism will no longer do. We need both dispersal and concentration in cities—places to get away from each other, and places to gather—and it's time to stop assuming that one necessarily precludes the other.

The old hierarchy of center and periphery, of downtown and suburb, which both Daniel Burnham and Le Corbusier believed in no matter how different their urban visions, is being replaced by something else—something diffuse, amorphous, and held together, as J. B. Jackson has suggested, by a system of roads and highways and, one could add, by a system of telephone wires, television cables, and computer links. According to Jackson, what was once a composition of well-defined physical places has been replaced by vague zones of influence; accessibility, not permanence, is what characterizes the metro area. If getting somewhere is as important as being somewhere, then mobility affects our very sense of place. "It can be said that a landscape tradition a thousand years old in our Western world is yielding to a fluid organization of space that we do not entirely understand, nor know how to assimilate as a symbol of what is desirable and worth preserving," Jackson writes. If he is right, North American cities will continue to become less and less like the cities of the past.

The urban future can be glimpsed in new, fast-growing cities like San Diego, Dallas, and Jacksonville, which are developing a dynamic kind of home-grown urbanism based on movement and accessibility, decentralization, and a complete reliance on private cars rather than on public mass transportation. It is these cities that are the new economic powerhouses. The city of San Jose proper, whose population almost quadrupled between 1970 and 1990, is the only American city with more than a quarter of its workforce engaged in manufacturing; the median household income is the highest of any of the major cities. Cities like San Jose are characterized by an extremely low overall urban density, much lower than that of the nineteenth-century industrial cities. Phoenix, which has grown through vigorous annexation, now extends over more than 400 square miles; Houston over more than 500 square miles, about four times as large as the area of Philadelphia.

Once we accept that our cities will not be like cities of the past, it will become possible to see what they might become. Combining lessons from the past with the present will not produce a unified city, but a combination of disparate elements, old and new, dense and diffuse, private and public: Frank Lloyd Wright's Broadacre City meets Jane Jacobs's Greenwich Village. This will please neither the advocates of traditional urbanism nor the edge-city boosters, but its chaotic, ideological impurity may be a more truthful accommodation to the way we live today.

* * *

I take the train to work, the same line that Henry Houston convinced the Pennsylvania Railroad to build in 1882. The stop where I get on has only a platform with a small, open shelter to protect waiting passengers from inclement weather. One morning I read a notice calling for volunteers to clean up the grounds around the railroad stop. The following Saturday, I joined my neighbors in what I discovered is a semiannual event. The anomalous sight of a retired business executive raking leaves, and a turbaned matron chain-sawing dead trees seemed slightly ridiculous and also discouraging. After all, this was the sort of maintenance traditionally held to be the job of the public authorities, whose inability to perform even such humdrum tasks seemed to me evidence of serious urban decline. But on second thought, I changed my mind. Decline there might be, but our efforts were not worthy of ridicule. Here were citizens reaffirming a small measure of control over their shared physical surroundings, and demonstrating a sense of community, which is part of what cities are about—or should be.

As I was heaving branches into the Dumpster, I was reminded that the city of the future, whatever form it takes, will depend on the goodwill of its citizens for its well-being. Planners and architects lay out the avenues and expressways and build public monuments and civic symbols, but these don't add up to much if a strong sense of urban community doesn't take root. A sense of community has nourished Savannah and ensured that James Oglethorpe's beautiful streets and squares are still used today. It has sustained large parts of the center of Philadelphia as residential neighborhoods, despite the decline of that city's manufacturing base, and if it is not exactly "a green country town," as Penn wished, it remains a good place to live. A sense of community enabled the people of Chicago to rebuild after the fire of 1871, and to create so many architectural masterworks. A sense of urban community is also visible in Yorkship Village, whose inhabitants have tended and preserved Electus Litchfield's modest and humane architecture, like good gardeners.

"A town is always a town," Braudel observed. He might have added, had he been writing about North America, "even when it doesn't appear to be." The first crude settlements, isolated in the wilderness of the New World, up and down the Atlantic coast and on the banks of the inland rivers, were certainly towns; despite their size, so were the hamlets of New England, like Woodstock, which resembles a miniature town in its civilized urbanity; so were the hastily built, grandiloquently named "cities" of the western frontier. Like Annapolis and Williamsburg, all are properly called towns because the intentions of their makers were ambitiously but explicitly urban. City life continued to evolve in unexpected places: in the temporary plaster-covered pavilions of the White City, which opened the door to a new vision of the city; in the town centers and along the leafy streets of the garden suburbs, where escapees from the industrial city created a new kind of urbanism; and today in the shopping malls, where a promenading version of city life is reappearing.

Yes, the fortunes of cities rise and fall. This was—is—especially true in the New World, where there is little urban stability and some cities grow while others decline. This very instability, however, seems like a native condition of our cities. It is a reflection of a society that has embraced change and transformation, and which continues to fashion and refashion its surroundings. Mistakes will be made, as they have been in the past, technological change will continue to surprise us, and ambitions will frequently outstrip reality—and vice versa. But the expectations will continue to be, as they always were, urban.

NOTES

CHAPTER ONE: WHY AREN'T OUR CITIES LIKE THAT?

17 the Duc de Broglie: Eugen Weber, *France: Fin de Siècle* (Cambridge, Mass.: Harvard University Press, 1986), 58.

18 "American comforts": Siegfried Giedion, *Mechanization Takes Command: A Contribution to Anonymous History* (New York: W.W. Norton & Co., 1969), 695–99.

21 "We will have achieved nothing": Mitterrand quoted in *Paris 1979–1989* (New York: Rizzoli, 1988), 11.

29 Pacific Electric Railway: Reyner Banham, *Los Angeles: The Architecture of Four Ecologies* (Baltimore: Penguin, 1971), 82.

29 Today trolleys are making a small comeback: Matthew L. Wald, "Key to Trolley Success: Connecting Popular Areas," *New York Times* (June 10, 1994), B2.

30 Best places: "The Best Places to Live in America," *Money* (September 1992), 110–124.

32 1992 Nobel Lecture: Derek Walcott, "The Antilles: Fragments of Epic Memory," *The New Republic* (December 28, 1992), 26–32.

33 Americans' restlessness: John Lukacs, *Outgrowing Democracy: A History of the United States in the Twentieth Century* (New York: Doubleday, 1984), 171.

34 "Similar, too, are the human qualities": Vincent Scully, *American Architecture and Urbanism* (New York: Praeger, 1969), 16.

CHAPTER TWO: THE MEASURE OF A TOWN

36 The grandly named Dodge City: Odie B. Faulk, *Dodge City: The Most Western Town of All* (New York: Oxford University Press, 1977), 72

37 Size of medieval German and French towns: Fernand Braudel, *The Structures of Everyday Life: The Limits of the Possible*, Siân Reynolds, trans. (New York: Harper & Row, 1981), 482.

38 The city was thought of as the seat of authority: see John Brinckerhoff Jackson, *Discovering the Vernacular Landscape* (New Haven: Yale University Press, 1984), 73.

40 So-called megacities: Eugene Linden, "Megacities," *Time* (January 11, 1993), 32–40.

41 The New Ghetto: Mary McCarthy, *The Stones of Florence and Venice Observed* (New York: Penguin Books, 1972), 254–55.
41 "When a man is tired of London": James Boswell, *The Life of Samuel Johnson* (London: Folio Society, 1968), Vol.2, 171.
42 Distinct ways of thinking about cities: Kevin Lynch, *Good City Form* (Cambridge, Mass.: MIT Press, 1981), 72–98.
47 Three distinctive stages in the early history of European towns: *The Structures of Everyday Life*, 515.
47 Pharaonic towns: Lewis Mumford, *The City in History: Its Origins, Its Transformations, and Its Prospects* (New York: Harcourt, Brace & World, 1961), 81.
49 "A town is always a town": *The Structures of Everyday Life*, 481.
50 "Urban development," he writes, "does not happen of its own accord": ibid., 520.

CHAPTER THREE: A NEW, UNCROWDED WORLD

54 William Bartram, quoted by Peter Nabokov and Robert Easton, *Native American Architecture* (New York: Oxford University Press, 1989), 104–105.
55 Size of Anasazi settlements: ibid., 361.
56 Palace of Knossos in Crete: Vincent Scully, *Pueblo: Mountain, Village, Dance* (New York: Viking Press, 1972), 117.
56 "The architectural principle": Vincent Scully, *Architecture: The Natural and the Man-made* (New York: St. Martin's Press, 1991), 5.
57 History of San Agostín: Albert Manucy, *The Houses of St. Augustine* (Saint Augustine, Fla.: The St. Augustine Historical Society, 1962), 8.
59 "The North American settlements of the Spanish colonial empire": John W. Reps, *The Making of Urban America: A History of City Planning in the United States* (Princeton, N.J.: Princeton University Press, 1965), 46.
59 "Spanish colonial efforts": ibid., 54.
59 Population of Montreal: *Opening the Gates of Eighteenth-Century Montréal*, Phyllis Lambert and Alan Stewart, eds. (Montreal: Canadian Centre for Architecture, 1992), 45.
61 Description of Montreal's fortification: ibid., 22–23.
64 Belonged to the Middle Ages: Christopher Tunnard and Henry Hope Reed, *American Skyline: The Growth and Form of Our Cities and Towns* (Boston: Houghton Mifflin, 1955), 31.
67 New Haven influenced by Vitruvian principles: Anthony N. B. Garvan, *Architecture and Town Planning in Colonial Connecticut* (New Haven: Yale University Press, 1951).
68 "avoid the undecent and incommodious irregularities": "A Contemporary View of Carolina in 1680," *The South Carolina Historical Magazine*, Vol. 55 (1954), 153–54.
71 All the hallmarks of the American small town: see Jaquelin T. Robertson, "The House as the City," *New Classicism*, Andreas Papdakis and Harriet Watson, eds. (London: Academy Editions, 1990), 234.
73 "Let every house be placed": Samuel Hazard, *Annals of Pennsylvania, from*

the Discovery of the Delaware, 1602–1682 (Philadelphia: Hazard & Mitchell, 1850), 527–30.

73 "The Improvement of the place": *The Making of Urban America*, 167.

75 "The streets of Philadelphia intersect each other at right angles": quoted by Richard L. Bushman, *The Refinement of America: Persons, Houses, Cities* (New York: Alfred A. Knopf, 1992), 139.

78 "Since in America they do not like to live crowded": Christopher von Graffenried, *Account of the Founding of New Bern*, Vincent H. Todd, ed. and trans. (Raleigh, N.C.: Edwards & Broughton Printing Co., 1920), 377.

81 "an idealized, even mythic, domesticity": "The House as the City," 237.

CHAPTER FOUR: A FRENCHMAN IN NEW YORK

84 "We went to see the town": Quoted by Richard Reeves in *American Journey: Traveling with Tocqueville in Search of Democracy in America* (New York: Simon & Schuster, 1982), 30.

88 "Almost all the houses are charming": Alexis de Tocqueville, *Journey to America*, J. P. Mayer, ed., George Lawrence, trans. (London: Faber & Faber, 1959), 202.

88 "the ultimate *individual*": ibid., 152.

88 "Americans love their towns": Alexis de Tocqueville, *Democracy in America*, J. P. Mayer, ed., George Lawrence, trans. (New York: Harper & Row, 1988), 278–79.

89 According to local tradition the green represents: see John W. Reps, *The Making of Urban America: A History of City Planning in the United States* (Princeton, N.J.: Princeton University Press, 1965), 132.

89 "The visual satisfaction one discovers": ibid., 132.

92 From a map of the town as it was in 1869: see Beers, Ellis, and Soule, *Atlas of Windsor County, Vermont* (New York, 1869) reproduced in ibid., 134.

93fn "Technicians of today": Camillo Sitte, *The Art of Building Cities: City Building According to Artistic Principles*, Charles T. Stewart, trans. (Westport, Conn.: Hyperion Press, 1991), 30.

94 "Cincinnati presents an odd spectacle": *Journey to America*, 265.

97 "They have already rooted up trees": *Democracy in America*, 469.

97 The symbolic iconography of the city's plan: see Allan Greenberg, "The Architecture of Democracy," *New Classicism* (London: Academy Editions, 1990), 70.

97 "External appearance of the town": *Journey to America*, 164.

98 "All the edifices are neat": Quoted in *American Journey*, 252.

98 "One feels one has escaped": *Journey to America*, 203.

98 "To a Frenchman": Quoted in *American Journey*, 315.

98 Letter to Chabrol: Alexis de Tocqueville, *Selected Letters on Politics and Society*, Roger Boesche, ed., James Toupin and Roger Boesche, trans. (Berkeley, Calif.: University of California Press, 1985), 43.

99 "As an aid to speculation": *The Making of Urban America*, 299.

100 Manhattan street levels: William Rathje and Cullen Murphy, *Rubbish! The Archaeology of Garbage* (New York: HarperCollins, 1992), 35.

101 "Quantity increases": *Democracy in America*, 468.
101 "Democratic peoples . . .": ibid., 465.
102 There is evidence that, beginning in the 1720s: Richard L. Bushman, *The Refinement of America: Persons, Houses, Cities* (New York: Alfred A. Knopf, 1992), 84.
105 "America has not yet any great capital": *Democracy in America*, 278–79.
105 "I view great cities": quoted by Christopher Tunnard, *The City of Man* (New York: Charles Scribner's Sons, 1970), 34.
106 "Money is the only form of social distinction": *Journey to America*, 157.
107 "Neither the Park nor the Battery": Quoted in *The Refinement of America*, 165.
107 "condemned by law and opinion": *Democracy in America*, 69.
108 "Toward the end of the [eighteenth] century": *The Refinement of America*, 168.
108fn "This may be changing." See Heather MacDonald, "San Francisco Gets Tough with the Homeless," *City Journal* (Autumn 1994), 30–40.
109 "Individualism is a calm and considered feeling": *Democracy in America*, 506.
109 "An American . . . changes his residence ceaselessly": *Selected Letters on Politics and Society*, 39.

CHAPTER FIVE: IN THE LAND OF THE DOLLAR

112 "When you leave the main roads": Alexis de Tocqueville, *Journey to America*, J. P. Mayer, ed., George Lawrence, trans. (London: Faber & Faber, 1952), 334.
113 Monticello and the Hôtel de Salm: *Jefferson and Monticello: The Biography of a Builder* (New York: Henry Holt & Co., 1988), 210.
113 "point of maximum concentration": Lewis Mumford, *The Culture of Cities* (New York: Harcourt Brace Jovanovich, 1938), 3.
114 About 10 percent of the total population living in towns is the threshold: Fernand Braudel, *The Structures of Everyday Life: The Limits of the Possible*, Siân Reynolds, trans. (New York: Harper & Row, 1981), 484.
116 "little more than a dozen or so log cabins": Quoted in John W. Reps, *The Making of Urban America: A History of City Planning in the United States* (Princeton, N.J.: Princeton University Press, 1965), 300.
116 Losses of the Chicago fire: see Ross Miller, *American Apocalypse: The Great Fire and the Myth of Chicago* (Chicago: University of Chicago Press, 1990), 18.
117 Electric lights in a Prairie Avenue mansion: Harold L. Platt, *The Electric City: Energy and the Growth of the Chicago Area, 1880–1930* (Chicago: University of Chicago Press, 1991), 34.
119 The first complete steel frame was erected in 1890: see T. K. Derry and Trevor I. Williams, *A Short History of Technology: From the Earliest Times to A.D. 1900* (Oxford: Oxford University Press, 1960), 416.
121 Nearly nine out of ten Chicagoans were first- or second-generation immigrants: American Social History Project, *Who Built America? Working Peo-*

ple and the Nation's Economy, Politics, Culture, and Society, Volume 2: *From the Gilded Age to the Present* (New York: Pantheon, 1992), 17.

121 "Chicago is conscious that there is something in the world": Quoted in *American Apocalypse*, 112.

122 "That a city had any other purpose": Lewis Mumford, *Sticks and Stone: A Study of American Architecture and Civilization* (New York: Horace Liveright, 1924), 109–10.

122 "self-consciously setting out to ennoble commerce": Daniel Bluestone, *Constructing Chicago* (New Haven: Yale University Press, 1991), 150.

123 "an aesthetic that created a necessary connection": ibid., 140.

128 "the first effectively planned complex of public buildings": Robert A. M. Stern, *Pride of Place: Building the American Dream* (Boston: Houghton Mifflin, 1986), 307.

129 Described the White City as reactionary and subversive: James Marston Fitch, *American Building, 1: The Historical Forces That Shaped It* (New York: Schocken Books, 1973), 210.

130 "sanitary wonder": William H. Wilson, *The City Beautiful Movement* (Baltimore: Johns Hopkins University Press, 1989), 57.

130 A Tower of Light with ten thousand Edison bulbs: *The Electric City*, 62.

CHAPTER SIX: CIVIC ART

131 "Chicago was the first expression of American thought as a unity": Henry Adams, *The Education of Henry Adams* (Boston: Houghton Mifflin, 1918), 343.

132 "Against chaos and anarchy in architecture": Werner Hegemann and Elbert Peets, *The American Vitruvius: An Architect's Handbook of Civic Art* (New York: Princeton University Press, 1988). 1.

133 "a devotion to clarity and order": John Brinckerhoff Jackson, *Discovering the Vernacular Landscape* (New Haven: Yale University Press, 1984), 67.

133 Olmsted's all-important influence: see William H. Wilson, *The City Beautiful Movement* (Baltimore: Johns Hopkins University Press, 1989), 33.

134 Criticisms of the enlarged mall: see *The American Vitruvius*, 293.

136 The term "City Beautiful" emerged in 1900: *The City Beautiful Movement*, 128.

137 Focal points for the expression of civic values: see Sally A. Kitt Chappell, *Architecture and Planning of Graham, Anderson, Probst and White, 1912–1936: Transforming Tradition* (Chicago: University of Chicago Press, 1992), 29.

140 "architectural design cult": Jane Jacobs, *The Death and Life of Great American Cities* (New York: Random House, 1961), 375.

141 Reps on Burnham Plan: John W. Reps, *The Making of Urban America: A History of City Planning in the United States*. (Princeton, N.J.: Princeton University Press, 1965), 517.

142 Burnham's original draft incorporated reforms: see Kristen Schaffer, "Fabric of City Life," introduction to Daniel H. Burnham et al., *Plan of Chicago* (New York: Princeton Architectural Press, 1993), viii–xiii.

142 "We have found that those cities": ibid., 22.

143 There was no pressure to build tall buildings: see Jonathan Barnett, *The Elusive City: Five Centuries of Design, Ambition and Miscalculation* (New York: Harper & Row, 1986), 29.

146 Zoning changes along North Michigan Avenue: John W. Stamper, *Chicago's North Michigan Avenue: Planning and Development, 1900–1930* (Chicago, University of Chicago Press, 1991), 39.

147 "North Michigan's transformation": ibid., 27.

147 According to Wilson, the newly established associations of professional city planners: *The City Beautiful Movement*, 285.

148 "At the First National Conference on City Planning": ibid., 287.

148 "the bourgeois interlude": John Lukacs, *Outgrowing Democracy: A History of the United States in the Twentieth Century* (New York: Doubleday, 1984), 159.

CHAPTER SEVEN: HIGH HOPES

152 A City Beautiful conference was held in Liverpool: Frank Jackson, *Sir Raymond Unwin: Architect, Planner and Visionary* (London: A. Zwemmer Ltd., 1985), 107.

152fn Anthony Sutcliffe, *Paris: An Architectural History* (New Haven: Yale Architectural Press, 1993), 88.

153 First true New York skyscraper: see Robert A. M. Stern, *Pride of Place: Building the American Dream* (Boston: Houghton Mifflin, 1986), 255–56.

154fn The first New York City apartment buildings: Elizabeth Hawes, *New York, New York: How the Apartment House Transformed the Life of the City (1869–1930)*. (New York: Alfred A. Knopf, 1993), 37.

156 "We saw the mystic city of the new world": Charles-Edouard Jeanneret, *When the Cathedrals Were White*, Francis E. Hyslop, Jr., trans. (New York: McGraw-Hill, 1964), 109.

157 "the beautiful stone slabs of the floor": ibid., 79.

159 "Between the present skyscrapers": ibid., 191.

159 "a period of arrested urban development": Jon C. Teaford, *The Twentieth-Century American City: Problem, Promise, and Reality* (Baltimore: Johns Hopkins University Press, 1986), 74.

161 More than half of the entire proposed budget of $50 billion: Bernard J. Frieden and Lynne B. Sagalyn, *Downtown, Inc.* (Cambridge, Mass.: MIT Press, 1991), 21–22.

163 For a number of reasons, including an earlier federal court decision: Michael H. Schill and Susan M. Wachter "The Spatial Bias of Federal Housing Programs," Research Impact Paper #3, Wharton Real Estate Center, University of Pennsylvania, December 1994, 2–3.

164 Between 1957 and 1968, the Chicago Housing Authority: Raymond J. Struyk, *A New System for Public Housing: Salvaging a National Resource* (Washington, D.C.: The Urban Institute, 1980), 27.

165fn Jane Jacobs cites a number of residential studies: see Jane Jacobs, *The Death and Life of Great American Cities* (New York: Random House, 1961), 203.

167 Entrants were asked: "Architecture Competition for Public Housing," *Chicago Tribune* (March 1993), 11.
168 "One must avoid the danger": Nathan Glazer, *The Public Interest* (Number 7, spring 1967), 38.
169 Vincent Lane, the activist chairman: see Don Terry, "Housing Chief Pushes a Wrecking-Ball Plan," *New York Times* (February 14, 1994), A14.
169 Newark public housing: see Rachelle Garbarine, "Razing, and Remaking, High-Rise Public Housing," *New York Times* (May 8, 1994), 10/9.
170 "one of the largest and most rapid mass internal movements": Nicholas Lemann, *The Promised Land: The Great Black Migration and How It Changed America* (New York: Vintage Books, 1992), 6.

CHAPTER EIGHT: COUNTRY HOMES FOR CITY PEOPLE

174 "After a stimulating cocktail": Charles-Edouard Jeanneret, *When the Cathedrals Were White*, Francis E. Hyslop, trans. (New York: McGraw-Hill, 1964), 86–87.
174 "Fernand Braudel once wryly observed": Fernand Braudel, *The Structures of Everyday Life: The Limits of the Possible*, Siân Reynolds, trans. (New York: Harper & Row, 1981), 557.
175 "There is a suburban look and character": Quoted in John R. Stilgoe, *Borderland: Origins of the American Suburb, 1820–1939* (New Haven: Yale University Press, 1988), 5.
175 Henry C. Binford, *The First Suburbs: Residential Communities on the Boston Periphery, 1815–1860* (Chicago: University of Chicago Press, 1985), 2.
175 Rutgers historian Robert Fishman dates the first West Philadelphia suburbs: Robert Fishman, *Bourgeois Utopias* (New York: Basic Books, 1987), 140–41.
175 The rate of urban growth slowed to almost zero: "Urbanization," *Encyclopaedia Britannica* (Chicago, 1949), Vol. 22, 894.
175 Use of streetcars and buses: Jon C. Teaford, *The Twentieth-Century American City: Problem, Promise, and Reality* (Baltimore: Johns Hopkins University Press, 1986), 66.
175 Boston loses population: John Lukacs, *Outgrowing Democracy: A History of the United States in the Twentieth Century* (New York: Doubleday, 1984), 161.
175 "Chicago," *Encyclopaedia Britannica* (Chicago, 1949), Vol. 5, 447.
178 "women and men who established these communities": *Borderland*, 308.
178 "without the joys of genuine city life": ibid., 154.
178 On Jamaica Plain: Alexander von Hoffman, *Local Attachments: The Making of an American Urban Neighborhood, 1850–1920* (Baltimore: Johns Hopkins University Press, 1994).
178 "During the second half of the nineteenth century": ibid., 24.
179 "The suburb is . . . a state of mind": Robert A. M. Stern, "La Ville Bourgeoise," in *The Anglo-American Suburb*, Robert A. M. Stern and John Montague Massengale, eds. (London: Architectural Design, 1981), 5.

180 Origins of Llewellyn Park: see Kenneth T. Jackson, *Crabgrass Frontier: The Suburbanization of the United States* (New York: Oxford University Press, 1985), 76–79.

182 There are currently some 130,000 such developments: Evan McKenzie, *Privatopia: Homeowner Associations and the Rise of Residential Private Government* (New Haven: Yale University Press, 1994), 12.

182 He has estimated that by the year 2000: Evan McKenzie, "Welcome Home, Do as We Say," *New York Times* (August 18, 1994), A23.

182 "are not only the present but the future of American housing": ibid., 177.

184 "Barnett saw the new suburb": see Frank Jackson, *Sir Raymond Unwin: Architerct, Planner and Visionary* (London: A. Zwemmer Ltd., 1985), 98.

185 "It was not deemed enough": Quoted in ibid., 89.

185 "the jewel in the suburban crown": *The Anglo-American Suburb*, 42.

185 The largest annexation in American history: David R. Contosta, *Suburb in the City: Chestnut Hill, Philadelphia, 1850–1990* (Columbus: Ohio State University Press, 1992), 1.

186 Which he heard about in meetings of the National Housing Conference: ibid., 104.

187 "So long as we are confined": Raymond Unwin, *Town Planning in Practice: An Introduction to the Art of Designing Cities and Suburbs* (New York: Princeton Architectural Press, 1994), 353.

187 Commissioned about 180 houses: *Suburb in the City*, 112.

187 He sent his young architects: ibid., 109.

187fn Designed by H. Louis Duhring in 1910: ibid., 106.

187fn Wright first proposed this idea in 1913: John Sergeant, *Frank Lloyd Wright's Usonian Houses: The Case for Organic Architecture* (New York: Whitney Library of Design, 1975), 72.

190 Garden suburbs in Montreal and Toronto: see John Sewell, *The Shape of the City: Toronto Struggles with Modern Planning* (Toronto: University of Toronto Press, 1993), 52.

191 Two public housing projects in Bridgeport: see Mark Alden Branch, "Two Villages, Two Worlds," *Progressive Architecture* (December, 1993), 50–53.

193 "We have become so used to living": *Town Planning in Practice*, 11.

195 The second Levittown also included: see *The Twentieth-Century American City*, 102.

195 Amenities of Levittown house: see *Crabgrass Frontier*, 235–36.

196fn Robert Gutman, *The Design of American Housing: A Reappraisal of the Architect's Role* (New York: Publishing Center for Cultural Resources, 1985), 56–57.

CHAPTER NINE: THE NEW DOWNTOWN

198 Description of nineteenth-century Plattsburgh: *Plattsburgh 1897* (Plattsburgh: Plattsburgh Daily Press, 1897), reprinted 1978, Corner-Stone Bookshop, Plattsburgh.

199 On Plattsburgh streetcars: see Roger Borrop, "Plattsburgh Traction Company," *Transportation Bulletin* (No. 78, September 1970–December 1971).

201 Patronage of non-commuter passenger trains: Jon C. Teaford, *The Twentieth-Century American City: Problem, Promise, and Reality* (Baltimore: Johns Hopkins University Press, 1986), 112.

202 On Piggly Wiggly and King Kullen: Phil Patton, *Made in USA: The Secret Histories of the Things That Made America* (New York: Grove Weidenfeld, 1992), 256–64.

203 "The automobile—especially the commercial automobile": John Brinckerhoff Jackson, *A Sense of Place, a Sense of Time* (New Haven: Yale University Press, 1994), 184.

203 From 1960 to 1970, more than eight thousand new centers opened in the United States: International Council of Shopping Centers statistic.

205 "with the advent of more civilized times": Quoted by Donald W. Curl, *Mizner's Florida: American Resort Architecture* (New York: The Architectural History Foundation, 1984), 113.

205 On Farmers Market chain: See Peter G. Rowe, *Making a Middle Landscape* (Cambridge, Mass.: MIT Press, 1991), 120–23.

206 In 1946 there were still only eight large shopping centers: Kenneth T. Jackson, *Crabgrass Frontier: The Suburbanization of the United States* (New York: Oxford University Press, 1985), 259.

206 Probably the first such center was Northgate: Margaret Crawford, "The World in a Shopping Center," *Variations on a Theme Park: The New American City and the End of Public Space*, Michael Sorkin, ed. (New York: Noonday Press, 1992), 20.

206 About 3,700 only a decade later: International Council of Shopping Centers statistic.

206 One of the largest was Northland: see *Making a Middle Landscape*, 126.

207 Cited the glass-roofed, nineteenth-century *gallerias*: Victor Gruen, *The Heart of Our Cities: The Urban Crisis, Diagnosis and Cure* (New York: Simon & Schuster, 1964), 194.

208 The Sports Museum of New England; Eben Shapiro, "Even City Hall Has Moved to the Mall," *New York Times* (July 30, 1992), D1.

208 The Board of Education of Ottawa: Nicholas Ionides, "Bringing the Classroom to the Student," *Globe & Mail* (November 19, 1992), D1.

208 Pittsburgh's new airport: Chriss Swaney, "Airport Mall Flying High," *New York Times* (December 13, 1992), R9.

209 Robert L. Sorensen: Quoted in Heidi Gralla, "Public Access Private Property," *Shopping Centers Today* (November 1991), 24 and 26.

211 Expect it to outdraw Walt Disney World: Neal Karlen, "The Mall That Ate Minnesota," *New York Times* (August 30, 1992), V5.

212 Invited in only three days a year: Allan Braham, *The Architecture of the Enlightenment* (London: Thames & Hudson, 1980), 157.

212 "in half an hour he would be most beautifully attired": Quoted by Mark Girouard, *Cities and People* (New Haven: Yale University Press, 1985), 204.

212fn "Fast food and takeouts are taking their toll of traditional French life": Marlise Simons, "Starved for Customers, the Bistros Die in Droves," *New York Times* (December 22, 1994), 2.

213 "They cater exclusively to middle-class tastes": *Crabgrass Frontier*, 260.

214 "In ambiance and retail mix": Bernard J. Frieden and Lynne B. Sagalyn, *Downtown, Inc.* (Cambridge, Mass.: MIT Press, 1991), 66.

214 The splendid GUM department store: see *Cities and People*, 291–93.

216 Large enough to qualify as a so-called regional mall: see Isadore Barmash, "For Shopping Centers, Less Is Becoming More," *New York Times* (September 27, 1992), F5.

216fn The New Jersey Supreme Court based its 1994 decision: "Excerpt from the Ruling on Free Speech at Malls," *New York Times* (December 21, 1994), B6.

CHAPTER TEN: THE BEST OF BOTH WORLDS

219 A 1989 Gallup poll: Quoted by Andres Duany and Elizabeth Plater-Zyberk in "The Second Coming of the American Small Town," *Wilson Quarterly* (Winter 1992), 21–22.

220 Recommends between 5,000 and 10,000: Christopher Alexander et al., *A Pattern Language: Towns, Buildings, Construction* (New York: Oxford University Press, 1977), 71–74.

222 The fastest-growing, wealthiest, and most educated areas: Alecia Swasy, "America's 20 Hottest White-Collar Addresses," *Wall Street Journal* (March 8, 1994), B1.

224 Commuting *out* to the surrounding suburban counties: David R. Contosta, *Suburb in the City: Chestnut Hill, Philadelphia, 1850–1990* (Columbus: Ohio State University Press, 1992), 266–67.

226 Only half as many Americans nationwide were making the traditional suburb-to-city trip: James Trefil, *A Scientist in the City* (New York: Doubleday, 1994), 123.

228 "The bottom line is": David Rusk, *Cities Without Suburbs* (Washington, D.C.: Woodrow Wilson Center Press, 1993), 75.

228 "The situation is not hopeless": David Rusk, *Cities Without Suburbs: Data Supplement* (Washington, D.C.: December 1993). Unpublished report. Unpaginated.

230 Planner and architect Andres Duany: "The Seaside Debate," *ANY* (July/August 1993 Number 1), 28.

230 "We're only reacting to the fact": Peter Applebome, "Basketball Tournament Vivifies Charlotte's Downbeat 'Uptown,' " *New York Times* (April 2, 1994), 1.

231 For Peter Calthorpe's projects: see Thomas Fisher, "Do Suburbs Have a Future?" *Progressive Architecture* (December 1993), 36–41.

231 For Duany and Plater-Zyberk's Markham project: see Albert Watson, "Born-Again Urbanism in Canada," *Progressive Architecture* (November 1994), 51–52.

232 "Policy for the coming decades": Moshe Safdie, *The City After the Automobile* (Unpublished ms, 1994), 38.

233 "It can be said that a landscape tradition": John Brinckerhoff Jackson, *A Sense of Place, a Sense of Time* (New Haven: Yale University Press, 1994), viii.

INDEX

Adams, Henry, 131
Adams, John Quincy, 88
African-Americans, 68, 85, 107–108, 113, 157, 170–72, 176; urban migration, 170–72, 200
African cities, 40, 44, 45, 83*n.*, 85, 111
Agriculture, 83*n.*, 113; colonial, 52, 53, 78; sharecropping, 170–71
Airports, 27, 32, 138, 201, 208, 228
Albany, N.Y., 87, 105
Alexandria, Va., 69, 72, 74, 76, 131
American cities. *See* city planning, American; *specific cities*
American Civic Association, 136
American Civil Liberties Union, 167*n.*, 208–209
American Institute of Architects, 136
Amsterdam, 64, 65, 72, 83, 100, 116
Amusement parks, 154–55, 211
Anderson, Pierce, 137, 138
Anderson, Sherwood, *Winesburg, Ohio*, 221
Annapolis, Md., 69–72, 76, 82, 103–105, 112, 235
Apartment buildings, 82, 120, 151, 164, 224; high-rise public housing, 164–70; New York, 154 and *n.*, 159; Parisian, 151–52 and *n.*, 154
Architecture. *See* city planning, American; *specific architects, buildings, cities, periods, and styles*
Aristocracy, 20–24, 48, 65, 74, 101, 107
Aristotle, 36–37, 93, 220
Arizona, 55
Art Deco, 28, 138, 155
Art Nouveau, 151
Arts and Crafts style, 185, 204
Asian cities, 39–45, 83*n.*, 113. *See also specific cities*
Athens, 37, 47
Atlanta, 45, 229
Atterbury, Grosvenor, 189–90, 196
Atwood, Charles B., 128
Australia, 43, 202
Automobiles, 32, 34, 77, 97, 109, 112, 145 and *n.*, 173, 189; city, 46–47, 162, 202–207; mass ownership of, 145*n.*, 162, 189–93, 200–207, 230, 233; suburban, 189–95

Baltimore, 11, 96, 104, 105, 115, 139, 170, 172, 204, 215, 226
Barnett, Henrietta, 184
Baroque design, 48–49, 69, 103, 149
Bartram, William, 54–55
Battery Park, New York, 107, 215
Beaumont de la Bonninière, Gustave-Auguste de, 84–86, 93, 96–98, 111
Beautification, urban, 101–109, 122–24, 131–48, 159–60
Beeby, Thomas, 168
Behrens, Peter, 139
Bennett, Edward H., 141–48, 151
Berkeley, Ca., 140, 177, 179
Berlin, 27, 43, 46, 61, 65, 100, 105, 142
Binford, Henry, 175
Bluestone, Daniel, 122–23
Boston, 66, 68, 87, 105, 116, 117, 156, 230; city planning, 64, 66, 98, 102, 124, 178; nineteenth-century, 178–79; population, 64, 115, 121,

Boston (*cont.*)
175, 226; shopping malls, 215; suburbs, 175, 178–79
Branch, Mark Alden, 191–92
Braudel, Fernand, 47–50, 105, 114, 174, 235
British Columbia, 36, 105*n.*
Broadacre City, 229–30, 233
Brooklyn, N.Y., 94, 124, 125, 165*n.*, 175, 177
Brunner, Arnold, 136–37
Buffalo, N.Y., 18, 30, 40, 57*n.*, 87, 115, 124; Pan-American Exposition (1901), 138
Burgs, 37, 48, 53
Burnham, Daniel, 119, 122, 127–28, 132–38, 141–48, 152–53, 155, 162, 232; *Plan of Chicago*, 136, 141–48
Burnham Brothers, Inc., 147
Bushman, Richard L., 108

Cable cars, 117–18
Cabrini-Green, Chicago, 164–70, 196
California, 58, 205, 209, 213
Calthorpe, Peter, 231
Cambridge, Mass., 66–67, 177, 208
Canada, 11, 20, 23–27, 29, 36, 57, 59, 97, 105*n.*, 190, 202, 207, 213, 219, 220, 225, 226, 231; French colonization in, 59–64. *See also specific cities*
Canals, 46, 47, 64, 99
Capital cities, 38, 40, 43, 104, 134–35, 143; American and European, compared, 104–105 and *n.*
Capitol, Washington, D.C., 95–97, 134
Carolina, 52, 54, 68, 78
Carrère, John, 132
Cathedral towns, 38, 80
Central cities and metro areas, relationship between, 224–33
Central Park, New York, 81, 99, 124, 125, 154
Champlain, Samuel de, 59
Champs-Elysées, Paris, 24, 25, 145, 146
Charleston, S.C., 64, 80, 82, 97, 223, 230; city planning, 68, 76, 77, 95
Chestnut Hill, Pa., 185–91, 223–24
Chicago, 11, 29, 38*n.*, 40, 57*n.*, 81, 110–30, 139, 151, 156, 170, 227, 228; Burnham plan (1909), 136, 141–48; city planning, 45, 76, 106, 110–11, 115–32, 136, 138, 141–48, 164–70, 234; civic beautification, 138, 141–48, 160, 162; Columbian Exposition (1893), 127–32, 133, 137, 138, 151–52, 167; fire of 1871, 116–17, 234; growth of, 115–21, 175–76; nineteenth-century, 110–11, 115–32; parks, 124–26, 141–43, 145; population, 111, 115, 116, 121, 175–76, 226; public housing, 164–70; skyscrapers, 110–11, 115, 118–20, 123–24, 126, 143–48, 153; suburbs, 175–76, 182–83, 190, 204–205, 207; transportation, 117–20, 130, 141–43, 145; twentieth-century, 141–48, 154, 155, 160, 164–70, 175–76
Chicago Tribune Cabrini-Green competition, 167–69
China, 39, 43, 48, 83*n.*
Chrysler Building, New York, 155
Cincinnati, 28, 87, 172; city planning, 45, 93–94 and *n.*, 95; population, 93–94, 115; suburbs, 188–89
City, definition of, 36–38 and *n.*, 39, 79, 113, 176
City Beautiful movement, 136 and *n.*, 137–48, 152, 153, 160, 165
City planning, American: civic beautification movement, 131–48, 162; colonial, 51–83, 101–103, 113, 129; downtown, 73–74, 90–92, 115–24, 143–48, 163–64, 197–217, 228, 230–32; European cities compared to, 15–27, 61, 64–65, 69, 78–83, 101, 104–107, 113, 120–22, 129, 132–33, 144, 145, 149–53, 193, 211–15; future of, 230–35; metro area and central cities, compared, 224–33; Native America, 52–57, 81; nineteenth-century, 84–109, 110–30, 131–48, 178–79, 199–200; and politics, 19–22, 44–45, 48–49, 65, 101, 104–105, 117, 122, 136, 147–48, 158, 160–72, 209–10, 226; and population, 36–42, 63–64, 75,

100, 111–15, 220, 223–28; street layouts, 42–47, 50, 66–67, 72–76, 81–82, 106, 162, 188; suburbs, 173–96; twentieth-century, 27–34, 140–48, 153–72, 173–217, 218–35; urban renewal, 160–72. *See also specific cities*
Civic art, 131–48, 162, 196
Civic centers, 136–37, 141–42, 160
Civil War, 77, 116
Classicism, 128–29, 132–34, 139–41, 155, 157
Cleveland, 76, 106, 115, 121, 136–38, 144, 170, 172, 189, 226
Cobb, Henry Ives, 128
Code, building, 146–47
Codman, Henry Sargent, 127
Colonial Revival, 129
Colonial urbanization, 44, 51–83, 101–103, 113, 129
Colorado, 55, 209, 222
Columbian Exposition (1893, Chicago), 127–32, 133, 137, 138, 151–52, 167
Commissioners' Plan of 1811, 99, 106
Congrès Internationaux d'Architecture Moderne (CIAM), 158, 192
Congress, 95, 96, 143, 160
Connecticut, 66, 67, 87, 105, 174, 177, 191–92, 209
Corbusier, Le, 156–59, 164, 173–77, 192, 229, 232; Voison Plan, 157–59; *When the Cathedrals Were White*, 156–57, 174
Country and town, relationship between, 47–49, 113–14, 127, 177–78, 219–29
Country Club Plaza, Kansas City, 204–205, 215
Country houses, 113–14, 173–96
Cram, Ralph Adams, 139
Cret, Paul Philippe, 189, 190
Crime, 18–19, 29, 31; nineteenth-century, 108 and *n.*, 109; twentieth-century, 156*n.*, 166–67, 192, 200, 223
Crystal Palace Exhibition (1853, New York), 118, 215
Culture, urban, 40, 41, 50, 111–13, 149; civic art movement, 131–48; nineteenth-century, 102–107, 112–15, 122–23, 131–48; twentieth-century, 148, 154, 157, 164, 172, 217

Dallas, 32, 134, 135, 233
Davis, Alexander, 180–81
Défense, La, Paris, 21, 22, 24
Deindustrialization, 172, 199, 200
Democracy, 47, 80, 86, 90, 93, 101–102, 106–107
Denver, 81, 134, 135, 137
Depression, 155, 159–60, 194, 200, 206
Detroit, 30, 41, 57, 62 and *n.*, 65, 76, 97, 115, 154, 156, 170, 172, 206, 226
Disease, urban, 96–97, 100, 125
Domesticity: colonial ideal of, 81–83; nineteenth-century, 102–103
Downing, Andrew Jackson, 181
Downtown, commercial, 66, 73–74, 76, 90–92, 115–24, 132, 143–48, 154, 163–64, 179, 197–217, 228, 230–32; decline of, 197–201; shopping mall replacement of, 207–17
Duany, Andres, 230, 231
Duhring, H. Louis, 187 and *n.*
Dutch colonization, 64, 82–83

Economy, 29, 30, 57, 73, 114, 222; and architecture, 30, 48, 148, 162; nineteenth-century, 99; and population, 39–42, 114; twentieth-century, 148, 161–62, 171–72, 200–201, 214
Edison, Thomas Alva, 117, 180
Eiffel Tower, Paris, 26–27, 144, 151
Electricity, 117–18, 123, 130, 151, 152, 178, 199
Elevator, 118–19
Ellicott, Andrew, 96
Emery, Mary M., 189
Empire State Building, New York, 155, 158
English cottage style, 181, 187
Edge cities, 229
European cities, 12, 15–27, 33, 113, 230; American cities compared to, 15–27, 61, 64–65, 69, 78–83, 101,

European cities (*cont.*)
104–107, 113, 120–22, 129, 132–33, 144, 145, 149–53, 193, 211–15; early history of 36–43, 47–50, 53–54, 64–66, 78–83, 149; nineteenth-century Paris, 149–52 and *n.*; parks, 124–25; population, 36–42; postwar, 202, 212 and *n.*, 225, 227. *See also specific cities*
Evelyn, John, 66
Expositions, 118, 127–33, 138–39, 151–52
Eyre, Wilson, 189, 190

Fairmount Park, Philadelphia, 126, 135
Farmers Markets, 205–206
Faubourg, 60, 63
Faulkner, Don, 168–69
Federal-Aid Highway Act (1956), 160–61
Federal style, 103, 129
Ferguson, Frank W., 139
Fires, urban, 66, 78, 101, 116–17, 120 and *n.*, 135, 143, 234
Fishman, Robert, 175
Fitch, James Marston, 129–30
Flatiron Building, New York, 153
Florence, 48, 53, 54
Florida, 41–42, 53, 54, 57–58, 231
Food, 19, 150, 176, 211; mall, 212–14, 217; production, 52, 78; supermarkets, 201–202
Forest Hills Gardens, N.Y., 189–90
Fortified towns, 61–63, 65
France, 12, 15–27, 37–39, 48, 60–61, 83–87, 96, 97, 104, 113, 125, 149–52, 155, 174, 187, 211, 214, 221; city planning, 23–27, 46, 61, 149–52, 211–12; colonial urbanization in New World, 51, 57, 59–63, 65, 76. *See also specific cities*
Fuller, Buckminster, 163, 168

Gabriel, Jacques-Ange, 135
Galleria, Houston, 207–208, 210
Gardens, 31; colonial, 69, 71–73, 78, 81–82, 83 and *n.*; nineteenth-century, 120, 124–26; Parisian, 22, 24, 107, 125, 150, 211–12; suburbs, 182–94, 204–205, 223–24; twentieth-century, 164, 182–94
Gare d'Orsay, Paris, 20, 151, 152
Garnier, Charles, 150
Garrison towns, 51, 57–58, 61–63, 74
Georgia, 54, 75–77, 222
Georgian style, 102–103
Germany, 16, 37, 38, 43, 48, 61, 75, 105, 125, 155, 165. *See also specific cities*
Gilchrist, Edmund, 187, 189
Glazer, Nathan, 168
Goodhue, Bertram, 139, 190, 196
Graffenried, Baron Christopher von, 78–79
Graham, John, Jr., 206
Grand Central Station, New York, 138, 157, 174
Great Britain, 16, 20, 37–39, 73, 75, 80, 86–87, 102–103, 104, 116, 214, 221; city planning, 45, 46, 65–66, 82, 83, 124–25, 152–53; colonial urbanization in New World, 51, 58, 60, 63–70, 80, 99, 113; garden suburbs, 183–87. *See also specific cities*
Greece, ancient, 36–37, 47, 93, 132
Greek Revival, 98, 129
Greenwich Village, New York, 165*n.*, 233
Grid planning, 44–46, 50, 106; colonial, 58, 60, 62 and *n.*, 63–83, 106, 188; nineteenth-century, 95–100, 103, 106, 120, 125, 126, 131, 135, 136; twentieth-century, 147, 157, 164, 169, 189
Griffin, Walter Burley, 43
Gruen, Victor, 207; *The Heart of Our Cities*, 12
Guerin, Jules, 141–46
Guimard, Hector, 151

Halles, Les, Paris, 25, 150, 157
Hampstead Garden Suburb (Great Britain), 184–88, 194
Hartford, Conn., 66, 67, 102
Haskell, Llewellyn, 180–82
Haussmann, Baron Georges-Eugène, 24, 27, 150–52 and *n.*, 161, 162

Hegemann (Werner) and Peets (Elbert), *The American Vitruvius*, 132, 136*n.*, 148
Highways, 27, 29, 47, 95, 141, 160–61, 201–203, 206
Hispanics, 176; colonial urbanization, 44, 51–59
Historic preservation, 28, 136
Hittorff, J. I., 150
Hoffmann, Josef, 139
Holland, 64, 75, 82–83, 116
Holme, Thomas, 72
Hood, Raymond, 146
Hotels, 28, 198, 201, 203
Houses, 223; colonial ideal of, 81–83; country, 113–14, 173–96; nineteenth-century, 102–104, 177–79; numbered, 72, 94; outlying residential, 120 and *n.*,–21, 173–96; private, 82–83 and *n.*; public housing, 29, 159, 160, 163–72, 191–92; standardized, 195
Housing Act (1937), 163
Housing Act (1949), 160, 163
Houston, 28, 47, 139, 177, 190, 207–208, 225, 233
Houston, Henry, 185–8, 223, 234
Houston, Sam, 88
Howard, Ebenezer, 193; *Garden Cities of Tomorrow*, 183–84
Howard, John Galen, 137, 140
Howell, John Mead, 146
Hunt, Jarvis, 138
Hunt, Myron, 190
Hunt, Richard Morris, 128, 132, 138
Hygiene: personal, 102–103; public, 17–18, 88 and *n.*, 96, 100–101, 130
Hypermarché, 212–213

Illinois, 115–21
Immigration, 42, 74–75, 78, 79, 108, 115, 121–22, 153, 228
Income, 222, 227–28, 233
India, 39, 40, 43, 44, 153
Indianapolis, 76, 106
Indoor shopping malls, 207–17
Industrial cities, 32, 39, 40, 41, 49, 78, 99, 116–22, 125, 150, 170–72, 193, 199, 226, 233
International Style, 156–59
Interstate highway system, 160–61
Iroquois Confederacy, 52–53, 57–59
Italy, 26, 27, 38, 40–41, 48, 65, 82, 144, 207, 214, 221. *See also specific cities*
It's A Wonderful Life (movie), 220, 221

Jackson, J. B., 133, 203, 232–33
Jackson, Kenneth, *Crabgrass Frontier*, 213, 215
Jacobs, Jane, 140, 165*n.*, 193, 233; *The Death and Life of Great American Cities*, 163–64
Jamaica Plains, Mass., 178–79, 185
Japan, 39, 40, 43, 83*n.*
Jefferson, Thomas, 20, 62*n.*, 96, 97, 105, 113, 128, 134, 139
Jenney, William Le Baron, 122, 128
Jerde, Jon, 215

Kansas City, 57*n.*, 135, 138, 155, 189, 204–205
Kentucky, 94

Labrouste, Henri, 150
Lake Forest, Ill., 183, 190, 204–205, 231
Lakes, urban, 81, 141
Land: availability, 78–79, 179; ownership, 60, 74, 83, 162; values, 78, 83, 119, 120, 145–47, 162, 165
Land Ordinance, 106
Landscaping, suburban, 181–94
Latin America, 39–45, 51–52, 158
Laws of the Indies, 44, 58, 62, 65, 67, 80
Layouts, urban, 42–47, 50, 66–67; automobile city, 46–47; organic, 46, 59, 64, 67; practical, 43–46; symbolic, 42–43, 46. *See also specific cities and designs*
Le Moyne, Jean-Baptiste, 62–63
L'Enfant, Pierre Charles, 70, 95–97, 106, 115, 134
Le Nôtre, André, 22, 24
Letchworth Garden City (Great Britain), 183–84
Levitt, William, 33, 184, 195

Levittown suburbs, 195
Litchfield, Electus, 191, 235
Literature, small towns depicted in, 220–21
Llewellyn Park, West Orange, N.J., 180 and *n.*–82
London, 12, 27, 69, 104, 118, 131, 142, 144, 174, 183, 184, 214; city planning, 46, 61, 66, 70, 83, 107, 124, 125, 149, 152–53; Great Exposition of 1851, 152; Great Fire of 1666, 66, 78; population, 38–41
Long Island (N.Y.) suburbs, 33, 181, 184, 195
Los Angeles, 18, 27, 58, 170; city planning, 45, 46; shopping malls, 215–16; suburbs, 190; transportation, 29 and *n.*; zoning, 143
Louis, Victor, 211
Louisbourg (Cape Breton Island), 61, 62, 65
Louis XIV, King of France, 20–24, 48, 127
Louis XV, King of France, 61
Louisiana, 53, 62–63
Louis-Philippe, King of France, 86
Louvre, Paris, 21, 22, 24, 157
Lukacs, John, 33–34, 148
Lutyens, Edwin, 153, 184, 185, 194
Lynch, Kevin, 42–47, 50, 67

Mall of America, Bloomington, Minn., 210–11, 213
Malls, shopping, 28, 176, 207–17, 228, 230, 232, 235; free speech in, 208–10 and *n.*; regional, 216; tourism in, 210–13
Manhattan, 57*n.*. *See also* New York
Mansart, Jules-Hardouin, 22
Mariemont, Ohio, 188–89, 191
Marina Village, Conn., 191–92, 196
Market Square shopping center, Lake Forest, Ill., 204–205, 215, 231
Maryland, 69–70, 104
Mason, George, 113
Masonic Temple Building, Chicago, 110, 119
Massachusetts, 66–67, 87–88, 105, 209
Massachusetts Bay Colony, 85
Mass media, 154, 228
Mass transit, 27, 29 and *n.*, 30, 46, 175, 200*n.*, 231, 233
Mathews, Maurice, 68
McFarland, J. Horace, 136
McGoodwin, Robert Rodes, 187, 189, 196
McKenzie, Evan, 182
McKim, Charles Follen, 128, 132, 134, 137, 138, 151
McKim, Mead and White, 128, 137, 139, 181
Medieval cities, 37–41, 46–49, 53–54, 60, 64–66, 76, 79, 93*n.*, 144
Megacities, 39–42
Memphis, 87, 93, 202
Metropolitan areas and central cities, relationship between, 224–33
Mexico, 51
Mexico City, 39–40, 44, 52, 151
Meyer, Frederick H., 137
Miami, 29, 36, 41–42, 57*n.*, 190, 231
Michigan, 62 and *n.*, 87
Middle class, 103, 106–13, 124, 148, 154, 165, 171–72, 178, 183, 188, 191, 213, 216, 227
Mies van der Rohe, 165–66
Mills, Robert, 134
Milwaukee, 28, 57*n.*, 115
Minneapolis, 28–30, 81, 177, 206, 210
Minnesota, 223
Mission towns, 51, 52, 58
Mississippi, 53–54
Missouri, 53–54
Mitterand, François, 19–24, 27
Mizner, Addison, 205, 215
Modernism, 129, 164, 165, 196
Modern urbanism, 162–72
Monticello, 113
Montreal, 23 and *n.*–27, 81, 87, 97, 105*n.*, 125, 164, 190, 198, 201, 219; city planning, 24–28, 45, 57, 59–61, 62, 72, 124, 162, 164; French colonization of, 59–62, 64; population, 226
Morris, William, 186
Movies, 28, 32, 33, 154–55, 163, 164, 198, 204, 220–21

Mumford, Lewis, 47, 122
Munich, 48, 194
Museums, 28, 156

Names: city, derived from Indian words, 57 and *n.*; street, 72, 94 and *n.*, 109
Naples, 65, 82, 214
Napoléon Bonaparte, 24
Napoléon III, 87, 149–51
Native Americans, 34, 113; settlements, 52–57, 81
Nelson, Jim, 168–69
Neoclassicism, 28
Neo-Gothic style, 155
New Amsterdam, 64
New Delhi, 43, 153
New France, 52, 59–63
New Haven, Conn., 67–69, 117
New Jersey, 31, 94, 209; suburbs, 180–82, 191
New Mexico, 55, 56
New Orleans, 29, 45, 72, 87; city planning, 62–63, 68, 97–98, 106; population, 115
Newport, R.I., 66, 84–85, 102
New Spain, 51–59, 60
New York, 18–19, 25, 27, 35, 37, 38*n.*, 66, 68, 81, 85, 87, 92, 95, 104, 105, 112, 117, 132, 170, 199, 201, 228, 230; British rule, 64, 99; city planning, 45, 64, 66, 98–102, 106, 107, 137, 138, 153–60, 164, 165*n.*; civic beautification, 137, 138, 160; Commissioners' Plan (1811), 99, 106; Crystal Palace Exhibition (1853), 118, 215; grid layout, 45, 64, 99–100; nineteenth-century, 98–102, 107–108, 116; parks, 81, 99, 124, 125, 153; population, 39, 40, 64, 75, 99–100, 111, 115, 121, 153–54, 176; public monuments, 99; riots, 108; shopping malls, 215; skyscrapers, 144, 153–60; social class distinctions, 107–108; suburbs, 174, 175, 177, 180, 189–90; transportation, 30, 174; twentieth-century, 153–60, 164, 172, 176; zoning, 143
New York State, 52–53, 197–200
Nichols, Jesse Clyde, 104
Nicholson, Frances, 69–71, 75, 104
Nineteenth-century American urbanization, 84–109, 110–30, 131–48, 178–79, 199–200
Nolen, John, 132, 134, 189–90, 196
Northland shopping center, Detroit, 206, 207
North Michigan Avenue, Chicago, 144–47, 162
Nouvel, Jean, 21
Numbered houses, 72, 94
Numbered streets, 109

Oglethorpe, James, 75–77, 234
Ohio, 53, 76, 93–95, 106, 189
Oklahoma, 55
Olbrich, Joseph Maria, 139
Olmsted, Frederick Law, 124–27, 132–34, 139, 141, 182–83, 185, 190, 204
Olmsted, Frederick Law, Jr., 132–37
Olmsted, John C., 132–35, 190, 204
Oregon, 209
Otis, Elisha G., 118
Ottawa, 57*n.*, 105*n.*, 208

Palais Royal, Paris, 211–12
Palm Beach, Fla., 205, 215
Paris, 12, 15–27, 33, 35, 38, 40, 54, 60–61, 65, 70, 92, 96, 99, 99, 104, 113, 122, 131, 142, 144, 149–52 and *n.*, 173, 175, 212 and *n.*, 214, 225; city planning, 23–27, 46, 61, 82, 90, 107, 125, 127, 135, 149–52 and *n.*, 161, 194, 211–12; *Grands Projets*, 19–22, 23; Second Empire, 87, 149–52 and *n.*
Parker, Barry, 183–85
Parking lots, 28, 202–207
Parks, 81, 99; Chicago, 124–26, 141; nineteenth-century, 102, 107, 108, 116, 124–26, 133, 135; twentieth-century, 141–43, 154–55, 164, 211
Parkways, 126, 133, 135, 141
Paxton, Sir Joseph, 124–25
Pedestrian movement, 28, 29, 46, 47, 162, 164, 166, 205–207, 230–32
Peets, Elbert, 132, 190

Pei, I. M., 21
Penn, William, 33, 72–75, 78, 80, 81, 96, 111, 135, 188, 223, 234
Pennsylvania Station, New York, 138, 157
Perrault, Claude, 22
Philadelphia, 11, 25, 29, 31, 33, 72–75, 81, 82, 87, 105, 117, 156, 170, 221–26, 230, 233; city planning, 50, 72–75, 76, 77, 94*n.*, 96, 98, 102, 106, 124, 135, 138, 162, 165*n.*, 188, 234–35; civic beautification, 138; colonial, 64, 72–77, 80; parks, 125–26, 135; population, 64, 74–75, 111, 115, 176, 226–27; riots, 108; suburbs, 175, 185–91, 195, 223–26; twentieth-century, 154, 155, 162, 172, 176, 185–91, 223–24
Phoenix, 32, 41, 47, 233
Pittsburgh, 37, 62, 87, 115, 116, 121, 154, 156, 208
Place de la Concorde, Paris, 24, 61, 135
Plantation mansions, 113–14
Plater-Zyberk, Elizabeth, 231
Plattsburgh, N.Y., 36, 197–201, 216–17
Policing, 18–19, 31, 108, 227
Politics, and city planning, 19–22, 44–45, 48–49, 65, 101, 104–105, 117, 122, 136, 147–48, 158, 160–72, 209–10, 226
Pollution, 31, 49
Pompidou, Georges, 19–20, 27
Pope, John Russell, 198
Population, 36–42, 78, 111–15, 220; African-American, 170–72; growth, 31–32, 41–42, 60, 63–64, 67, 74, 77, 93, 111–15, 121, 153–54, 170–71, 175, 200, 233; metro area, 224–28; nineteenth-century, 100, 111–15, 121; size, 36–42, 63–64, 75, 100, 111–15, 220, 223–28; suburban, 175–76; twentieth-century, 153, 175, 223–28
Portland, Or., 29, 30, 231
Post, George B., 128
Postmodernism, 28
Poverty, 29, 40, 44, 60, 78, 106–108, 163–72, 227–28
Presidios, 51, 58
Prisons, 86, 87
Promenades, 48, 61, 68, 107, 125, 145, 235
Providence, R.I., 66, 67
Public housing, 29, 159–60, 163–72, 196; Cabrini-Green (Chicago), 164–70; garden-suburb planning, 191–92
Public Works Administration, 159–60
Pueblos, 51, 55, 56, 58

Quakers, 73–74, 80
Quebec, 23, 26, 36, 59, 63, 219, 230
Quebec City, 59, 87, 97

Racial groups, 170–71, 176, 200
Racial zoning, 180 and *n.*
Railroads, 27, 29 and *n.*, 30, 42, 90, 95, 116–20, 130, 134, 141–43, 179, 186, 198, 201, 231, 234; commuter, 174, 178, 179, 183, 186, 190, 194, 201, 234; decline of, 201–203; stations, 20, 137–38, 140, 151, 152, 154, 198–99, 201, 202
Reed, Henry Hope, 175
Reid, John, Jr., 137
Religion, 38, 80, 90; mission towns, 51, 52; tolerance, 74, 80; in urban layouts, 42–43, 46
Reps, John W., 59, 89, 99, 141; *The Making of Urban America*, 99
Residential neighborhoods, outlying, 120 and *n.*, 121, 173–96. *See also* Suburbs
Revolutionary War, 60, 85, 99, 103
Rhode Island, 66, 67, 84–85, 105
Richmond, Va., 29, 104, 118
Rittenhouse Square, Philadelphia, 11, 165*n.*
River cities, 94–95, 104, 235
Robertson, Jaquelin, 81–82
Robinson, Charles Mulford, 136
Rochester, N.Y., 93, 137
Roebling, John Augustus, 94
Rome, 12, 37, 38, 39, 43, 47, 65, 66, 67, 75, 118, 131, 132, 137, 138, 149, 161
Roosevelt, Franklin D., 20
Root, John, 119, 122, 127

Rouse Company, 209, 215
Rudolph, Paul, 163
Rusk, David, *Cities Without Suburbs*, 227–28
Ruskin, John, 186
Russia, 38, 48, 96, 214

Safdie, Moshe, 232
Saint Augustine, Fla., 57–58, 230
Saint-Gaudens, Augustus, 130–34
Saint Louis, 29, 53, 116, 170–71, 227; city planning, 62, 137; civic beautification, 137, 139; Louisiana Purchase Exposition (1904), 139; population, 115, 226; transportation, 29–30
San Diego, 30, 41, 58, 215, 233; Panama-California International Exposition (1915), 139
San Francisco, 27, 29, 58, 108*n.*, 116, 117, 154; city planning, 45, 106, 124, 125, 135, 137, 165*n.*; civic beautification, 137, 139; Panama-Pacific International Exposition (1915), 139; parks, 125; population, 115, 225, 226; suburbs, 231
Savannah, Ga., 75–77, 82, 97, 104, 223, 234
Scott, M. H. Baillie, 185
Scully, Vincent, 34, 56
Seaside Village, Conn., 191–92
Seattle, 27, 81, 108*n.*, 116; Alaska-Yukon-Pacific Exposition (1910), 139; city planning, 45; suburbs, 206
Senate Park Commission, 134
Sewage, 44, 100–101
Shaw, Howard Van Doren, 190, 204
Shopping bazaars, 214–15
Shopping centers, 28, 176, 201–17
Shopping villages, 203–206
Sioux Falls, S.D., 30–32, 57*n.*
Sites and services projects, 44–45
Sixtus V, Pope, 66, 149, 161
Skyscrapers, 28, 153, 157, 227; Chicago, 110–11, 115, 118–20, 123–24, 126, 143–48, 153; New York, 144, 153–60
Slavery, 68, 85, 107–108, 113, 170
Slums, 41, 44, 107–108, 120, 160–64
Small towns, American preference for, 219–23
Social class distinctions, 235; nineteenth-century, 101–109, 112–15, 148, 151, 178; twentieth-century, 148, 154, 160–72, 176, 182, 188, 190–91, 202, 216–17, 227, 235. *See also specific social classes*
Social reform, 49, 148, 163–70
Southdale shopping center, Edina, Minn., 206–207
Spain, 38, 44, 105; colonial urbanization in New World, 44, 51–59, 63, 65, 76
Speer, Albert, 43
Squares, central, 48, 58, 67–69, 73–78, 93*n.*, 102, 106, 193, 194
Stamper, John W., 147
Steamboats, 94, 101, 115
Steel-frame construction, 119
Steevens, G. W., *In the Land of the Dollar*, 121–22
Stern, Robert A. M., 128, 179
Stilgoe, John, 175, 177–78
Stock market crash (1929), 200
Streetcars, 117–18, 178–79, 194
Street layouts, 42–47, 50, 66–67, 72–76, 81–82, 106, 162, 188. *See also specific cities and designs*
Strip development, 202–204, 229
Subdivisions, postwar, 194–96, 206
Suburbs, 23, 30, 31, 33, 44, 48, 49, 60, 79, 113–14, 120, 161, 163, 172, 173–96, 204–205, 235; annexed, 177–79, 185, 233; exclusive enclave, 181–82, 188, 204; garden, 182–94, 204–205, 223–24; growth, 145*n.*, 206; metro area relationship to, 225–33; postwar, 194–96, 206; shopping centers, 204–16; terminology, 176–78
Sullivan, Louis, 110, 119, 123, 128
Supermarkets, 201–203, 206
Supreme Court, 209
Symmes, John, 93–94

Taxes, 31, 172, 227
Technology, urban, 12, 49, 117–19, 130, 133, 151, 152, 161–62, 196*n.*, 199

Telephone, 117, 118*n.*, 199
Terminology, urban, 36–41, 176–78, 225
Texas, 61, 222
Third World cities, 39–40, 44, 121
Tocqueville, Alexis de, 84–109, 111–16, 156, 157, 220; *Democracy in America*, 86–87, 101, 109*n.*
Todd, Frederick, 190
Topography, 45, 56, 89, 92, 153, 180–81, 185, 188
Toronto, 11, 27, 29, 57 and *n.*, 81, 105*n.*, 106, 190, 208, 225, 231
Tourism, 41–42, 85, 199, 201, 210–13, 228
Town, definition of, 36–39
Transportation, 27–30, 46–47, 73, 77, 90, 94–95, 100–101, 109, 117–20, 130, 137–38, 140–43, 151, 155, 160–62, 199–201, 227, 231; commuter, 174–80, 183, 186, 189–95, 201, 226, 234; mass automobile ownership, 145*n.*, 162, 189–93, 200–207, 230, 233. *See also specific types of transportation*
Trolley cars, 27, 29, 30, 100, 117–18, 120, 199, 200*n.*
Trucking, 202–203
Tuileries gardens, Paris, 22, 24, 107, 125
Tunnard, Christopher, 175
Twentieth-century American urbanization, 140–48, 153–72, 197–217, 218–35

Unemployment, 49, 78, 160, 170–72, 199, 227
University campuses, 138–40, 199
Unwin, Raymond, 183–87, 193, 196; *Town Planning in Practice*, 193–94
Urban, definition of, 37–38
Urban renewal, 160–72
Utah, 55, 208

Vanderbilt, George, 18
Varro, Marcus Terentius, 36
Vauban, Sébastien Le Prestre de, 61, 65
Vaux, Calvert, 125–27, 141, 182
Venice, 27, 40–41, 46, 227, 230
Vermont, 89–93, 199
Versailles, 48, 86, 96
Vienna, 40, 48, 65, 82, 100, 142, 227
Village, definition of, 38
Virginia, 68–72, 103–104
Vitruvius Pollio, Marcus, 67
Von Hoffman, Alexander, 178–79

Walcott, Derek, 32
Walkways, elevated, 28
Walled cities, 37, 47–48, 54, 59–60, 64, 79
Washington, D.C., 27, 87, 95–97, 105, 116, 139, 198; city planning, 43, 70, 95–97, 105–106, 134–35, 137, 143, 152; civic beautification, 134–35, 137; population, 115
Washington, George, 96, 113
Washington Monument, 134
Weber, Eugen, 17
Webster, Daniel, 88
Welfare, 167*n.*, 171, 227
West Edmonton Mall, Alberta, 207–13
White House, 20, 43, 95–97, 134
Williamsburg, Va., 70–72, 77, 78, 82, 103, 104, 112, 230, 235
Willis, Nathaniel Parker, 175
Wilson, William, 136, 147
Wisconsin, 28, 106, 115
Woodfield shopping center, Chicago, 207
Wood-frame construction, 116, 120
Woodstock, Vt., 89–93, 155, 235
Woodward, George, 185–89, 193, 223
Woodward, Judge Augustus, 62*n.*, 76
World War I, 154, 156, 191
World War II, 42, 159–60, 194, 206
Wren, Christopher, 66, 70, 153, 185
Wright, Frank Lloyd, 187*n.*; Broadacre City, 229–30, 233

Yorkship Village, N.J., 191–92, 231, 235

Zeckendorf, William, 33
Zoning, 44, 79, 92, 143–44, 164; racial, 180 and *n.*; single-use, 164 and *n.*